Maurice Chevalier

The Authorised Biography

Other titles by David Bret published by Robson Books

Elvis: The Hollywood Years
George Formby
Marlene: My Friend
The Mistinguett Legend
Tallulah Bankhead: A Scandalous Life
Valentino: A Dream of Desire
Gracie Fields
Piaf: A Passionate life
Errol Flynn
Freddie Mercury
Maria Callas: The Tigress and the Lamb
Morrissey: Landscapes of the Mind

Maurice Chevalier

The Authorised Biography

David Bret

ROBSON BOOKS

This book is dedicated to
Marlene Dietrich
and
Jacqueline Danno

N'oublie pas . . .
La vie sans amies
c'est comme un
jardin sans fleurs

First published in Great Britain in 1992 by Robson Books,
64 Brewery Road, London, N7 9NT

This edition first published 2002

A member of the Chrysalis Group plc

British Library Cataloguing in Publication Data
A catalogue record for this title is available from the British Library.

ISBN 1 86105 499 8

Printed by Creative Print & Design (Wales), Ebbw Vale.

Contents

Chevalier was the truest friend I ever had.

His devotion to me was forever.

When I was named on the famous "Box-Office-Poison-List", Hollywood invented, he gave up a brilliant successfull career out of deep disgust over the disgrace my name received.

He left the United States never to return. I could not stop him. As I was in good company on that list I took the rebuff calmly and went on a European vacation. until Joe Pasternak lured me back. and my new career as a 'Western' star began.

My deep friendship with Chevalier continued through those years.

His illness at first did not seem serious, but I watched the event from afar and finally flew to Paris when the danger of death seemed near.

I was not allowed to see him, He had given orders to that effect. The reason was his fear that the sight of his death-ridden appearance would make me too sad to bear.

That's the kind of man he was. He gave up his own last joy for me

Marlene Dietrich

Foreword
by Marlene Dietrich

Chevalier was the truest friend I ever had. His devotion to me was forever.

When I was named on the famous 'Box-Office-Poison-List', Hollywood invented, he gave up a brilliant successful career out of deep disgust over the disgrace my name received. He left the United States never to return. I could not stop him.

As I was in good company on that list I took the rebuff calmly and went on a European vacation until Jo Pasternak lured me back and my new career as a 'Western' star began. My deep friendship with Chevalier continued through those years.

His illness at first did not seem serious, but I watched the event from afar and finally flew to Paris when the danger of death seemed near.

I was not allowed to see him. *He* had given orders to that effect. The reason was his fear that the sight of his death-ridden appearance would make me too sad to bear.

That's the kind of man he was. He gave up his own last joy – *for me.*

Acknowledgements

Writing this book would not have been possible had it not been for the help, inspiration, criticism and love of that very select group of individuals whom I will always look upon as my true family and *autre coeur*. Barbara, Irene Bevan, Marlene Dietrich, Roger Normand – *que vous dormez en paix*, René and Lucette Chevalier, Jacqueline Danno, Héléne Delavault, Tony Griffin, Betty Paillard, Annick Roux, Monica Solash, Terry Sanderson, John and Anne Taylor, François and Madeleine Vals, Axel Dotti, Caroline Clerc and Charley Marouani.

Especial thanks go to Odette Meslier, Jean-Christophe Averty, François Bellair and the late Sylvie Galthier, the late Michel Guyarmathy, Claudine Kirgener, the late Damia, André Bernard, the late Fernand Lumbroso, Claire Hudson of the British Theatre Museum, the late André Rivollet, Pierre-Yves Garcin of EMI France, the late Jean-Paul Neu.

Finally an immense *chapeau-bas* to my agent, David Bolt, to Jeremy Robson and his munificent team . . . and to my wife, Jeanne, still the keeper of my soul!

Introduction

Maurice Chevalier was the supreme professional. His career, spanning almost seventy years, was effectively a marriage with his beloved public, and in this way was similar to the careers of his contemporaries Edith Piaf, Mistinguett and Joséphine Baker. Yet it was not always an easy union, for woven into the thread of the complex tapestry of Chevalier's life was the weird and wonderful collection of stars that formed his first show-business family; his struggle for acceptance in a music-hall world that initially wanted little to do with him; his rise to success and his capture by the Germans during World War II and his subsequent incarceration in a prisoner-of-war camp; the tense and arduous rebuilding of his career only to have this very nearly destroyed in one fell swoop by the collaborationist charges levelled against him in World War II.

Then there are the innumerable relationships: the passionate but frequently soul-destroying ones with Fréhel, Mistinguett and Patachou; the tender ones with Martin Kenny and Marlene Dietrich; the controversial ones with Nita Raya and Joe Bridge; the much maligned *amour de coeur* with Odette Meslier, to whom Chevalier bequeathed much of his fortune.

Despite his chirpy and cheerful stage-screen persona, Chevalier was not always a happy man: like fellow 'clowns' Tony Hancock, George Formby and Tommy Cooper, there were tears lurking behind the mask. Chevalier was often tormented by lengthy periods of self-doubt even at the height of his fame – brooding unnecessarily on best-forgotten aspects of his past, progressively worried about his future.

As an artiste Chevalier was tetchy, difficult and almost fanatically discerning, as so often happens when one is trying to maintain one's position at the top. As a showman, he was without equal. As a man, he was warm, thoughtful, caring and generous to a fault, sometimes giving an impression of almost Scrooge-like meanness while secretly donating many thousands of pounds to charity.

Maurice Chevalier was an institution, not just in his native France but as his country's entertainments ambassador around the world. To many he will always be *le grandpère éternel*. This is his story.

Patapouf

When Joséphine Bossche married Charles-Victor Chevalier during the last quarter of the last century, little did she know what she was taking on. By profession, Charles-Victor was a shop- and house-painter, and he worked exceedingly hard. In common with many of his fellow inhabitants of the Paris suburb Belleville-Ménilmontant, he compensated for his long working hours by bouts of heavy drinking, though fortunately for his seemingly ever-pregnant wife, he was not much of a womanizer. The couple lived in the rue du Retrait, in an area rarely frequented by the tourists who, towards the end of 1888, began flocking into the city to watch the preparations for the 1889 Great Exhibition to commemorate the centenary of the Revolution. Indeed, with the exorbitant cost of public transport in pre-Métro Paris, where few of the poorer classes ventured beyond the confines of their own *quartier*, it is unlikely that Joséphine or her husband ever watched the progress of Gustave Eiffel's iron monstrosity in the Champs de Mars, where, in a blaze of publicity, it was already half-way towards becoming the symbol of Paris. Nor, it may be said, would they have cared. Joséphine, thirty-six years of age and not in the best of health was well into her ninth confinement, though only two of her brood, Charles and Paul, had survived infancy. Charles, it was decided, would inherit his father's mantle and become a house-painter; Paul was to be an apprentice metal-engraver. However, the son born on 12 September 1888, and baptized Maurice, was destined for greater things. He would very soon revolutionize not just the French music-hall but the entertainment scene in general all around the world.

Maurice was a plump but pasty baby, and for this reason alone his mother nicknamed him Patapouf; he never called her anything but La Louque. When asked in interviews why this was, he would usually respond haughtily, 'Because I did!' That he was something of a mother's boy goes without saying. That La Louque was the most important person in his life is also undeniable; even Chevalier's legendary affair with Mistinguett had to get her official seal of approval. In 1941, in her memory, he sang a song called 'Toi, toi, toi', which he had written with Henri Betti, and which remains one of his most moving.

> *Pourtant ce soir il faut que j'ose*
> *T'ouvrir mon cœur à plein flot,*
> *Et j'sais bien que mon existence,*
> *Se passera à te vénérer . . .*

> (And yet tonight I must venture
> In full flood to open my heart to you,
> And I know well that my existence,
> Takes place to worship you . . .)

When Maurice was five or six years old, the Chevaliers moved to an apartment at 15 rue Julien-Lacroix, just two streets from the rue du Retrait. It was not a move for the better. La Louque had just borne and buried her tenth and last child, and she was suffering from acute post-natal depression. This was made worse by her husband's rapidly increasing addiction to absinthe, and the fact that he was bringing in less and less money each week. She was forced to supplement her own meagre income as a braid-trimmer by taking a variety of cleaning jobs, and Charles-Victor, who felt strongly that a woman's place was in the home, took this badly. One evening when he did not arrive home to join the rest of the family round the dinner table, La Louque sent her son Charles on a tour of the local bars to find him. The boy was told that his father had left Paris and would not be coming back. Neither La Louque nor her sons shed many tears.

As head of the household, Charles was hardly better than his father. He too drank a lot, and gave his mother little by way of board. He also bullied his brothers, especially Maurice, who, though still affectionately known as Patapouf, was growing up weak and spindly. Maurice's stature also made him the butt of jokes at his school, the Ecole des Frères, on the rue Boyer, and thinking himself incapable of taking on his tormentors physically, he would either set his brother Paul on to them or make some ribald wisecrack which, more often than not, would result in his receiving a good hiding. This went on for more than a year, and ended only one evening when Maurice was collecting coal for his mother in a squalid back-alley near their home. He was suddenly set upon by the local gang and, because his brother was not there to protect him, Maurice found himself taking on the gang's leader. In a fit of ferocious temper, he bloodied the boy's nose, and far from there being any unpleasant repercussions, the rest of the gang hoisted him on to their shoulders and proudly carried him back to the rue Julien-Lacroix. The next morning, at school, he was nominated 'cock' of his class.

This incident also earned Maurice the respect of his brother Charles, and when the latter left home to get married the brothers were almost good friends. With Charles gone, however, the financial situation within the Chevalier household deteriorated rapidly. What her oldest son had handed over each Friday had at least enabled La Louque to keep her head above water; now, even with Paul bringing in seven francs a day – not a bad wage for an apprentice in turn-of-the-century suburban Paris – she found it practically impossible to make ends meet. In 1896 she suffered what appears to have been a severe mental breakdown, which resulted in hospitalization for several months. Maurice, aged just eight, was sent to a children's home at Denfert-Rochereau. This was still in Paris but, as far as the timid and impressionable child was concerned, it could have been on the other side of the world. Many years later he would tell a reporter that this was the worst period of his life, worse even than his years as a prisoner of war, and that he had endured the cold, grey dormitory and the ruthlessness which often came with such a religious institution only for his mother's sake. He would also have known, of course, what happened to those who tried to run away, as many did: they were sent to a house of correction.

Fortunately for everyone concerned, La Louque made a complete recovery and by the summer of 1897 the family were reunited. In many ways, they were happier now than ever before, and certainly more affluent, since Paul had passed the first part of his apprenticeship and been given a pay rise. This extra cash enabled the trio to indulge in occasional visits to local music-halls: the Cirque Médrano, La Commerce and the Palais du Travail at 13 rue de Belleville – notorious for the thick fog of smoke that welcomed the gallery clientele, and for its difficult audiences. Maurice's favourite establishment, however, was the famous Cirque d'Hiver in the rue de Crussol, not far from the République. Here, sitting in the cheapest seats, he would marvel at the feats of the acrobats and clowns, and in particular the Fratellinis. He also adored the antics of the two most popular French comedians of the day, Dranem and Polin.

The former, born Armand Ménard in 1869, had changed his stage name after looking at a poster of his in the mirror. He specialized in absurd songs such as 'Ah! Les petits pois', which Chevalier once sang. Polin, who had begun his professional career at around the same time as Dranem, was a speciality act who would rush on to the stage wearing a railwayman's uniform and waving a checkered flag. Whenever he was about to utter something obscene, he would hold this up as a cue for the ladies and prudes among the audience to cover their ears. No one was ever offended, of course, though it is doubtful if such a ridiculous act could take root today, even in the age of alternative comedy. However, Maurice was very impressed by what he saw, and by the time he was ten he was determined to work on the stage, making people laugh.

Initially, Maurice's ambition was to become an acrobat, and in this venture he was supported by his brother Paul; indeed, it was Paul who decided that they should form a double act under an English name, The Chevalier Brothers. He even agreed to pay for their 'training' sessions at the Arras Gymnasium, a project that was quickly dropped not just because the other weightlifters and boxers laughed themselves silly every time Maurice took off his shirt, but also because the gymnasium manager raised his charges to the then astronomical amount of five francs a day, which was a third of Paul's daily take-home pay. Not to be deterred, Paul rented an allotment on a spare plot of land in Ménilmontant for twenty-five francs a year, and the pair trained here, in the open air and mindless of the weather, until Paul was satisfied that they had reached audition standard. Even so, they were turned down by the Palais du Travail, and for several months played to passers-by on pavements, or to courtyard crowds on Sunday mornings. The partnership ended abruptly when another friend joined the act, forcing Maurice to form the apex of a human pyramid. Losing his balance one day, Maurice fell, breaking his ankle and incurring the wrath of La Louque – probably for the first and last time.

Undeterred, and with his ankle still in plaster, Maurice made up his mind that he would perform comedy songs, like Polin. One of La Louque's friends was a man called Georgel, a local nightwatch-man who on Saturday nights could be found delivering his comedy patter at the Café des Trois Lions, on the boulevard de Ménilmont-ant. Georgel told Maurice that Saturday night was also audition night, and that a number of famous acts had started after being discovered by the great entrepreneurs of the day, such as Madame Rasimi and the Marchands, who often called by in search of new talent. This was not so, however, and when Maurice went to see the manager he was promptly shown the door. For several weeks he persisted, though, and one evening the manager's wife took pity on him and wedged him in in between a juggling act and an alpine yodeller. As cocky as ever, he asked to be billed as 'Petit Chevalier, Comique Miniature', and for ten minutes he impersonated Carlos, a bumbling, country-peasant comic who was known for singing vulgar ditties. His big hit was 'V'la les croquants', which he always sang in knickerbockers, a bright-blue shirt and white gloves. One can only guess at what the puny, eleven-year-old Maurice Chevalier looked like in this attire, and the fact that throughout his first song he was half a bar in front of his pianist, who in despair got up and walked off the stage, can't have helped. It was also alleged that during his second song 'even the navvies blushed'. Even so, he proved the hit of the evening, and Carlos's most famous song would for many years rank among his favourites.

> *Je suis venu à Paris,*
> *Pour voir la capitale,*
> *Mes yeux en sont ébahis,*
> *Ma joie est sans égale . . .*

(I came to Paris,
To see the capital,
My eyes are flabbergasted,
My joy without equal . . .)

Maurice's payment for his first 'recital' at the Trois Lions, unimpressive but no doubt appreciated, was a bowl of soup – not enough, La Louque convinced him, to ensure his future in music-hall circles! Even so, he was determined to earn his living and be in a position to support his mother if and when Paul left home, and a few months after his début he told her that he would be leaving school at the end of the current term. La Louque did nothing to stop him. Maurice left the Ecole des Frères on the Friday and began working the very next day as an electrical apprentice. This lasted but a few weeks: he was fired for causing a short circuit. There then followed a variety of jobs, including sweeping the floor in a factory, working for a printer, and being an errand boy in another factory which made drawing pins, and then a doll-painter. The last he liked most of all because it afforded him direct contact with his 'clients'. One of these was a young girl not much older than himself, Georgette Lucas.

According to André Rivollet, who in 1927 wrote one of the earliest Chevalier biographies, Georgette and Maurice fell head-over-heels in love when they first met in April 1900. Georgette was a large, plain and unhappy girl whose parents quarrelled incessantly. She was also led to believe that Maurice was fifteen, and this was confirmed by his employer – the boy had added three years to his age to ensure the regular adult wage of fifteen francs a day, and the shopkeeper had believed him, no doubt because La Louque backed up his story when she accompanied her son to his interview. It seems likely that Maurice and Georgette experienced some kind of fumbling sexual relationship. She told him that she had often watched her parents making love after their frequent rows, and in order to express her undying love for him, Georgette would invite Maurice to crawl under a public bench with her outside the church in the main square of Ménilmontant when it was dark and there was no one around.

He looked upon Georgette as his little wife [wrote Rivollet], and he badly wanted to fight someone for her honour. He dreamed of how it would be, kissing sloppily and making up after an argument, the way married people did. Then one day they passed a church just as the wedding-party was leaving. The droning of the organ reminded Maurice of a Polin song and Georgette grabbed him by the hand and dragged him towards the door. In the spirit of the moment, they would become betrothed! And then, quite unexpectedly the church door slammed shut, crushing his finger and causing him to utter a high-pitched scream. Later on, while having his injury tended to at the local hospital, he sang the Polin song to himself again and decided that he would give up his 'wife' in order to pursue his career, which he considered a worthier cause.

Maurice lost more than Georgette over the incident at the church: when the owner of the paint-shop discovered him 'dilly-dallying' with another local girl instead of getting on with his duties, he was fired on the spot.

Maurice's next and, he claimed, most important job was errand-boy in a shop that sold sheet-music. Again, he spent much of his time dreaming and gazing at the pictures of famous music-hall stars on the walls. Harry Fragson was already a major force on the French entertainment scene, as were Pauline Darty and Félix Mayol. Occasionally, Maurice would be given concessionary tickets to see them at the Eldorado, or at the Scala on the boulevard de Strasbourg, and of course he always took La Louque. He also had an adolescent crush on a popular charm singer of the day, Lise Fleuron, but almost nothing is known of this apart from the fact that she went into the shop one afternoon to buy some music. Expecting a hefty tip, as was customary, Maurice was surprised to find that his reward for helping her to make her selection was a peck on the cheek – and this set a precedent for him in later life. Maurice Chevalier rarely tipped waiters or hat-check girls. A kiss or a handshake from him, he once said, was worth much more than a few coins! He may well have been right, but as far as many French people were concerned, he was displaying only his meanness.

Maurice's ten-minute performances at the Café des Trois Lions ended abruptly when the establishment closed down, but this set-back did not prevent him from seeking engagements elsewhere. He was not immediately successful. Some entrepreneurs found him too cheeky and arrogant, and many were used to booking even minor acts through agents. It was probably thanks to Georgel, the nightwatchman, that he was invited to audition at the Folies-Popincourt, not far from the Cirque d'Hiver. Here the laughter was of a different kind, for the decidedly rougher-edged audiences of the République area did not take kindly to being provoked by child prodigies.

In December 1901 Maurice sang two songs at an amateur night at the Elysée-Montmartre. This was hosted by an artiste known as Le Mayol des Tourelles, an elderly has-been homosexual singer with a penchant for under-age boys. Maurice may have refused the older man's advances, but he certainly took his advice and tried out his Carlos impressions on Monsieur Rithier, the proprietor of the Casino des Tourelles near the Lac Saint-Fargeau, where Le Mayol was artiste-in-residence. Rithier was so impressed that he engaged him for a three-week season, during which there would be twelve performances – and a total salary of thirty-six francs. La Louque was delighted, but still not convinced that her pre-cocious son would be able to make a living from the music-halls. He therefore promised to return to the Ecole des Frères should there be no engagements after the Casino des Tourelles.

In fact, the young Maurice took his career very seriously and at once assumed the stance of a hardened campaigner. He gave up his job with the music shop, and spent most of his days visiting publishers in search of new material. For any up-and-coming entertainer, this would have been a difficult task; for an occasion-ally obnoxious child-star, it was impossible. New songs cost a great deal of money to launch, and were almost always given only to established stars. Everyone else had to take pot-luck, and usu-ally ended up with castoffs not worth the paper they were printed on. If Maurice was lucky, he was shown the door; if not, he was given a clout for his impudence. In the end he decided that as he would have to stick with his two Carlos songs for the time being, it was more important to change his image. Therefore, using his meagre savings, he went to a secondhand shop and bought himself a checked jacket and trousers, and a ridiculous-looking Girondin hat – making him something of a precursor to Stan Laurel. Also, he changed his attitude, becoming more snooty, so much so that many of the friends who had admired him for standing on his own feet now refused to have anything to do with him. Indeed, one evening while on his way home, a bunch of hooligans set upon him, ripping his clothes and trampling his hat in the gutter. This was in fact the best thing that could have happened to him: the next evening he walked on to the stage wearing his everyday clothes and a flat cap, and he was an instant success!

In an age where many of the major stars of the day were playing as many as four different theatres each evening – forty minutes was the usual time allotted in a bill for the *vedette*, the star attraction, and one-man shows were virtually unheard of – Maurice discovered that it was very easy to find work once he had become established. Maintaining his popularity, on the other hand, was not so simple. He did well at the Concert du Commerce, but failed miserably at the Ville Japonaise on the boulevard de Strasbourg. This was one of the most unusual café-concerts in Paris, decorated with lanterns, fans and various *objets d'art* from the Far East. It was also known as a society pick-up joint, with regulars ranging from the outrageous *horizontalistes* Liane de Pougy and Emilienne d'Alençon to some of the better-class whores who had made their way on foot or by Métro from the Pigalle.

Maurice might have fared slightly better at the establishment had he remembered the house rules banning any kind of fraternization with the clientele. But he did not, and one evening he fell foul of an angry pimp who accused him of trying to pick up one of his girls without paying. Needless to say, the management asked him to leave. Many years later Chevalier wrote about the incident in his memoirs, probably with a disingenuous naïvety.

La Louque was an innocent being who never saw bad in anyone. Paul, too, was possessed of an inconceivable purity. I had no one to guide me morally. I saw singers insulted while they were on stage, and watched the poor buggers weeping in their dressing-rooms. The fact that I was not devoured entirely by this needless cruelty gave me enough confidence to follow my destiny.

At this time there were problems once more with Maurice's brother Charles, who visited his mother more often after she and Maurice moved to a better apartment, on the sixth floor at 118 boulevard Saint-Martin (Paul had not moved with them owing to his impending marriage). Charles had seen one of Maurice's offerings at the Concert du Commerce, his only comment being that Maurice had 'looked gormless, with his bottom lip sticking out like that of a Negro'. Maurice never forgave him and, as head of the household now in Paul's absence, told him that he was no longer welcome in the family home.

After the Ville Japonaise, Maurice was engaged by La Fourmi, in Barbés-Rochechouart, for the princely sum of thirty-five francs for three performances. Here he met his first agent, a man called Dalos, who, though probably doubling as a pimp, did at least find him some decent engagements. Thus, early in 1903 he was sent on his very first provincial tour, playing flea-pit cinemas, minor music-halls and cafés in Tours, Amiens and Le Havre. Although the two songs by Carlos still figured in his act, he had broadened his repertoire a little by adding one or two Fragson songs, some absurd monologues written by a comedian called Claudius, and an engaging number by Christiné, 'L'enfant du cordonnier', which he would sing for many years.

> *Je suis le fils du gniaff, gniaff, gniaff,*
> *Qui fait des ribouis,*
> *Et fait d'orthograph 'graph 'graph,*
> *Je connais peau de zébie . . .*

The Swiss-born composer Henri Christiné was one of the most important figures in the early years of the French music-hall, supplying standards for Josephine Baker, Mistinguett, Dranem, Mayol, Harry Fragson and Yvonne Printemps – and, of course, Maurice Chevalier, who did as much to propagate his legend as anyone. 'L'enfant du cordonnier', like so many of his works, was fashioned around a very tricky Parisian argot which would make any attempt at translation grossly unfair to the original.

In July 1903 Maurice returned to Paris, where he was engaged as an extra at the Concert de l'Univers on the avenue Wagram. Such was his appeal, now that he had been brought back down to the level of the people, that a three-day contract was extended to eleven weeks. Again, he had changed his appearance, this time dirtying his face and hands, and wearing a tattered shirt over a striped sailor's pullover, tight-fitting trousers which were several inches too short, and a tiny hat. His other songs, which would today be regarded as ridiculously outdated, included 'Le trottoir roulant', which had been written in the year of his birth to commemorate one of the tourist attractions of the Great Exhibition.

Because his act took place during the first half of the show – more often than not he was second or third on – Maurice hardly ever stayed for the finale, and this enabled him to catch up with whatever was going on in the rival theatres. Strangely for a fifteen-year-old filled with *joie de vivre*, one of his favourite actresses was Eve Lavallière, whom he had seen at the Scala. Born in 1866, she was neurotic to the point of absurdity, and an extremely possessive bisexual with a mortal fear of stepping outside her apartment. Whenever she had a show to do, the taxi-cab would always back up to her door so that she would not be seen leaving, and she always wore her black, jewelled peignoir until the moment came for her to put on her costume for the stage. Some of her costumes rivalled those worn by the *meneuses de revues* at the Moulin-Rouge, but she was always at her happiest in male attire. There was a sound reason for her intense neurosis. As a child, she had watched her father's messy suicide after he had attempted to strangle her mother. Lavallière was married to the impresario Samuel Louveau, known to friends and enemies alike as Samuel le Magnifique, and it was he who had directed her in successful seasons at the Théâtre des Variétés, where her co-star had been the English-styled comedian and dancer Max Dearly, who subsequently became her lover. Maurice was well acquainted with Louveau, having auditioned for him several times, and he had met Lavallière on various occasions. Max Dearly he did not know, though he soon would, and in regrettable circumstances. Towards the end of July 1903, when he was more confident than ever that Louveau would engage him for one of his revues, Maurice went to meet him backstage at the Eldorado. It was here, quite by chance, that he first encountered the woman who would transform his life.

Jeanne-Marie Florentine Bourgeois – later to be known as

Mistinguett – had been born at Enghien-les-Bains, 12 miles north of Paris, in April 1875 and, like Maurice, she had never really wanted to be anything but a music-hall star. Her professional début had taken place at the Casino de Paris in 1893, since which time she had gradually worked her way up the bill in theatres all over Paris, before becoming resident *vedette* at the Eldorado. When she met Maurice she was about to leave for Brussels, where she had been signed up to play the lead in Georges Feydeau's *La dame de chez Maxim*. This most momentous of meetings was reported by André Rivollet.

> Maurice saw her waddle on to the stage, singing 'J'suis une gamine'. He saw her forget-me-not eyes, and her wonderful, wonderful legs. He saw her magnificent smile and imagined her beautiful, full-blown breasts, and dreamed of getting to know her some day. They met that same night, and quite by chance. Maurice had gone backstage to meet his friend, one of the chorus boys, and he was talking to her dresser when the door opened. Her language was shocking, though not lacking in humour. Maurice was introduced, and she asked him where he was appearing. He told her, and she suddenly leaned forwards and pinched his cheek. The orchestra, now that the interval was over, was playing her introduction, and she said, 'Don't worry, my boy. Your future seems very secure – you've got a pretty little mug!'

Impressed as he must have been at meeting the greatest star in France, Maurice was sensible enough to realize that dreams did not put food on the table. In fact, when his contract with the Concert de l'Univers expired at the end of the year, he found it so difficult to obtain work that it was almost necessary for La Louque to ask for help from the Public Assistance. 'Every day, for weeks, we lived on boiled potatoes and tea brewed from cherry leaves,' he wrote. And then, when he had all but lost hope of ever performing again and was dreading having to keep his promise to La Louque and get himself a regular job, out of the blue an offer came for him to join the chorus of *Satyre bouchonne* (a pun on the French word for corkscrew), which was due to open at the Parisiana in February 1904.

This famous theatre, which stood on the boulevard Poissonnière, was then owned by the Isola Brothers, who were renowned
for putting on some of the best revues in Paris, while paying stingy
fees to the artistes. Even so, working the Parisiana could be enormously advantageous for any up-and-coming star wishing to be
observed and possibly 'discovered' by the higher echelons of the
music-hall fraternity. Many spectators attended its premières to
see not who was performing on the stage but who happened to be
sitting in the audience. Maurice's first important première was a
good example, for the 'guests of honour' included King Léopold
II of Belgium and his mistress Cléo de Mérode, La Belle Otèro,
and the writer Colette, accompanied by her husband, Monsieur
Willy. None of these celebrities would have noticed him at all had
it not been for the fact that he was a good head shorter than
anyone else on the Parisiana stage – something that amused Harry
Fragson, whom the Isolas had invited to supplement the show on
an *ad hoc* basis.

This talented young man, the son of a Belgian brewer, had been
born in London in 1869. Known affectionately as the Entente
Cordiale Comedian, his most famous song was 'Hello, Hello,
Who's Your Lady Friend?', which he introduced towards the end
of his brief but glorious career. An extremely ugly, bucolic-looking
individual, Fragson had some rather unsavoury habits. These
included drinking the water which he had used to wash his feet
in, urinating on passers-by from his apartment window and, worst
of all, sending 'chocolates' to his rivals which had been fashioned
from his faeces. Maurice, however, was merely amused when Fragson commented on his stature, adding, 'Put some horse-muck in
your shoes, my boy. That should do the trick!' It is not known
whether the youngster took Fragson's advice, but incredibly, when
he left *Satyre bouchonne* six months later, he had grown a good
6 inches.

Maurice's next major series of engagements did not take place
in Paris but in nearby Asnières. The venue was the Eden Music
Hall, and he was paid twelve francs per performance. His act had
not changed. He was still singing such silly ditties as 'Amours et
haricots', but some of the great Chevalier vehicles were just around
the corner. A great many of his admirers were middle-aged
women, no doubt because he looked so fragile and, as one critic

put it, 'motherless'. One of these matriarchs was so moved to pity by him one night when he walked on to the stage that she cried, 'Look, he's like little Jesus!' The name stuck, and the next day Maurice asked the management to have 'Le Petit Jésus d'Asnières' added to the posters outside the theatre. The ruse worked, and his contract with the Eden was extended by three months.

'After the Eden, I never had to look for work again. It was the turning point in my career,' he wrote in his memoirs. His good fortune also made him more appreciative of money. For every ten francs that he earned, six were always set aside 'for a rainy day', even if it sometimes meant having to go without. Little wonder, then, that he very quickly developed a reputation for meanness which was sometimes carried to the point of absurdity.

At the Eden, Maurice celebrated his sixteenth birthday. Being well away from central Paris allowed him to take the risk of performing numbers which were still the exclusive property of their owners. He introduced a Dranem song into his act, 'Le beau momignard', which was apparently such an innovation that each night the sweetseller would shut up shop and refuse to serve anyone while he was on stage. Another song, on the other hand, was so downright filthy, even if it was all *double entendre*, that some people walked out of the theatre in disgust.

> *Je l'ai trempée dans l'amidon,*
> *C'est un excellent remède . . .*
> *Comme ça elle est restée raide*
> *Pendant huit jours environ . . .*
>
> (I steeped it in starch,
> It's an excellent remedy . . .
> Like that it remained stiff
> For about a week . . .)

At the end of 1904 Maurice appeared at the Scala in Brussels. His nightly fee of twenty francs was the same as the average weekly wage of a workman. He stayed there for four weeks, and this led to his being offered and accepting a three-month tour of France taking in Lille, Amiens, Rheims and Toulon, culminating in second-billing at the Alcazar in Marseilles. This particular theatre was known for its difficult audiences, and even hardened campaigners like Dranem, Polaire and Fragson had been whistled at while working there. Maurice suffered stage fright for the first time in his career, particularly when the *chanteuse* preceding him was pelted with orange peel and booed off the stage after drying up. In fact, he almost did fail. His opening number met with stony silence and the second, meant to be a romantic love song, had everyone rolling in the aisles.

After Marseilles, he returned to Paris to play in short seasons at the Casino Montparnasse and the Casino Saint-Martin, but if La Louque was expecting him to rest for a while, she was to be disappointed. Maurice gave her the bulk of what he had earned, asked her to put most of it away, and then promptly set off on another tour. He was still working freelance, and during the spring of 1905 he played in Lille. People continued to taunt him because of his puny physique, so he began taking boxing lessons and working out at a gymnasium. It is interesting to note that his very first amateur match was against a promising fourteen-year-old called Georges Carpentier, who in 1914 would become heavyweight champion of the world.

Although undeniably French in everything that he had done so far, Maurice was greatly impressed by the English music-hall scene, which had recently taken off in Paris. The proprietor of the Alhambra was Lord Baradsford, a flamboyant homosexual who tried to book as many English acts as he could, and one or two French ones if they were handsome enough to get past the casting-couch! Baradsford had done much to further Fragson's career, and he had also brought over Little Tich from London. Maurice saw Little Tich for the first time in 1905, and called him the greatest innovator of his day. 'He did more to lift my spirits than all the French comics put together,' he wrote. '[He] was my first teacher.'

Born Harry Relph in 1868, the man whom the French also called Little Big Boots had made his Paris début in the year of Maurice's birth. He chose his stage name because of his resemblance to the claimant of the Tichborne inheritance, and in doing so added a new word to the English language. Standing little more than 4 feet tall, his act was so utterly ridiculous that it became a sensation. Wearing a deadpan expression and a pair of boots

whose soles were longer than he was tall, he would deliver monologues and tell vulgar jokes, or just clown around. He also sang
such songs as 'The Best Man Gets the Best of It' and 'Since Poor
Father Joined the Territorials' in a voice which was not at all bad.
A founder member of the Water Rats Society, he also did a great
deal of good work for the organization.

Another artiste who influenced the young Maurice was an
English-Canadian dancer-comedian called Norman French, who
made his début at the Alhambra in 1905 but only really came into
his own when given top billing at the Scala the following year.
Something of a precursor to Jack Buchanan and Fred Astaire, and
described by Lord Baradsford as 'my perfect English rose', French
was a tall, muscular young man with blond hair, perfect blue eyes,
an elegant mien and an ever-ready smile. He always wore black
evening dress on stage, and carried a top hat and cane, and it was
he who introduced the one-step and the cake-walk to the French.
That Maurice Chevalier was fascinated by him goes without saying. 'I was overwhelmed. It was as if a huge window had opened
up on the horizon!' he later enthused. Thus it was that he decided
to combine his boxing and acrobatic skills with an off-key imitation of Norman French, and when he toured again in 1907 his
audiences observed a marked improvement in his act.

In 1907 Maurice worked briefly with Toulon-born Félix Mayol,
who at twenty-five was already a music-hall veteran. This
interprète-extraordinaire has been variously described as a genius
and a turn-of-the-century punk, owing to his curiously tufted hairstyle. His most famous songs were 'Elle vendait des petits gâteaux'
and 'La paimpolaise', which he always sang while mincing up and
down the stage, twiddling the tails of his jacket. He was a very
great friend of Mistinguett, who admired him for his rampant
homosexuality and for his knack of making a public spectacle of
himself. Mayol was an initiator of the custom known as '*le privi-
lège du cape*', whereby any man unable to find a *pissoir* in the
street had the right to stop a gendarme and request that he extend
his cape. It was a convenient way of soliciting for sex, and sometimes, if the gendarme was young and good-looking, Mayol would
pretend to be drunk in the hope that he might be given assistance
with his flies. Surprisingly, the ruse often worked. If not, Mayol

would simply wet his victim's feet and slope off, seaching for another candidate.

In 1907, at the Bouffes de Bordeaux, Maurice found himself not just on the same programme as Mayol but sharing top billing. What was more, the great comedian, who no doubt considered the young man a more than worthy catch, actually allowed him to sing two of his most famous songs 'Cousine' and 'La mattchiche'. According to Roger Normand, however, Mayol had engineered this: 'Mayol was an unsavoury character with a penchant for young boys. Maurice was not yet twenty, too old for him, and at that time was keen on Paul Ardot, an absolutely ravishing specimen – well-built, tall, with a blond ducktail haircut like the one sported many years later by Elvis Presley. Mayol was consumed with jealousy. Paul Ardot and Norman French were besotted with Maurice, but neither of them could stand Mayol. So, unable to seduce Maurice in the more conventional way, Mayol paid the theatre director to move Maurice right to the top of the bill, hoping that he would end up sleeping with him, even if just the once out of gratitude. It's possible that Maurice *did* sleep with French and Ardot – but would he have slept with Mayol when competition was so strong? I don't think so.'

A few weeks after their revue, Maurice and Mayol met up again after the latter's show at the Olympia: they were actually spotted by a journalist, holding hands and laughing, en route for Mayol's favourite eatery. It was, however, but a brief, one-sided flirtation at the most – a sexless 'date' with the irascible young charmer, for Maurice had already begun to show an avid interest in a pretty little mannequin who had that summer arrived on the Paris social scene.

Fréhel, Mistinguett and
the Folies-Bergère

In the summer of 1907 the great comedian Dranem, who had been performing at the Eldorado since 1899 (and would subsequently play there off and on until the First World War, when he left to star in operettas and films), was taken ill, and the management set about searching urgently for a replacement. Under normal circumstances top billing would have passed to the *vedette-américain* – this was the secondary artiste who closed the first half of the show – but in this case it went to a tall, horse-faced comedian named Montel who specialized in humorous and sometimes vulgar monologues. From the theatre director's point of view, however, Maurice's youth, vivacity and now immense appeal were firmly on his side, and so it was that he and not Montel stood in for Dranem. Needless to say, there were heated arguments backstage, and one of these was so serious that the pair actually came to blows in the wings. Astonishingly, Maurice was able to use even this situation to his advantage, careering backwards on to the stage after ducking under Montel's fists and continuing the fight with an imaginary sparring partner. Success was instant.

Maurice was now earning 1,000 francs a month, and the critics agreed unanimously that he was worth every centime. The troublesome Montel was replaced on the bill by Maurice's old chum Georgel. More important for Maurice, when Dranem came to see the show with his nurse, he gave his act the 'official' seal of approval.

Another spectator was Paul-Louis Flers, the producer for the Folies-Bergère, who was looking for 'stars with a difference' for a forthcoming winter revue at the famous theatre on the rue Richer. Then as now, the Folies was not accustomed to engaging French stars for its revues, which were aimed at titillating the tourists, many of whom did not care for the smoky and often rowdy café-concerts and more traditional music-halls favoured by the stars themselves. Flers may not have liked the Chevalier voice, but he did recognize the extraordinary talent and personality which went with it, and the following evening he watched the show again with the theatre-director Clément Bannel, who had just acquired the lease to the Folies-Bergère and Jacques-Charles, a man who within a few years would be recognized as the greatest revue writer of his generation. Flers was all for negotiating the contract with Maurice there and then, but Bannel did not initially agree with him, particularly as one of the leading critics of the day, Fernand Nozière of *Le Figaro*, had dismissed him as 'the most laborious and painful comic ever to appear as the lead in any first-class production'. In the end, however, a compromise was reached and Maurice was signed up for three years – not as a lead but as a featured artiste, with an impressive salary which began at 1,800 francs per month and was guaranteed to rise after two years to 2,500. Maurice, meanwhile, continued at the Eldorado, and it was here, a few weeks after signing the contract for the Folies, that he met the woman soon to be known throughout most of Europe simply as Fréhel.

Described as 'an angel with a mouth like a sewer-worker', this highly original artiste had been born Marguerite Boulc'h in 1891, near Cap Fréhel in Finistère. Tender or aggressive, depending on her mood – or on what she had snorted or drunk before going on to the stage – she created *le rétro* long before the word had been invented. Vibrating to the strains of the famous Médinger accordions, more essential to her than the piano, her unusual voice and timbre transferred her enormous *joie de vivre* into even the saddest of songs. Her dialogue between songs, if there was any, was often sprinkled with vulgar asides. The Fréhel catchphrase was, 'I am as I am and so is a stone, them as don't like me can leave me alone!' Her apprenticeship had been in the rough-and-ready *salles des beuglants* (literally 'bawling halls') so few of her true admirers were genuinely offended. In her heyday, when she was one of the most popular singers in France, she had little regard for money;

what she earned she squandered on her friends or on living life to the full.

Like many phenomena of the early music-hall, little is known of Fréhel's upbringing. She had no time for the media, rarely gave interviews and jealously guarded her private life. She was fond of telling everyone that she had begun singing in cafés and bars at the age of five, accompanied by a blind accordionist. One of the customers who had been taken with the pretty, curly-haired child had baptized her La Pervenche, after the periwinkle-blue of her eyes, and the name had stuck. Shortly before meeting Maurice she had made her professional début at the Concert de l'Univers, singing one song. To support her meagre income, Fréhel also worked as a mannequin, modelling for various fashion houses in and around Paris, and it was in this capacity that she met the young man who, in her own words, 'would fuck up my whole life'. This was not entirely fair. To a certain extent, Maurice may have been partially responsible for what happened to Fréhel a few years later, but so were a number of others, as will be seen. One could also add that the singer was her own worst enemy. At sixteen she was renowned as the '*coqueluche*' or darling of the Montmartre nightclub set, collecting jewels and furs from a succession of wealthy young lovers who never failed to be shocked the moment this beautiful creature opened her mouth to regale them with some filthy anecdote.

La Louque, although rarely present at her son's performances, did manage to keep a close check on his activities, and she was particularly keen on protecting his morals – obviously, she had been told nothing of his friendships with Norman French and Félix Mayol. Therefore she reacted strongly when informed of Maurice's involvement with Fréhel. Having made numerous inquiries, she had learned of the mannequin's mania for money, and of her reputation for breaking young men's hearts and bank balances. One or two of these hapless lovers, she had also discovered, had committed suicide rather than face total ruin, and La Louque was terrified that her son would end up in the same situation. Maurice, however, would not listen to her advice and he flatly refused to believe that Fréhel was as dangerous as everyone said she was, claiming that when they were together she had eyes for him alone. It never occurred to him, of course, to ask Fréhel where the fancy clothes came from, or how she could afford to pick up the tab whenever they dined at a plush restaurant or visited an expensive club. Being paid for was obviously more important to him than the fact that he was being led on by one of the classiest whores in Paris.

For several months, Fréhel followed Maurice everywhere and still managed to keep up a double life. When he was spending time with La Louque, she was usually with someone else. When he was working or rehearsing, she would hang around backstage, trying to work out if *he* was seeing someone else. Her jealousy, as well as her great beauty, drove him wild. André Rivollet, who was forbidden to use her actual name in his biography, referred to her as *'le mystère des fortifs'* and 'an hallucination of a lover, oscillating between danger and idolatry'. Colette, who met her when she accompanied Maurice to Lyons, where he had an engagement at the Casino Kursaal, found her 'attractive but uninteresting'. Chevalier, on the other hand, she despised; though she used him as the basis for her character Cavaillon in *La vagabonde*, what she wrote about him in her memoirs was not at all flattering.

> Maurice Chevalier is a tall young man who walks like a boneless human snake. His fists are too heavy for his frail wrists. Indeed, he is a fragile being, dumb and ever-conscious of his loneliness, and with an anxious, wandering pale-blue gaze which tells of acute neurasthenia.

Maurice is said to have been incensed by Colette's description of him. And yet, when he wrote about her many years later, he was unusually complimentary even though she had been dead for some years, so had he wished he could have been more 'honest'.

> Colette was a superb example of the 1908 beauty. She was plump, broad-shouldered and a trifle stocky. And yet she was without surplus fat, and she had a high, full, shapely bosom. A bosom which was – here goes – the most exciting and the most appetizing bosom in the world!

Maurice's first revue at the Folies-Bergère opened in September 1909, and sitting in the audience was the British impresario C B

Cochran, who had first seen him at the Eden Music Hall in the company of Ercole, the French agent of the American showman P T Barnum, who was always on the lookout for exciting new talent.

> I was interested in a young man with his hat pulled down to his ears, very thin and with a long neck, the length of which he exaggerated with a movement of throwing his head forward like a cock crowing. A few years later P-L Flers was producing a revue at the Folies in which he introduced tableaux representing English sporting prints, a number of which I had collected for him in London. I recognized 'Le Petit Jésus', and three of those taking part in the revue were to become great friends of mine later on. I saw him again a few years later, by which time he had discarded the garb of the café-concert comic, proving that he could still be funny with a clean face and a well-cut suit.

The three stars favoured by Cochran were Yvonne Printemps, at fifteen already a music-hall veteran, the conjuror Morton, and the star of the show, Jane Marnac. This beautiful brunette came very close to rivalling Mistinguett in popularity, wooing her audiences with cleverly rehearsed tomboy gestures. Then, quite suddenly, she gave up the musical revue for the legitimate stage and was a smash hit in a large number of productions, including Henri Bataille's *Manon*, which played at the Théâtre Madeleine. Cochran may have nurtured similar ideas for Maurice Chevalier. He certainly discussed the possibility of borrowing the star from Flers for a brief season – until, that is, he read Fernand Nozière's most recent criticism in *Le Figaro*.

> Who let this big gangling lout loose on the boards of the Folies-Bergère? Who hired this painfully unfunny comic to do his worst in what otherwise would be the best sketch in the whole revue? Chevalier's vulgarity and total lack of talent are too obvious to mention. One of his songs in particular is pure *filth*. He is, altogether, a repulsive exhibition!

This article gave Flers a brainwave. If his young protégé *was* to be regarded as a figure of controversy, then why not build on this side of his act by putting him into a revue with the most famous *horizontaliste* of them all, Gaby Deslys? The idea is said to have delighted Maurice, though not so one of P-L Flers's conditions, which was that he should rid himself of the troublesome Fréhel before signing the contract. For once, no doubt because a great deal of money was involved, Maurice began to take notice of what his mother and his friends were saying about Fréhel, and one evening after his show he had her followed to a nightclub, where she was observed 'having a good time' with one of his friends. Even so, he was reluctant to let her go, and only after someone convinced him that money had exchanged hands did he eventually give her her marching orders. Little did he know, at the time, that Fréhel would make him regret his decision time and time again over the next ten years.

As for Gaby Deslys, she was regarded on both sides of the Channel as the original 'tart with a heart'. A fickle young woman, she came to prominence initially only via the casting-couch; having achieved a measure of fame, she nurtured it by being in the wrong place at the right time and by toppling a monarchy, and finally became a living legend thanks to Harry Pilcer, the young man she brought back with her from America, who was responsible for their becoming for a time the most celebrated couple on both the French and the English stage. Born Gabrielle Caire in Marseilles in 1881, Gaby made her Parisian début at the Scala in 1903, but because of her strong southern accent she was booed off the stage. The following year she appeared in a sketch written for her by Jacques-Charles, turning the tables on her critics by scoring a great success. This brought her to the attention of George Edwardes, the director of the London Gaiety Theatre, who then cast her in *The New Aladdin*. In 1907 she partnered Max Dearly at Les Ambassadeurs, and in June of that year she met and fell for Prince Manoël of Portugal, then aged seventeen and on his first official visit to Paris. In December 1907 she returned to London to star in an operetta, and Manoël's letters were redirected to the theatre. It was here, in February 1908, that she received the news of the uprising in Lisbon which culminated in the death of King Don Carlos and his twenty-year-old heir, Lúis-Filipe, at the hands of the Republican Party. In Britain she also incurred Winston Churchill's wrath when a young peer of the realm, whose advances she had spurned, flung himself under the wheels of her car. Subsequently, Churchill ordered her to leave the country.

Back in Paris, Gaby starred in her own revue at the Moulin-Rouge during the winter of 1908, and it was here that Maurice saw her for the first time. She was still very much in love with Manoël, now king of Portugal, and would meet him secretly after her shows. Such was his infatuation that he gave her enough jewels to sell to enable her to purchase a house on the rue Henri de Bornier, although the house had already been paid for by Mariano, an Argentinian millionaire whom she had been using as a convenient meal-ticket for some time. Early in 1909 she was invited to play in a series of charity recitals in Lisbon, aimed at raising money for poor children. Manoël installed her in his private villa, and even there she cheated on him, having an affair with one of his best friends. Then she played a short season in Berlin, and this was followed by *Les caprices de Suzette* at the London Alhambra. It was here, in April 1910, that she was told about the proposed revue with Maurice Chevalier.

Sans rancune was written by P-L Flers and Rip – the latter's real name was Georges Thenon, and like Flers he was not averse to utilizing the casting-couch as a means of procuring dancers for his chorus or the occasional leading lady, although this time it does not appear to have been necessary. Nor did the lovely Gaby have to try too hard to woo Maurice into her bed, for she made a point of insisting that the preliminary rehearsals for the revue should take place at her house.

It was a very frustrating few weeks. Gaby was extremely demanding, and did not care how much a particular costume cost once she had decided to wear it. Her favourite designer was Paul Poiret, who, with Erté, was one of the most flamboyant men of his day. Claiming that he was a reincarnation of an Eastern prince, he held wild parties on his floating restaurant – a precursor of the present-day *bâteaux mouches* – which he camouflaged as painting exhibitions. Janet Flanner, an American correspondent who specialized in reporting some of the more controversial aspects of French society and show business, was once invited to his mansion in the faubourg Saint-Honoré, to a scene which Poiret had been playing for twenty years. Each of the guests was presented to mine host, immensely fat, wearing a sultan's robes and seated upon a throne of pure gold.

Three hundred guests stayed to see the dawn come up in his garden. Black slaves served dishes at tables 75 feet long, and paler female slaves lay feigning sleep on an immense golden staircase erected beneath the trees. De Max, the actor, recited poems, his costume shivering with the shaking of thousands of pearls. Among electric blossoms live parrots were chained to the bushes. Rug merchants, beggars and sweetmeat-sellers, hired to whine, strolled among the crowd. Thousands of shrimps were consumed, 300 lobsters, melons and goose livers, and 900 litres of champagne.

Costume-design was not Poiret's only art form, although some of his designs for the great *meneuses de revues* made him legendary. He designed an all-black, windowless room for Isadora Duncan and even made a film with Colette. And yet, despite his exorbitant fees, he squandered away his fortune and died almost penniless. For the revue with Maurice, Gaby asked for a short mauve muslin skirt, over which would be worn a gold-lamé basque and a plumed train. She also told Poiret to add some of the rarer feathers to the diamond collar which Manoël had given her, and he complemented the ensemble with a cloth-of-gold torque decorated with four bird-of-paradise feathers. Maurice accompanied her to the first fitting, and was present when she dropped the bombshell to Poiret that the costume would have to be ready within a week. Before the première of *Sans rancune* she had promised to do another charity gala in Lisbon.

Most of Gaby's friends were delighted at this sudden change in character, the fact that for the first time in her life she was doing something for others and not herself. Maurice, however, advised her not to make the trip. Not only did he disapprove of her relationship with Manoël; he also pointed out that Portugal, two years after the assassination of its last king, was again on the verge of revolt, and that, moreover, this time she alone was the cause of the unrest. For a while, Maurice seemed to be winning his battle. Gaby succumbed to an attack of influenza which laid her low for two weeks. Maurice, who had arranged for a Parisian press agency to receive and translate a number of Portuguese newspapers, was able to advise her that even Manoël's family had joined forces with his government in denouncing their affair, and that one of the revolutionary groups had vowed to assassinate her should she set foot in the country.

Gaby, however, was not to be swayed, and the première for *Sans rancune* was delayed for one week as she set off on her perilous journey. Her recital, in the poor district of Alcantara, was a disaster. As soon as she walked on to the stage she was greeted with a tirade of hisses and filthy words. Her first song, not a very sensible choice, was 'Je chante la gloire de la parisienne' and 100 or so of the spectators sitting in the stalls clambered over the orchestra to get at her. Some drew weapons, but incredibly the theatre management refused to call the police and Gaby had to be rescued from her dressing-room by Manoël's friends. The king himself had been locked in his bedroom by his mother, who, Gaby later learned, had been behind the plot to kill her. The actress had to be smuggled from the theatre into an old car and was eventually placed on a train which would take her safely to the Spanish border.

From here she sent a telegram to her mother, who at once contacted Maurice. The pair met her at the Gare d'Austerlitz, along with dozens of reporters and press photographers. Most of them had seen the lighter side of Gaby's affair with Manoël, and one wrote, 'Gaby Deslys is a latter-day national heroine, a Joan of Arc reborn on the banks of the River Tagus!' The great star posed amid a sea of flowers, but not with Maurice. When he took her back to her house and showed her the massive bunch of orchids sent by the Portuguese embassy she broke down and wept. Hidden among the blooms was a priceless diamond and emerald bracelet from Manoël. For Maurice, this was the last straw and when *Sans rancune* finally opened at the Théâtre des Capucines, it was without him.

Maurice was happier now than he had been for some time, working hard to perfect his act and in love with no one in particular – except his mother, who is alleged to have found Gaby Deslys even more obnoxious than Fréhel.

By this time Fréhel had, in fact, married her impresario, a young man called Edouard but who would be known to early French music-hall circles as Roberty. 'I settled for Roberty not because he was good-looking, but because he'd gone and got me pregnant,' she later said. Sadly, the child, who could quite easily have been anybody's, died, and for reasons known only to herself Fréhel blamed Maurice. A few months later, when she began making records, she chose a song called 'Comme une fleur', claiming that it told the story of how Maurice had seduced her against her will. This was, of course, pure fabrication.

> *Je lui donnais tout mon cœur,*
> *J'trouvais que la vie était douce,*
> *J'en fichais pas une secousse . . .*
> *Mais il effeuilla ma pudeur,*
> *Comme une fleur . . .*

> (I gave him my whole heart,
> I found that life was sweet,
> and didn't mind the shock . . .
> But he stripped away my petals of modesty,
> Like a flower . . .)

To compensate for Maurice's disappointment at not being able to work with Gaby Deslys, P-L Flers told him that he was organizing a 'surprise' revue, but as this would take some time, would he mind working Les Ambassadeurs with one of the young starlets from his recent season at the Folies-Bergère? Maurice was more than delighted, since the artiste in question was the sixteen-year-old Yvonne Wigniole. At the Folies she had been billed simply as 'La Petite Yvonne'. Everyone had been so taken with her sunny attitude towards life – despite the fact that her parents had split up and she alone was supporting her invalid mother – that they had baptized her 'Printemps'. Thus it was that as Yvonne Printemps she made her impact on Parisian audiences, supporting Maurice Chevalier and singing a handful of delightful little songs in her pleasant, soprano voice. Maurice said of her, 'For a Frenchwoman, her skills as a dancer are unique, and that pretty little mouth of hers was enough to damn all the saints in Ménilmontant!'

In spite of her tender years, Yvonne seems to have been yearning for a relationship with an older man, particularly as at this stage in her career most of her fellow artistes treated her like a child, bringing her gifts of sweets, pretty clothes and dolls. Madame Wigniole, however, though not always able to visit the theatre personally, did make a point of getting to know what was going on, and hovering constantly over her daughter's head was the invisible caution, 'Look by all means, but do not touch!'

Maurice was absolutely delighted when P-L Flers's long-awaited surprise was finally announced, even if he did have to read it on the noticeboard backstage at the Folies-Bergère, for his new partner was none other than the great comedienne Polaire.

This truly remarkable young woman, said by Colette to put 'all other women in the shade', was billed for a number of years as having the smallest waistline in Europe, measuring as it did an astonishing 15¾ inches. The two women were intimate friends which in itself was unusual, considering the actress's mania for never discussing her private life with anyone. Moreover, when Colette's phenomenally successful *Claudine* books were transferred to the stage, she insisted that Polaire play the title role every time. As a *diseuse*, she rivalled Yvette Guilbert, although her voice had no strength to speak of. Preferring harsh refrains with subject matter concerning drugs, debauchery and failed love, she would occasionally sing a request from someone in the audience wearing an expression, as Colette put it, 'as if sucking on a lemon'.

Initially, Maurice was terrified of her, especially when he learned that she had expressed disapproval of his style of dancing. Therefore, during the last three days leading up to their meeting he took lessons in step-dancing with the famous Jackson Boys. In effect, he had wasted his time, and his money. Polaire, when introduced to him, was bowled over by his youthful charm, dashing good looks and natural ability.

Paul Pitron, a café-concert comedian who later changed his name to Paul Derval, and who would in 1918 take over at the Folies-Bergère from Clément Bannel, admitted that he was madly in love with Polaire though always from a suitably safe distance, given her reputation for losing her temper.

If Colette was the typical beauty, Polaire was an exact reverse. She was so slim that she looked as though she was going to snap in two at any moment. She was as flat-chested as any boy and never used make-up except on her eyes – these were enormous, with incredibly long lashes. She was such a bag of nerves that her whole body seemed to quiver when she was on the stage.

Maurice's description of Polaire was less complimentary. 'She had a mouth full of gums, protruding teeth, and no tits. In our sketch together, I felt so utterly ridiculous.' This called for a lively gypsy dance, in which Polaire wore a short, low-cut taffeta gown by Landolff and black silk stockings. Later in the revue, she executed one of the immensely funny sketches which had made her a household name. This was '*Le portrait du petit chat*', which she always performed dressed as a little girl. One evening, however, the great Polaire slipped up and forgot her usually impeccable manners. Skipping on to the stage, she tripped over her skipping-rope. She sprawled headlong and all but toppled into the orchestra pit. Then, looking up, she muttered, 'Fuck me!' Henceforth, the phrase would be expected of her whenever she appeared on a stage, and Polaire rapidly endeared herself to a new section of the public.

Working with Polaire may not have been an enjoyable experience, but it was enormously advantageous as far as Maurice's career was concerned. Then, as if announcing the fact that his protégé had passed his 'test', P-L Flers pinned another announcement on the Folies-Bergère noticeboard. Maurice's next leading lady would be none other than Mistinguett.

Maurice had seen Mistinguett dancing the *valse-chaloupée* with Max Dearly at the Moulin-Rouge during the autumn of 1909. This was an extremely passionate piece in which traditional dance-steps were secondary to sensual body movements, in many ways transferring to the stage Dearly's violent machismo, thus far seen only in the bedroom. The action took place in a cheap bar, with a slut entering and tucking the night's takings into the top of her stocking. There then followed a battle with Dearly the pimp – a lengthy tirade of slaps and kicks until, tossing her over his shoulder like a sack of coal, the man left with his prize. With Mistinguett and Dearly the drama of the *chaloupée* had been acted out for real; away from the theatre, they barely spoke to each other. More tension followed early in 1910 when the couple were invited to play in London. Mistinguett refused point-blank, and Dearly had taken his new protégée, Marie-Loiuse Damien. A few years later, as Damia, she would be hailed as the greatest of the French *réaliste* singers, and Mistinguett would hate her for the rest of her life.

Maurice had not, however, seen much of Mistinguett on a personal level since the meeting at the Eldorado. They did not move in the same circles socially, and in any case she had been tied up in a battle with the courts and a certain Monsieur de Lima in an attempt to get back their son Léopold, whom de Lima had seized and spirited out of the country to Brazil. Furthermore, while Maurice was enthusing to friends and colleagues that Mistinguett was 'my inaccessible star', the lady herself was raucously dismissing him as 'gormless and effeminate'. Her opinion of him changed, of course, once she saw how he had developed physically.

Such was Mistinguett's power in the music-hall that she was given full licence over the new production at the Folies-Bergère. This allowed her to audition and employ the cast, from co-star down to chorus. Her methods were distinctive, and would remain so for another forty years. The girls had to be tall, leggy and, above everything else, unattached. The boys had to be good-looking, slim and strong, and if they were homosexual, this was to their advantage. Gay men, Minstinguett declared, were more reliable than the 'other' sort in that they loved in-house relationships but never got anyone pregnant. She also found it very much of a personal quest to attempt to convert a gay man back to what she believed was 'the straight and narrow' – invariably failing. Roger Normand, my godfather, who danced with her in 1943 and whose impersonation of Mistinguett was even more lifelike than the real thing, told me:

Miss adored beauty in a man, but she encouraged them to get off with each other by some of the tricks she used to play. You remember how she used to go under the bridge at Enghien with the local *voyous*, armed with a ruler and a notebook? Well, she sometimes did the same thing backstage at the theatre. In my day, a devishly pretty guy called Jean Clément always walked off with the first prize. And it was woe betide anyone who couldn't manage to stand to attention –

they got the sharp end of the ruler. As for Chevalier, Miss reckoned that he was like the dancer Harry Pilcer. In other words, she couldn't get it all to fit on to her ruler!

According to Mistinguett herself, P-L Flers was against hiring Maurice for his production, and had suggested Max Dearly. This led to an outburst in his office in which she threatened to boycott the revue unless the younger man was hired for exactly the same fee. In the end, Flers let her have her own way. In order to compete with Max Dearly and Marie-Louise Damien, who had scored a triumph with the *chaloupée* in London and were now filling the Théâtre de Châtelet, Mistinguett had devised a dance of her own, the *valse-renversante*. Though not as rough and damaging to the partner as the *chaloupée*, the new sketch was hazardous to whoever was sitting on or near the stage while it was taking place. The setting was a typical Parisian *bistrot* with tables, chairs, crates, the bar and several customers wearing street clothes. The dance began with the pair standing on a table, their feet sending bottles, glasses and the ashtray flying. Then, leaping down from the table, they tore around the stage like things possessed, executing a succession of cartwheels and leaps and sending every stick of furniture, not to mention the spectators, careering into the wings. By this time, all that was left was the carpet, and the dance would end with Maurice and Mistinguett at opposite ends of this. Then, after a final couple of somersaults they would fling themselves on to the floor and roll themselves up in the carpet as the curtain fell.

The first time this happened in rehearsals, Miss ended up with a split lip and more than her share of bruises. During the next rehearsal, she got carried away. Squeezed up against Maurice in the dusty carpet, she unbuttoned his flies to find out if the rumours she had heard about his being 'well endowed' were true. Maurice is alleged to have called her a filthy little harlot, though needless to say he enjoyed the experience and expected it to happen again at the next rehearsal.

Mistinguett summed Maurice up in just four words: '*Il a du fluide*.' That she worshipped the very ground he walked on goes without saying. The huge paragraphs about him in her memoirs make very poetic reading, although from Maurice's own angle the relationship was more complicated. There is no doubt whatsoever that initially he *did* love her; the sentimentality of her memoirs speaks for itself. Sex and success, however, did progress beyond the bedroom and Maurice knew from the very start that he was not indispensable. The lovers in Mistinguett's life, before and after her Chevalier phase, always had to submit to competition being flaunted in their faces, often in public. This woman, though arguably the greatest star the music-hall has ever known, was absolutely incorrigible and never made any secret of her appetite for mean and moody men. Nor did she act like a lady when things were not going her way. Maurice, like everyone else, had to swear that he had eyes for her alone, while turning a blind eye himself to tantrums, bad language and occasionally almost psychotic attacks of jealousy.

Mistinguett credited herself with teaching Maurice how to behave in public – how to dress, how to eat, how to drink and, above all, how to walk without mincing. She also persuaded him to take her to his new apartment on the boulevard de Strasbourg to meet La Louque. Strangely, the two women got on well, and there were regular family get-togethers around the dinner table. Mistinguett loved every moment of it, and called the period her second youth. What she did not know was that Maurice had resumed his affair with Fréhel (after the death of her baby the *chanteuse* had left her husband, although he was still acting as her impresario). And yet in spite of her torrid affair with Momo, as she called him, Mistinguett never had any particular desire to live with him. She was also very quick to scotch rumours that they were planning to make their union permanent by marrying. 'I'm already married – to my public!' she would say. This, of course, was true, and so over the next two years the pair spent much of their time furthering their respective careers.

The *valse-renversante* was filmed by Charles Pathé, although no decent print seems to have survived. At around this time, June 1912, Maurice was starring with the future film-actor Raimu and Régine Flory at the Cigale. In the November, Mistinguett appeared with Yvonne Printemps at the Folies-Bergère, where Maurice was conspicuous by his absence. P-L Flers had for some reason decided not to renew his contract, and so he returned to the Cigale. Meanwhile, Mistinguett was playing in an operetta, *Milord l'arsouille*, at the Scala. There then followed a temporary period of unemployment during which Maurice appeared in a number of amateur boxing contests aimed at raising money for Ris-Orangis, the retired actors' home which had recently been founded by Dranem.

Being officially named as Mistinguett's 'main lover' in May 1913, an announcement which coincided with the ending of her season at the Scala, would do Maurice few favours professionally – for now, he was told, he would be expected to make his own way up the fickle music-hall ladder. Whereas Mayol had forked out money to move Maurice *up* the bill in the hope of acquiring his sexual favours, La Miss paid theatre directors – most especially P-L Flers – *not* to hire him in halls where she was appearing because, she claimed, another success like the *valse-renversante* would only make him too big for his boots! Normally, this would have made sense: overnight sensations were extremely uncommon in the French and British music-halls and artistes were expected to work their way through the ranks before seeing their names in large letters or lights. Much as she is supposed to have loved him, of course, Mistinguett was being typically selfish, terrified of him getting more attention than herself, and that she chose to be partnered instead by a series of less-talented leading men almost forgotten today – Dorville, Morton, Boucot – was only doubly insulting for up and coming young star.

'Maurice needs to work a little more on his acts,' Mistinguett told a press conference, the evening the curtain came down on her Scala revue. 'He isn't ready for the big time, not for the moment!'

It was a phrase that would be repeated many times over the next seven years.

Operation Villefleur

In mid-May 1913 Maurice and Mistinguett spent several days in London. Mistinguett knew the British capital well. Some ten years before she had stayed there with her baby son when she had played La Môme Pee-Oui in a disastrous production by C B Cochran, who had since vowed never to have anything to do with her again. For Maurice, the trip was a revelation. Since his début at the Trois Lions, he had been fascinated by English entertainers, and he was looking forward to seeing some of his favourites on their home ground. He also badly needed to escape, for a little while at least, from the constant hustle and bustle surrounding Mistinguett. As Roger Normand has said, 'Whenever Miss arrived anywhere, they always treated it as though the circus had come to town.' So each morning Maurice rose long before she did and spent an hour or so happily strolling through the streets of London, confident that no one would recognize him. It was, he confessed, his only chance of getting any rest, for although he had informed Mistinguett that she must take her pick of the sumptuous shows, plays and revues on offer, she insisted that they saw them all. Incredibly, they spent more than ten hours each day watching everything from *Richard III* to an impersonation of Gaby Deslys and Harry Pilcer – then by far the most popular duo on the London stage – by a couple of children at a local school.

Mistinguett and Maurice adored London, but for the time being both had contracts to fulfil in Paris. Maurice had signed for a new season at the Cigale, and Mistinguett had been engaged to appear in a film.

Between May 1913 and the end of 1916, Mistinguett made no fewer than fourteen films, most apparently so bad that even she was pleased that the prints did not survive. One or two, however, were better than average. In Albert Capellani's *Fleur de pavé*, she played an orphan who, after leading the harshest life possible, ends up as a successful actress. Her co-star was Prince, one of the unsung heroes of the French silent cinema, who in his hey-day, between 1910 and 1914, made four films every month. It was while shooting this little melodrama that Maurice accused her of sleeping with Prince, whom he slapped outside the film-lot. Mistinguett decided to get away from Paris for a while, but first of all there was the question of the 'duel', for Prince had not taken kindly to Maurice's attack. With a great deal of behind-the-scenes publicity, this showdown was organized to take place in the rue Saulnier, outside the actors' entrance to the Folies-Bergère. Paul Derval recorded the event.

At the appointed time, half the theatre folk of Paris were lurking tactfully in doorways as Maurice's adversary, pale with fury and impatience, paced up and down, muttering dire threats under his breath. Maurice appeared, wearing boxing gloves and a sweater. He tried to reason with his rival, but the man refused to calm down. Squaring his shoulders, Maurice advanced on him. A right hook, a straight left and a resounding uppercut, and his opponent lay groggy and bleeding on the pavement. Mistinguett emerged from a doorway, clasping her pet monkey to her breast, sailing forth to meet the victor.

Mistinguett, knowing for certain that Maurice was still seeing Fréhel, made various attempts to arouse his jealousy, though she went about it in such a way that she came dangerously close to losing him altogether. In those days the most fashionable resort in France was Trouville. Mistinguett opted for Deauville, which had yet to be discovered, because some of her more snobbish acquaintances had condemned it as '*ennuyeux à mourir*'. When she arrived there during the summer of 1913, Félix Mayol had already agreed to take part in a devious plot to bait Maurice. First of all, they began spreading rumours that they had just had a violent quarrel, and of course the town was immediately invaded by the press, hoping for some exclusive. What they discovered there absolutely astonished them. A 'press conference' had been arranged in the form of a dinner. The guests included the actor Louis Verneuil, the Russian bass Chaliapin, the songwriter Gaston Gabaroche, and a young journalist called Maurice Prax. During the meal, the two stars glared at each other constantly. Prax later reported that the atmosphere was extremely uncomfortable because everyone around the table had something to hide. Finally, Mistinguett banged her fist on the table and screamed for Mayol to leave. Rising, the comedian explained that his quarrel with Mistinguett had been little more than a lovers' tiff. Miss, never less than a great actress of the Bernhardt tradition, then burst into tears and craved forgiveness, after which her 'lover' got down on one knee and asked her to marry him. The act was so convincing that even Louis Verneuil, who *was* Mistinguett's lover off and on until 1917, believed it, and of course Prax's story appeared on the front page of his newspaper the next day,

LATEST SENSATION! MISTINGUETT AND MAYOL TO MARRY!
Félix Mayol, the well-known artiste, has fallen in love – with Mistinguett. The celebrated star claims he has always been the man of her dreams. Sensational, but true!

What Mistinguett hoped, of course, was that Maurice would be grossly offended by her 'relationship' with a man so obviously over-the-top in his effeminacy. In fact, he could not have cared less, although he did contact her to say that he would be willing to forgive her for cheating on him with Prince as long as she returned to Paris at once. This was not possible as she had a number of social and professional engagements there. Neither did the press believe her when she tried to explain that her 'marriage' to Mayol had been but a publicity stunt. Ultimately, Mayol himself tried to rectify the problem by inserting a piece in one of the local newspapers. This, in the form of a letter to Dranem, succeeded only in making matters worse.

My dear old chap! As one of the latest wonders of Tangoville let me explain why I have decided to give Mistinguett up as a bad job. Mind you, at first I *was* willing. I bumped into this deliciously alluring creature at the Potinière, and we had a tender conversation. We decided to get hitched – just like that. Then I thought about my public. You know what they're like! They would have expected me to have kids. So I told Miss that I wanted to remain a spinster. She was so understanding, old chap. We're happy together – and I shan't be getting into the family way after all.

Mistinguett did not see the funny side of Mayol's article and, cancelling her engagements and leaving even Louis Verneuil in the lurch, she packed her bags in the middle of the night and drove herself back to Paris. Several months later she patched up her differences with Mayol, and the pair remained close friends until his death in 1941. Her affair with Maurice was resumed, as if nothing had ever happened. Their happiness, however, lasted but a few weeks before the first in a chain of events which would later be described by both as 'our three years of sheer hell'.

In August 1913 Mistinguett opened at the Théâtre des Variétés in Alfred Capus's *L'institut de beauté*. Two weeks into the run she collapsed with stomach pains. Her doctor suspected appendicitis, but, as she had never suffered a day's illness in her life, Mistinguett refused to believe him, and, of course, with her there was no question of the cancelling the show. There was more talk of a joint revue with Maurice, but this was shelved when Mistinguett tried to persuade P-L Flers at the Folies-Bergère to double the salary Maurice had been paid before: 'Chevalier's good, but not that good,' came the curt reply. So for the time being Maurice returned to minor revues while Mistinguett tried to work out a viable way of improving his lot in the music-hall. She herself opened at the Olympia towards the end of the year in *La revue légère*, an extravaganza which certainly did not live up to expectations when she collapsed again. This time she was rushed to hospital, and compelled to undergo an emergency operation for a gangrenous appendix. Although she was deemed lucky to be alive, two days after surgery she rose from her bed to assist the nurses. The hospital was short-staffed because of a flu epidemic and in her memoirs she records movingly how one of her patients, a young man of nineteen, actually died in her arms. She had barely recovered from this ordeal when La Louque contacted her to say that Maurice had been called up for military service. He had been prevented from visiting her because of the epidemic, and now he felt 'too emotionally drained' to say goodbye.

Discharging herself from the hospital, Mistinguett spent two weeks with La Louque at the apartment on the boulevard de Strasbourg. From here she contacted Maurice's camp at Belfort, only to be told that she had no chance of visiting her lover, and even less of 'buying' him out of the army. The saving grace at Belfort for Maurice was a handsome, twenty-two-year-old soldier called Maurice Yvain. Their friendship would endure for many years and was especially important in that it resulted in Yvain meeting the formidably talented Albert Willemetz. Between them, this pair collaborated on literally hundreds of songs, many of them massive hits for Mistinguett and Chevalier. 'Dîtes-moi, ma mère', in which Maurice reflects upon his curiosity as a child, was first conceived in the army barracks at Belfort.

> *Quand j'étais petit*
> *J'étais naïf, j'étais gentil,*
> *Et chaque dimanche à mes sortis*
> *J'interrogais ma mère:*
> *'Dîtes-moi, ma mère,*
> *Pourquoi les chiens dans la rue*
> *Se montent dessus?'*

> (When I was small
> I was naive, a good boy,
> and on Sunday outings
> I interrogated my mother:
> 'Mother, tell me why
> The dogs mount each other
> In the street?')

The two Maurices talked later in life of their immense popularity among the other soldiers at Belfort. This might have been true to begin with, when the pair organized singalongs in the mess-room. They were, however, soon shown considerable favouritism, being invited to dine in the commanding officer's quarters, and while the others endured unpalatable rations of, at best, corned beef,

Maurice and his friend ate sausages, beefsteak and foie gras, and drank only the finest wines. That they deserved some small privilege for keeping up the morale of their fellows at a time when war clouds were gathering cannot be denied, though there must have been indignation from those who thought that 'star' treatment was being taken a little too far.

Back in Paris, Mistinguett was going through another crisis. Complications had set in after her operation and once again she was rushed to a clinic. This time she had a hysterectomy, and was reported to be on the brink of death. This gave Maurice real cause for concern, and maybe this time money did exchange hands, for he was transferred from Belfort to Melun, which was only a fifty-minute drive from the centre of Paris. A few days later, Mistinguett left the clinic and booked herself into a nursing-home at nearby Bois-le-Roi. Maurice had no difficulty whatsoever persuading his commanding officer to give him time off to visit her, and she reminisced over this happy time in her memoirs.

> Each evening they allowed us to dine together, and we were truly happy! Provisionally, we had few worries. For several hours, perhaps the most beautiful hours of my life, we were just like any other lovers. All our problems had vanished, enabling us to relax in the regulated security of our love.

Mistinguett and Maurice's temporary idyll was brought to an end by the dramatic event at Sarajevo on 28 June 1914, when a young patriot named Gavrilo Princip assassinated Archduke Franz Ferdinand, igniting a spark which would subsequently set fire to the world. This was followed by the murder of the French pacifist Jean Jaurès, by the aptly named fanatic Raoul Villain, at the Café du Croissant in the rue Montmartre. A few days later, on 1 August, mobilization began. Three days after that, Austria declared war on Serbia, which successfully appealed to the Russians for aid. France joined the side of her ally, and the men of the 31st Infantry marched off to fight.

La Louque and I were there to see him off, but after all my catastrophes I could think of nothing to say. They did allow us one last kiss before giving orders for the march to begin. Then, through eyes blinded by tears, we watched them disappear into the distance. Maurice's handkerchief was still waving, and then I lost sight of him and I knew that my soul had just died.

Mistinguett returned to Paris, to complete her season at the Olympia which had been curtailed because of her illness. It was not a success, and for a while she left Paris to concentrate, yet again, on getting her son back. Léopold had been illegally adopted by members of the de Lima family living in the Midi, but for some reason she had never taken them to court. For a while, she was reunited with him and the pair spent a happy few weeks in Deauville – as happy as Mistinguett could be without Maurice. Then the child had to be handed back and this had such a bad effect on her that she became ill again, suffering what appears to have been a nervous breakdown. Maurice never found out about this. Always on the move, Mistinguett's letters never caught up with him.

On 21 August Maurice's company halted at Cons-la-Grandville in the Meurthe-et-Moselle district. German troops had been spotted in the vicinity of nearby Cutry, and the commanding officer planned to take them by surprise. The manoeuvre backfired and very soon Maurice and his friends found themselves encircled. Though the men of the 31st Infantry were going down like flies, the commanding officer steadfastly refused to surrender, and soon only a handful remained. Maurice himself was felled by a bullet which passed through his pack before entering his chest and grazing his right lung. A German medic offered emergency treatment on the spot, almost certainly saving his life, while the surviving members of his detachment gave themselves up. The next morning the captives were unceremonially bundled into the back of a cattle truck and transported to the internment camp at Alten Grabow, near Magdeburg, some 75 miles south-west of Berlin. Here, with their families not knowing whether they were alive or dead, they would remain incarcerated, and outnumbered by often belligerent Belgian and Russian prisoners of war, for more than two years.

Although the prisoners were not on the whole badly treated, they were poorly fed. During the first few weeks they were made to eat cattle-feed, and their diet was changed only when several local farmers handed over the season's failed crop of blighted red cabbage. There was also a severe epidemic of typhus which all but wiped out some areas of the camp, and spasmodic outbreaks of dysentery. This resulted in Maurice being ousted from his bed in the infirmary, so although his wound healed over and he made a full recovery, the offending bullet was never removed. Like most of the other inmates, he also had his head shaved because the camp was riddled with lice and vermin. Even so, once he had convinced himself that he would have to put up with the indignity of being a prisoner of war, there were some lighter moments. He was befriended by a soldier from Durham called Ronald Kennedy, who had once seen him at the Folies-Bergère. Kennedy was also an enthusiast of the British music-hall, and it did not take the pair very long to discover that they had much in common. When Maurice commented that one of his ambitions had always been to sing on the London stage, not in French but in English, Kennedy agreed to teach him 'the language of Shakespeare', as Maurice later referred to it. This probably explains his dreadful vowel pronunciation, a fault which he successfully turned into an endearing quality.

Many years later, Kennedy would remember their meeting with affection, explaining in an interview for the BBC that he had been greeted with delight by a British sergeant-major who was feeling rather embarrassed by the persistent requests of a young Frenchman to teach him English. Kennedy added that Chevalier was a splendid pupil, already dreaming of a mighty career in America. 'The first time Maurice sang in English, in the dimly lit barrack room, the English lads lifted the roof with their applause.' Kennedy concluded.

Maurice's fake-seeming French accent when speaking or singing in English, and certain of his mannerisms off and on the stage, would of course be criticized for another fifty years. The controversial American author Martin Greif, in his racy and hilariously readable *The Gay Book of Days*, wrote:

So much did Chevalier ooze exported 'Frenchiness' that one began to suspect that the accent itself was fake, and that he had probably been born in Cedar Rapids. There was something of the runny cheese about him even in his youth, and he perfected a rakish wink . . . which was only slightly to the right of Liberace's. But the ladies loved Maurice, and that is all that mattered!

Professionally, Maurice's most important encounter at Alten Grabow was with a young man who arrived about a month after he did, Joë Bridge, a brilliant caricaturist who had already scored a hit in Paris with risqué pieces such as *Gueule d'empeigne*. The relationship they formed was alleged to have progressed beyond the platonic. With his powerful physique, blond hair, blue eyes and, above all, his extrovert personality, he reminded Maurice of his old friend Norman French. Joë was an expert boxer, had won prizes in fencing competitions and was also on friendly terms with the Germans. When he informed the guard in charge of his hut that he would like an audience with the kommandant, this was granted without too much fuss. He told the kommandant that a concert party would boost everyone's morale no end, and permission was given to go ahead. The Chevalier–Bridge acting troupe was formed, which, with his customary good humour, Bridge named 'La Boîte à Grabow', and over the next eighteen months the officers and prisoners at Alten Grabow were entertained by a series of music-hall sketches and satirical revues. As the latter were usually performed in poor English, the Germans did not know that they were being lampooned. Joë also made some 'pin money' with comic sketches of the kommandant – which he sold to the German officers! (His best-known caricature, however, dates from 1946, and depicts Chevalier in his famous *chapeau de paille* and with his equally famous jutting lip.) Maurice, of course, was the star of the show, singing old songs like 'Youp-youp larifla' and 'Sur mon bourriquet', while Joë Bridge played the piano, or danced around pulling faces and doing impressions. 'Direct from the Paris Opera' there was a dancer, Aveline, and a young actor called Louis Tunc added culture to the evening. Glamour was provided by 'Les Girls' – in other words, the youngest, prettiest members of the troupe, who put on drag and after lights-out 'entertained those soldiers who liked that sort of thing'.

Meanwhile, on 5 November 1915 Mistinguett appeared in a charity show at the Paris Olympia and broke down in front of an audience of wounded soldiers. Fourteen months after waving Maurice off, she still did not know whether he was alive or dead, and apart from a brief tour of Italy she had scarcely left La Louque for a moment. Towards the end of the month, she was approached by the writer Michel Carré and offered the lead in a new revue, *Taisez-vous, méfiez-vous*, or, in other words, *Shut up and Watch Out*. The show opened on 21 December at the Scala, not far from the Chevalier apartment. Alternating between the roles of an old has-been café-concert *chanteuse* and a chimney-sweep, she was an enormous success, and incredibly, between performances, she found time to make yet another film, *Mistinguett détective*, hailed as one of the best French silent films ever made.

It was one hour before going on stage at the Scala on the evening of 6 January that she was brought the distressing news of Maurice's plight within the prison camp at Alten Grabow. There was absolutely no question of 'the show must go on', and for the first and last time in her career Mistinguett cancelled a performance. She was unsure of the exact location of Maurice's camp, but she did know precisely what to do. The message had told her, without mincing words, that Maurice had had his hands cut off and his eyes put out. She was sensible enough to realize that this was probably an exaggeration meant to worry her, but on top of this she acknowledged the fact that in spite of his bravado and fighting skills, Maurice was not a regular he-man. She knew that if he had not been hurt physically, then mentally he would have been going through anguish.

The following afternoon, Mistinguett set off for Geneva, which, apart from housing the headquarters of the International Red Cross, was also a hotbed of counter-espionage. She had already worked with the young Dutch-Javanese dancer born Gertrud Zelle, who as Mata Hari had made a name for herself all over Europe, and when she set off for Switzerland Mata Hari's contacts with the German Secret Service were on the train. Thus, when the train pulled up at a level crossing outside Sens, it was boarded by

French soldiers carrying bayonets, and Mistinguett was arrested. Though she was unafraid of admitting the nature of her mission – among her papers was a document bargaining for Maurice's release – the soldiers ridiculed her. She was made to strip naked, was examined for 'evidence' and, after being given an old army sweater with which to cover herself, was locked up in a shed for the night; the commanding officer, she was told, was too busy to see her because he was in the middle of an important poker game. The next morning she demanded to see the local commissaire de police. Here, fate came to her rescue, for the commissaire knew her personally: many years before he had worked as a gendarme in Enghien. She was given back her clothes, and put up in a hotel for the night. The next morning, the same soldiers who had arrested her escorted her to the railway station. She tricked them into believing that she had had her handbag stolen, and while they were chasing after the 'thief', she sneaked on to the train bound for Geneva. Here she was granted an interview with the director of the Red Cross. He agreed to help her and booked her into the Hôtel Beaurivage. Three days later she was told that Maurice was safe and reasonably healthy, and at Alten Grabow. Simply having his address did not satisfy her, of course, so she arranged for a food parcel to be sent on to him and returned to Paris to take matters further. She had known Emile Buré, private secretary to the cabinet minister Aristide Briand, for some time. Briand's philosophy was that progress could be better made not by winning wars but by preventing them; even so, he considered it unfair to treat Maurice as a special case when thousands like him were in exactly the same predicament. Instead, he suggested that Mistinguett pen an appeal to the pacifist Spanish king.

Mistinguett and Alfonso XIII were already good friends. He and his queen had visited Paris in 1913, and one of the non-political highlights of their trip had been a personal invitation to see Mistinguett's new revue at the Théâtre des Variétés. After the show they had had supper together, and Mistinguett had been impressed when the handsome young king informed her that his pastimes included tennis, polo and making love to pretty women. He also showed her, during the course of the evening, some of the scars he had received during the numerous attempts on his life. The worst of these had taken place on his wedding day in 1906, when a fanatic had tossed a floral bouquet containing a bomb into the royal procession, killing seventy-five people. Mistinguett had expressed her disappointment, however, when after the repast Alfonso declined to accompany her back to her apartment on the boulevard des Capucines.

Now Alfonso worked quickly. He wrote to Mistinguett within the week informing her that 'Operation Villefleur' had already begun, and that Maurice would soon be released. Mistinguett then wrote Chevalier a long letter, but instead of mailing it or sending it by courier she decided to deliver it to the kommandant at Alten Grabow. She then set about ensuring the safety of her loved ones. Her mother and brother were brought over from Enghien, while La Louque fetched Mistinguett's son Léopold from the de Limas. The next morning she escorted everyone to the villa she had rented at Paramé. The enemy were now within 60 miles of Paris, and rumour had it that the city would soon be occupied. Then, on the outskirts of Paramé, she was arrested for the second time. For a month the local police had been searching for a female spy who had last been seen driving a grey Chrysler similar to Mistinguett's. Considering what happened next, it seems very likely that she was who everyone thought she was. This time she was subjected to a humiliating interrogation by the commissaire de police, and given a body search. She handled the situation well, giving away nothing, and was allowed to drive on to Geneva. Here, the message was waiting from Maurice: 'Tell Monsieur de Villefleur that I thank him from the bottom of my heart.'

Operation Villefleur had succeeded, and Mistinguett was told that Maurice would be released by the end of the month. As for her adventure in Geneva, this was far from over. At the Hôtel Beaurivage she was approached by a representative of the German ambassador and an attempt was made to pressgang her into spying against France. It was the only way, he told her, that she would see Maurice again. For twenty-four hours she agonized over what to do, become a traitor or lose the man she loved. Luckily, there was no need to choose. She told her story to an agent from the Deuxième Bureau and accepted a more 'lucrative' offer: while pretending to spy for the enemy, she would be working for the French!

Nothing whatsoever is known of Mistinguett's activities for the Deuxième Bureau, though we do now know some of the dangers she was exposed to. One evening she was invited to dine with the German chief of counter-espionage, revealed as a double agent and promptly arrested. Her trial was held in secret, and she was sentenced to face the firing squad. Her life was seemingly saved by the fact that a number of Germans had been taken hostage by her patriots in Geneva, including the wife and daughter of the Kaiser's secretary. Mistinguett was released, examined to check if she was still in good health and allowed to return to Paris. Two weeks later, in October 1916 and on the eve of the second phase of the Battle of Verdun, she and her lover were reunited.

One would have expected Maurice to have shown at least some gratitude towards this remarkably courageous woman who, in poor health at the time, had risked her own life in order to save his. He did nothing of the kind. Indeed, he had been back in Paris only a few weeks when he began revealing his true colours. Because the newspapers had reported nothing about Mistinguett's Swiss adventure, Maurice was able to circulate stories that he and Joë Bridge had organized their own 'escape' from the prison camp by falsifying their identity papers and posing as nurses, thus enabling them to be transferred to the Red Cross. Maurice had in fact assisted the doctors at Alten Grabow, mostly in the capacity of washing bodies in preparation for burial, or carrying the vessel for the priest to offer last rites. His repatriation, however, was solely due to the efforts of Mistinguett, and though their affair lingered on for several more years, she never forgave him.

I will never forget the train and the railway station that day. My heart was aglow, after twenty-six months of separation. At first we were no longer Mistinguett and Maurice Chevalier, but two reunited lovers. Then he asked me to leave him alone, and I thought I understood why. His spirit had been broken by his captivity and he knew that he would have to go back to square one with his career, and as he had no money of his own, he had no alternative but to accept my hospitality. I never minded helping him, and I tried to ignore the fact that when he finally found the one thing he had been searching for, he would not be sharing it with me.

Mistinguett had been offered another season at the Théâtre des Variétés, scheduled to open at the end of the year provided the terms were to her liking. Naturally she insisted that Maurice should be her leading man – for once she was even prepared to allow him shared top-billing. This was an unexpected volte-face, one where Mistinguett may be accused of allowing her heart to overrule her business sensibilities. Yet the directors were not keen. It was not simply a question of them believing Chevalier was not good enough and, after such a lengthy absence from the stage, quite possibly forgotten by many people; Mistinguett may have been an insufferable martinet, but they believed she was entitled to a little respect from the ingrate she had risked life and limb to bring home in one piece, only to have him cheat on her at once, first with Joë Bridge, then with a number of chorus girls.

Initially, the directors tried a tactful approach, suggesting that in view of his poor physical state, Maurice might not be strong enough to get through a major season. This she 'sorted' by having him examined by the best doctors in Paris and pronounced fit. Yet still the directors refused to have anything to do with him. Therefore, informing them that she would not set foot in their 'shit-tip of a theatre' again, Mistinguett called Raphael Beretta and Léon Volterra, giving them one month to find something for herself and Maurice in one or other of their establishments – either that or suffer the consequences, such was her power – and left Paris for a tour of Italy.

Two Dogs Fighting Over
the Same Bone

Had it not been for Mistinguett's generosity and support, it is very doubtful that Maurice Chevalier's 'second' career would have got off the ground. His spirits were broken, and so indeed was his earlier rapport with the public. In December 1916 he gave a series of recitals at the Casino Montparnasse, his old stamping ground, but even here he was poorly received. He was then sent on a brief tour of the provinces, where matters improved slightly, and he was engaged by Léon Volterra and Raphael Beretta to play two weeks at the Paris Olympia. This, however, proved such a disaster that Beretta vowed never to work with him again. In short, Maurice's sort of act had gone out of fashion.

During the winter of 1916–17, Mistinguett found herself turning down several promising revues because the writers and producers would not give Maurice second billing. As a last resort, she went to see the directors of the Folies-Bergère, who just happened to be Volterra and Beretta! The former was talking of renovating the Casino, whose takings had slumped since the start of the war. He himself did not mind Maurice, and acknowledged that it would take him a while to get back on his feet. But Beretta loathed him, and when Mistinguett barged into his office to ask why, she caught him in the worst mood possible. The impresario flatly refused to have Maurice anywhere near his theatre, let alone inside it. Mistinguett knew, of course, that in persisting she would be putting her own career on the line as far as any future productions with the Folies-Bergère were concerned, for neither of the new directors was as sympathetic to her as P-L Flers had been. She informed Beretta that Maurice was so desperate for money that he would be willing to work for 300 francs a night. Beretta retorted that he was not worth fifty. When his partner remarked, tongue in cheek, that Maurice's fee could be provided by supplying Mistinguett with one dress less for the prospective revue, Beretta actually compromised and 100 francs was offered on a take-it-or-leave-it basis. Mistinguett accepted the deal. She herself made Maurice's salary up to the 300 mark, and so far as is known he was never enlightened as to the fact.

La grande revue des Folies-Bergère opened on 15 March 1917. In effect, it managed to preserve the passionate side of Maurice's affair with Mistinguett for several months, although within a week of the première both had begun searching for more stable bedmates. Mistinguett was still seeing Louis Verneuil, and Maurice spent a lot of time with Joë Bridge, who had been given a small part in the revue. There was also an incident when she called on him at his apartment in the boulevard de Strasbourg and found a pair of pink knickers on his bedroom floor. Mistinguett reciprocated by instructing him that henceforth he must not enter *her* apartment unless there was a scarlet ribbon tied to the railings of her balcony. There was also a piece of paper pinned to her door which read, 'Enter, but at your own risk!' And in spite of all this, Mistinguett persisted in telling all and sundry that she was madly in love with her co-star.

At the Folies-Bergère Maurice and Mistinguett were clearly in their element, giving dozens of curtain-calls every night to an adoring public who knew absolutely nothing about the goings-on behind the scenes. According to Paul Derval, the stars would pose for photographers outside the theatre smiling vivaciously, only to begin tearing one another to pieces the moment the stage doors closed behind them. Relations between the two directors were equally strained, so much so that half-way through the run of the revue Volterra moved out of the theatre and finally took over the Casino. He then teamed up with Jacques-Charles, who was in the middle of writing what he declared would be the most exciting musical revue of all time. This was *Laissez-les tomber*.

Jacques-Charles consulted Mistinguett with regard to playing the lead in the new revue and she agreed to sign the contract, provided Maurice could be her co-star. Volterra, now no longer on Maurice's side after the débâcle with Raphael Beretta, would have nothing to do with the idea and even accused Maurice of sponging off Mistinguett. And, of course, the great star was so infatuated by her lover, in spite of their constant bickering, that she refused to work in any production without him. Even so, she kept Jacques-Charles hanging on for several weeks, until most of the costumes had been designed, before turning him down flat. As a last resort, the writer and Léon Volterra made plans to go to London, where they hoped they might be able to negotiate some kind of contract with Gaby Deslys and her American partner, Harry Pilcer. They left Paris during the first week of July 1917 after borrowing two soldiers' uniforms from the costume department at the Folies-Bergère. At Calais they boarded a steamer which was full of English troops on their way home. They then hired a car and drove up to London, where in fine style they used a suite at the Savoy Hotel as their base.

Deslys and Pilcer were packing the Globe Theatre every night with *Suzette*, and were contracted to stay in London until the end of September. Léon Volterra had always had a soft spot for Gaby, but Jacques-Charles went one step further by falling for Pilcer, who as things turned out only pretended to return his love in order to acquire his passport to the Casino. Mistinguett was so furious that she did her utmost to prevent the revue from taking place. When Gaby reached the Casino during the last week of October, she was stunned to find the building being picketed by the employees of Léon Volterra's former partner, Beretta. Until that moment Beretta had despised Mistinguett, but now he joined forces with her to hamper the workmen brought in to renovate the theatre. There were further problems too, when two weeks later Harry Pilcer arrived in France only to be immediately taken to the nearest police commissariat and accused of draft-dodging. Again, this seems to have been the result of Mistinguett's scheming, although she would soon change her attitude once she saw the irascible young dancer 'in the flesh', as she put it. For the time being he was rescued by Jacques-Charles. A few days later Pilcer's brother, the jazz-band innovator Murray, arrived in Paris and the scene was set for the showbusiness extravaganza which would knock the French capital sideways.

It has been alleged that Mistinguett watched some of the rehearsals for *Laissez-les tomber*, disguised as a cleaning lady. Given her character, of course, this was entirely possible, and she 'flipped her lid' when she saw Pilcer for the very first time – minus most of his clothes and perspiring in the wings. His big song in the revue was 'Roses of Picardy', which he had sung to the wounded soldiers in military hospitals in and around London with tremendous success. *Laissez-les tomber* was an extremely costly revue to produce – the chorus alone comprised some 300 dancers – and until a few weeks before the première there was some talk that it might not go ahead. Mistinguett was keeping her fingers crossed in this respect, for she had great plans regarding Harry Pilcer's future, which in effect meant that she intended to drop Maurice at the first opportunity. Momentarily, her aspirations were thwarted when Gaby Deslys told Volterra that if need be he could owe her her salary until the end of the season; on top of this, she invested some of her own money in the project.

Laissez-les tomber finally opened on 11 December 1917, with both Mistinguett and Maurice attending the première. Its most famous tableau was called '*Les échelles*' and comprised a dozen 30-feet-high ladders strategically positioned across the stage from which descended, in single file, 150 beautiful chorus girls, naked but for spangled G-strings, high heels and plumed head-dresses. Gaby Deslys wore a chiffon dress peppered with millions of francs' worth of diamonds, while Harry Pilcer appeared in a Roman tunic and very quickly danced out of it, bringing gasps of admiration from his legion of gay followers, including a young Jean Cocteau, and from Mistinguett.

The scene which caused the most controversy, however, had nothing to do with this ocean of naked flesh. Unable to hear his musicians during rehearsals on account of the constant hammering of the workmen, Murray Pilcer had introduced a whole range of noisy devices, including blank shots from revolvers and saxophone blasts. The first time these were fired, many of the audience panicked, thinking that it was an air raid. And then, emerging from behind the backdrop as if by magic, a huge staircase appeared, with, standing at the top, Gaby and Harry. This time she was drenched in carmine ostrich plumes and he was wearing tails. For more than thirty minutes the couple danced up and down the staircase, performing acrobatic routines the likes of which had never been seen before. The audience went absolutely wild with delight, and even the awesomely jealous Mistinguett was heard to mutter, '*Formidable!*'

Mistinguett decided, therefore, that she would have to have

Harry Pilcer in her next revue, and not Maurice, whom she said was beginning to tire her. In fact, there was more to it than this. As *La grande revue des Folies-Bergère* was drawing to its more than welcome conclusion, word was brought to her that Maurice had been sneaking back to the theatre after hours to meet Fréhel in his dressing room. She at once hired someone to keep tabs on him, and when this contact knocked her up in the middle of the night, she was so keen to exact her revenge that she left the apartment on the boulevard des Capucines with just a coat thrown over her nightdress. Under this she had concealed a meat cleaver!

The hapless Maurice was thus caught 'in the act', and when the gendarmes arrived a little later they found Mistinguett chasing him around the theatre, swearing that she would castrate him! All was resolved in the end. The gendarmes were so amused that they never charged her, and Mistinguett expressed her gratitude by offering them free seats to the show. What is remarkable, however, is that when Maurice explained that Fréhel had led him on, he was believed, and the young singer was so terrified of possible repercussions that she left Paris a few weeks later. It was during her exile, in 1920, that she was badly injured in a car crash, and when she eventually returned to Paris three years later she no longer posed a serious threat. Her weight had risen from eight to eighteen stones, and the fact that men no longer found her attractive – something which cropped up regularly in her songs – actually invoked Mistinguett's pity. The former rivals became good friends.

Fréhel never forgave Maurice for treating her badly, and over the next twenty-five years many of her songs would contain portentuous or damning lyrics obviously commissioned with him at the back of her mind. 'L'amour des hommes' told of the way he had used her, then dumped her. In 'Je n'attends plus rien' she expressed her loneliness and sorrow so movingly that the song brings a lump to the throat. In France even now, five decades after her death, Fréhel's more serious devotees switch off the radio whenever a Maurice Chevalier record is being played.

> *Je n'attends plus rien,*
> *Rien désormais ne m'appartient,*
> *Sans un ami qui me console,*
> *D'un geste ou d'une parole . . .*

(I wait for nothing more,
From now on nothing belongs to me,
Without a friend to console me,
With a gesture or a word . . .)

Four weeks after the première of *Laissez-les tomber*, Gaby
Deslys and Harry Pilcer were offered a staggering 200,000 francs
to leave the revue and sign a contract with the upmarket Folies-
Marigny. Pilcer turned the deal down on Gaby's behalf. Increasingly concerned for her failing health now that she had been
diagnosed consumptive, he advised her to rest for a while at her
villa in Marseilles. Léon Volterra was therefore left with a seemingly insoluble problem – how to find a replacement, and more or
less at a moment's notice. He knew that only one artiste was
capable of stepping into Gaby's shoes, and that was Mistinguett.
She refused because she knew that dancing with Pilcer would only
cause an eruption in her private life. Although Pilcer was bisexual,
and narcissistic to the extent that he would sometimes spend hours
gazing at his naked form in his dressing-room mirror before going
on stage, she realized that from a physical point of view he was
more attractive than Maurice could ever be. Volterra therefore
came to the most logical conclusion and asked Pilcer to leave the
show. This resulted in an extremely violent quarrel. Pilcer's temper
had always been unpredictable. In America he had once put a
theatre manager in hospital by hitting him over the head with an
electric heater when the man decided that his latest dance, which
he had introduced on stage in Chicago as the Pilcer Wank, was
immoral. And although a major star in Europe for only five years,
Pilcer did resent being upstaged by a man who, in his own words,
'couldn't sing or dance to save his mother's life'. For the rest of
his life he would hate Maurice and make no secret of the fact.
Occasionally, they would find themselves sharing the same bill,
and it is alleged that when they came to actual blows early in 1936
after a benefit for the widow of the famous clown Antonet, Pilcer
won. By this time, of course, Mistinguett was not amorously interested in either man.

Laissez-les tomber heralded the music-hall period referred to by
the French as '*Les années folles*', and if Mistinguett regretted not
being *meneuse de revue* in the original production, then she had

every intention of bettering anything done by Gaby Deslys. She did not, however, consider Maurice worthy of taking over from Harry Pilcer, especially as Léon Volterra had needed so much convincing to engage him for the Folies-Bergère revue. Therefore, she declared, he would have to prove his worth by playing in a minor revue. There was, it had to be said, a certain amount of method in her madness, and by now she did not really care whether she lost Maurice or not.

Gobette of Paris opened at the Bataclan early in 1918, but if Maurice was her co-star, most of the attention was focused upon Mistinguett, who stole the show by singing a poignant love-song to a life-sized porcelain bulldog. The lyrics, however, were very apt.

> *Elle ne l'aimait pas, lui non plus,*
> *Quelle drôle de chose qu'dans l'existence*
> *Deux amants peuvent faire connaissance,*
> *Mais ils ne s'étaient jamais vus . . .*

> (She didn't love him, he likewise,
> How funny that in life
> Two lovers can be acquainted,
> But unable to stand the sight of each other . . .)

The new *Laissez-les tomber*, which opened at the Casino in May 1918, came close to eclipsing the Pilcer–Deslys triumph, although many of the young men sitting in the stalls were disappointed to see Maurice replacing their handsome, hirsute hero. Mercifully, during the Roman sketch he kept his clothes on. There had been some problems with the songs: Pilcer threatened legal action if Maurice should attempt to sing any of his songs, especially 'Roses of Picardy', and Léon Volterra had summoned up enough courage to tell Mistinguett to her face that her kind of voice would murder 'Broken Doll', Gaby's big number in the show. Maurice's most popular sketch was entitled 'Jim Bouge, World Boxing Champion', for which he would run on to the stage as he had done so many times before and shout, 'I'm afraid of no one!' Big Bertha, so named after Krupp's daughter, was positioned in a wood near Crépy-en-Laonnois and had just begun shelling Paris when, by a strange twist of fate, Maurice uttered his opening line and immediately one of the air-raid sirens went off outside the theatre. Bang on cue, Maurice yelled back, 'I wasn't talking to *you*!' The audience gave him a standing ovation at once, and not one person left the theatre. The next day he was told that besides being assaulted by Big Bertha, Paris had been attacked by sixty planes! He and Mistinguett also agreed with one of the first-night critics that the revue should be awarded a touch of originality and rechristened *Boum!*; 'It was the only thing we ever did agree upon,' Mistinguett later said.

Astonishingly, Maurice and Mistinguett did work together again, even though they were gradually growing to detest each other. The next Jacques-Charles revue at the Casino, *Pa-ri-ki-ri*, caused so many problems that the writer walked out of the theatre during rehearsals and threatened to scrap the production unless the two warring stars agreed to call a truce. There were more cat fights when Maurice asked for his name to appear in letters the same size as those of his leading lady. For the time being, the terms of his contract would not allow this. Even so, he was aggressive and bitter towards Mistinguett, and she made matters decidedly worse by pretending to have an affair with Charles Gesmar, the young man who had been engaged to supply the costumes for the new revue.

When Gesmar was introduced to Mistinguett in 1918 he was still only seventeen years of age. A native of Nancy, he had arrived in Paris during the first year of the war, armed with just a box of crayons, and after hawking some of his brilliant designs around Paris, he was taken in by the actress Andrée Spinelly. Effeminate and neurotic, he had attempted suicide in her apartment after a lovers' tiff and she asked him to leave. Mistinguett proved much more understanding. While working with her on the designs for *Pa-ri-ki-ri*, he had told her the heartrending story of his life, and she was so moved that she unofficially adopted him.

Gesmar was so delicate and feminine that one angry word would have broken him in two. He was so good, poking fun at the 'real men' of the music-hall – the virile types who had everything down below, but nothing at all up top. He was like a son to me, and yet I was the one who used to call *him* Maman!

What angered Maurice the most about Gesmar, apart from the fact that he felt his nose had been put out of joint, was the young man's fondness for having a good time. 'I earn it, and I spend it!' was Gesmar's motto, and it served him well. He never paid for a taxi with anything less than a 100-franc note and he always told the driver to keep the change. He frittered away a fortune, as if aware of the fact that he would die young – he succumbed to a viral infection in 1928, when he was just twenty-seven. Maurice may also have hated him because of his constant 'tittle-tattling', and the fact that Gesmar might have guessed about his friendship with Joë Bridge and have been about to spill the beans to Mistinguett. In any case, Maurice very quickly decided that he had had enough, and promptly embarked on a brief affair with the singer Damia.

Since dancing the *chaloupée* with Max Dearly in London, Damia had done rather well for herself. Befriended by Harry Fragson, she had to a certain extent tamed him; he in turn had secured her engagements at the Alhambra and the Alcazar d'Eté, where she had worked with Maurice. Then, in December 1913, Fragson was shot dead by his father during a heated argument over a showgirl and Damia, grieving for the man she loved, decided to seek her fortune in America. She proved successful on Broadway, but in 1916 she returned to Paris, where she invested her savings into the establishment known as the Concert-Damia, in the heart of Montmartre. She was the first French singer to work with the spotlight directed on her face, and her reviews were sensational. Even Mistinguett admired her, although whenever her name was mentioned she was always referred to viciously as 'that fucking German' – when Damia was born in Lorraine in 1889, that area was part of Germany.

If Maurice was hoping that his affair with Damia would arouse Mistinguett's jealousy, then he was to be disappointed. Nor was the episode given much publicity. In an interview in 1969 Damia mentioned it briefly, and admitted that her fascination had lasted but a few weeks, 'until Maurice had gone off with Elsie Janis'.

Maurice first met Elsie Janis, then one of the most popular stars on the British stage, during his visit to London with Mistinguett in 1913. At that time she was rehearsing for *The Passing Show*, which had proved the city's biggest box-office draw during the summer of 1914. When they met again in Maurice's dressing room during the run of *Pa-ri-ki-ri* – Elsie was on holiday between seasons – he fell for her in a big way, although interestingly enough it was she who asked *him* out to dinner. During the course of the evening, feeling depressed after his latest fight with Mistinguett, Maurice poured out his heart to Elsie, who was moved to pity. She immediately asked him to leave his famous partner there and then and return with her to London, where, she assured him, they would have the pick of the revues. Maurice was tempted, especially when Elsie called him 'the most charming man I've ever met', but he did not let his heart rule his head. He realized that singing in a foreign country, even though he could speak the language relatively well, would be risky. Also, he had been contracted to appear in another revue with Mistinguett – something he was not looking forward to. Elsie did not press. She spent a week in Paris with Maurice, visiting the tourist attractions, and then, on the platform at the Gare du Nord, they swapped telephone numbers and promised to stay in touch.

Outside this music-hall arena, the hostilities in Europe were drawing to a close. Germany's downfall was hastened by the slow but sure collapse of her three great allies, Austria, Turkey and Bulgaria, and at the beginning of November 1918 fighting broke out among the German fleet at Kiel, quickly spreading to other ports. On 10 November the Kaiser abdicated, and the next morning, in a railway siding in the Forest of Compiègne, the Armistice was signed. Four hours later, the war was declared over. That evening, on stage at the Casino – and without Mistinguett's prior knowledge – Maurice sang Lucien Boyer and Charles Borel-Clerc's 'Le Madelon de la victoire' to one of the most emotional scenes Paris has ever known.

> *Madelon, emplis ton verre!*
> *Et chante avec Les Poilus!*
> *Nous avons gagné la guerre!*
> *Hein, crois-tu qu'on les a eus!*
>
> (Madelon, fill up your glass!
> And sing with the Tommies!
> We've won the war!
> You'd better believe it!)

For his bravery at Cutry – or, as some critics observed, simply because he was Chevalier – Maurice had been awarded the Croix de Guerre. The impulsive decision to sing the song was, however, a mistake because, as he later pointed out, it brought back only too clearly the horrors of the war. After just one week, it was dropped from his programme, though not before he had convinced himself that at long last he was on a level footing with Mistinguett, and thus entitled to equal billing. Not so! The incident, and what was said, was well publicized.

MAURICE: Either I have my name in lights, with letters
     the same size as yours, or I go for good!
MISS: please don't forget to close the door as you
     leave.

Even so, there was a last-ditch attempt to get the couple to patch up their differences. In May 1919, after *Pa-ri-ki-ri* had closed, Mistinguett rented a summer house for several weeks at Villerville. As Jacques-Charles was already half-way through writing her next Casino revue, he was invited along, as were his co-writers Albert Willemetz and Maurice Yvain. Maurice, it would appear, was 'overlooked'. Away from the music-hall, Mistinguett still loved to live life to the full, throwing wild parties, and this was even more the case now that 'jazz dances' were all the rage. At Villerville, however, she was suffering from the high blood pressure which had plagued her for some time. Jacques-Charles, unaware of this, assumed that her depression had something to do with Maurice's absence. He at once telephoned Paris, and the next day Maurice arrived, only to be met by a Mistinguett far angrier than he had ever seen her before. Later on, when she had calmed down and at least permitted him to speak, she took his advice – or rather La Louque's – that a long sea voyage might help her condition. This was another mistake, for she decided at once that she would conquer the United States.

Mistinguett's first visit to New York was not the success she had anticipated, although it did enable Jacques-Charles to finish writing the revue, which was given the title *La grande revue du Casino*. It opened in September 1919, just four weeks after Mistinguett docked at Le Havre. It was not one of her favourite shows, primarily because her co-star was Max Dearly, and it ran for just two weeks before Léon Volterra instructed Jacques-Charles to come up with something more substantial – in other words, to obey the demands of the public by supplying another Mistinguett–Chevalier vehicle on the same scale as *Laissez-les tomber*. He did exactly this with *Paris qui danse*, which opened in November 1919. This was an immensely successful revue, but from a personal angle an absolute horror, since one scene called for Mistinguett to kiss Maurice fully on the lips, not once but twice!

The story-line of *Paris qui danse* was uncomplicated. It told of the pupils of a select boarding school who for some reason had consulted the Confédération Générale du Travail and gone on strike. The dance-teacher is asked to single out his most promising student – Mistinguett, of course, playing the role of Miss Touffue, whose English counterpart is Miss Involved – and they then go on a world tour by aeroplane. Thus in front of an Amsterdam wind-mill she and Maurice jigged to 'Tulip Time' before collapsing on to a bed of animated tulips, and later they appeared in a copy of Ziegfeld's 'A Pretty Girl is Like a Melody'. And besides the dreaded kiss there was another 'embarrassing' sketch, this time aimed at Maurice by Mistinguett, who sang 'Comme une fleur', the song which had caused so much anguish during the Fréhel episode.

It was during the run of *Paris qui danse* that Maurice received news of the death of Gaby Deslys, who had passed away in a Paris clinic shortly after undergoing an operation to remove a tumour from her throat. He was heartbroken, and though he was unable to attend the funeral he did send a wreath. Mistinguett went one better. Having been told, probably by Gaby herself, about Harry Pilcer's 'exceptional endowment', and having found this out for herself by actually seducing the dancer, she sent a personal 'representative' to lead the mourners – a half-grown donkey called Harry.

Maurice's nerves were so badly affected by the backstage rows with Mistinguett that in April 1920, in desperation, he sent a cable to Elsie Janis in London, begging her to rescue him 'from complete madness'. He also confided in Jacques-Charles, who at that moment would have done almost anything to get back at Mistin-guett for robbing him of Harry Pilcer. Jacques-Charles therefore agreed to assist Maurice as much as he could, working behind the scenes with Sir Alfred Butt of the London Palace. Thus a few weeks later everyone at the Casino, including Mistinguett, was surprised when an extremely lucrative offer came 'from out of the blue', inviting Maurice to replace the British actor Owen Nares and star opposite Elsie Janis in *Hello, America!*

Maurice was not used to making snap decisions, and Butt's demand that he contact him within twenty-four hours to clinch the deal put him in a quandary. In spite of his love–hate relationship with Mistinguett, he did know that he was on to a winner working with her, even though an estimated 70 per cent of the ticket-buying public were paying to see her, not him. He also realized that in London the odds would be stacked against him, as Elsie Janis was a major star and he would be speaking as well as singing in a foreign language. And he was worried about opening in a new revue on a Monday, the traditional day off in the French theatre, and even more so about opening with an ordinary matinée performance instead of the usual star-studded première. Even so, he telegraphed Sir Alfred Butt to inform him that he would accept his offer, before summoning the courage to break the news to Mistinguett that he would not be working with her any more.

In effect, the great star could not have cared less, because she was desperately in love with Harry Pilcer. Some said that she had fallen for him on the rebound after her break-up with Maurice, and that he had sought her out as a convenient shoulder to cry upon after the death of Gaby Deslys. (It has been pointed out that Mistinguett did not write much about Pilcer in her memoirs, but in an interview in a London bookshop shortly before her death she said that she had 'overlooked' their affair simply because reflecting upon it caused her great pain.) Thus, while Maurice was getting ready to leave for England, she and her lover were ensconced at a retreat near Paris, safe from the prying eyes of the press. Mistinguett was so concerned for Pilcer's fragile health that she barred even his closest friends from visiting; the exceptions were Jacques-Charles and Léon Volterra, already scripting her next Casino revue, for which Pilcer had at long last been signed as co-star. For this reason, Maurice left Paris without saying goodbye to her. He told the French press, 'I've been Mistinguett's errand boy, dancer and partner for far too long. Now's the time to prove to myself what I'm worth!'

From London's Charing Cross Station, Maurice made his way straight to the Palace Theatre – rather than pay for a cab he walked, the way he usually did in Paris unless someone else gave him a lift home. He also gently reprimanded Sir Alfred Butt for booking him into the Savoy, when a simple boarding house would have sufficed. Butt was impressed by this all too obvious parsimony, and the fact that his latest star acquisition was not like his last French import, Gaby Deslys. Her demands even before setting foot on a stage had cost almost as much as her inflated salary! He was also amused to find Maurice wearing very light but distinguishable make-up, and clothes which may not have caused much of a stir on a Parisian boulevard, but which were decidedly too 'loud' for the streets of London. He was therefore introduced to the distinguished actors Maurice Farkoa and Sir Seymour Hicks, who advised him on what a 'gentleman about town' should look like. Maurice took them seriously, though not until after a humiliating incident had taken place. Rising early one morning, he decided to get to know some of the *'petit peuple'* of the city by taking a stroll down to the docks. In doing so he met a group of dockers on their way home from the nightshift and they gave him such a hard time that he decided, that very morning, to visit the bespoke tailor whom Sir Seymour Hicks had recommended. Here, he was further embarrassed to see photographs of one of the shop's more illustrious clients, Harry Pilcer, displayed in the window. Needless to say, he took his custom elsewhere.

Prior to taking over from Owen Nares, Maurice studied his performances minutely. Blue-eyed, blond and extremely good-looking, he was almost a teen-idol and it was not uncommon for some of the young ladies in the audience to scream whenever he walked on to the stage. Maurice instinctively knew that he would never be able to compete – his brother Charles's taunts about his bottom lip still rankled, even if Mistinguett had once described him as 'a handsome catch' – so he decided to do in England exactly what he had done in Paris. Working with the Palace scriptwriter, he adapted his part in *Hello, America!* so that it included his famous boxing sketch, and left out his reserved-for-the-French imitations of Mayol and Dranem. He also saw Elsie Janis on the stage, as opposed to the somewhat impersonal rehearsal room, for the first time and was astonished that she could bring her girl-next-door charm to the footlights with such comparative ease. He was in fact *so* impressed that when he met her in her dressing-room after the show, he told her that he had already made up his mind to return to Paris and the emotionally charged but nevertheless success-assured environment of the Casino. Elsie persuaded him to stay, in the usual way!

Attracted towards him as she obviously was, Elsie did not let Maurice off lightly when it came to preparing for his part in the revue. Considerably younger than Mistinguett, and as beautiful in his eyes though lacking much of her fire and what the French call *gouaille*, her energy seemed boundless. When Maurice asked her out to supper after her performance she declined, adding that she would rather put him through his paces. She certainly proved more difficult than Mistinguett in this respect, for he was kept on stage until two in the morning, and told to report for duty in seven hours' time. Maurice was a willing pupil, and not just to please the teacher he was bedding, but because he genuinely wanted to make a second career for himself in Britain. He was, of course, half-way there, with his natural ability to be funny and his curious but effective manner of attacking the English language. From Elsie's point of view, however, he was not a good dancer – certainly not from a romantic angle, for she announced that she was not interested in learning the *valse-renversante*! He was therefore taught the waltz, which he is said to have disliked as much as the smart fawn suit he was compelled to wear.

On the day of the première, when Elsie Janis brought the house down wearing a tuxedo and offering deadly accurate impersonations of Sarah Bernhardt and Max Dearly, Maurice was given a decidedly cool reception. Fortunately for him, as it was, in Sir Alfred Butt's words, an 'unimportant Monday matinée', there were no critics sitting in the audience. Maurice told Elsie and the manager that he would do things his way, or not at all. The next evening he went on stage wearing pretty much the same costume as he had worn at the Casino. During the afternoon he had persuaded Elsie to learn two of his songs, 'Just a Little Bit' and 'On the Level, You're a Devil'. They stopped the show!

The news of Maurice's London triumph winged its way across the Channel to Mistinguett's dressing room at the Casino, where she was preparing for *Paris qui jazz* with Harry Pilcer. She pretended not to be interested, although it is said that she was missing him – if only for their arguments! As for Harry, she was telling everyone that he was the greatest love of her life, just as she had done with Maurice ten years before. To prove this, she had written a song called 'Au fond de tes yeux', one of her rare excursions into the *chanson-réaliste* tradition.

> *Je vois un peu de peine*
> *Ou même un gros chagrin . . .*
> *Je découvre des pleurs parfois*
> *Qu'tu retiens au fond de tes yeux . . .*

> (I see a little pain
> Or even a great grief . . .
> Above all I discover the tears
> You hold back deep in your eyes . . .)

Mistinguett sang this song to Pilcer in *Paris qui jazz*, and later to a child in her only sound film, *Rigolboche*. Nothing compared, however, with another song from the revue, one that would be hailed throughout the world as her theme-tune. Jacques-Charles had now given up trying to tempt Pilcer into his bed, although several others had managed this, without Mistinguett's knowledge. He therefore made up for his disappointment by assisting Maurice Yvain and Albert Willemetz with the lyrics to 'Mon homme'. Much of his inspiration had come from Francis Carco's novel of the same name, but Jacques-Charles had opted not to change the title because this and the new lyrics expressed his love for Pilcer.

> *Sur cette terre,*
> *Ma seule joie, mon seul bonheur*
> *C'est mon homme!*
> *Quand il m'dit: 'Viens!'*
> *J'suis comme un chien,*
> *C'est comme un lien qui me retient.*
> *J'sens qu'il me rendrait infâme,*
> *Mais je n'suis qu'une femme,*
> *Et j'l'ai tellement dans la peau . . .*

(On earth my only joy and happiness
Is my man!
When he says: 'Come!'
I'm like a dog,
It's like a leash holding me back.
I sense he's making me infamous,
But I'm only a woman.
And I've got him under my skin . . .)

For the rest of his life Maurice would tell interviewers and reporters that *he* had been the sole inspiration behind Mistinguett's most famous song, particularly as the music had been written by Maurice Yvain, his old pal from his army days. There is no doubt, however, that when Mistinguett introduced it in *Paris qui jazz* – she sang it Damia-style, in a long black dress before a totally bare backdrop – she had eyes only for Harry Pilcer.

Some years later Maurice commissioned Albert Willemetz – 'at great personal risk' – to write him a parody of 'Mon homme'. The result was 'C'est ma bonne' ('She's My Maid'), and this infuriated Mistinguett to such an extent that she tried to prevent him from singing it. The original lyrics, however, might have applied to one of Maurice's more clandestine adventures during his first London season.

One evening whilst Maurice was on stage, a young man managed to get past the doorman and into the wings. That evening, Maurice had agreed to take Elsie Janis out to supper, but as soon as he recognized the young man he stood her up. Aged twenty-seven, his name was Martin Kenny and the pair had first met in the prison-camp at Alten Grabow. Needless to say, when Elsie Janis realized what was happening she threw a tantrum and swore she would never work with the Frenchman again. André Rivollet, who appears to have met Martin in Paris some time later, described him as 'muscular, blond and blue-eyed, and ever-blushing'. The ex-soldier lived with his sisters May and Sally in a bungalow on the outskirts of London – the garden of this actually backed onto the Thames, and compared with the grime and the fog of the city, the location was an idyllic setting for the development of the couple's relationship.

The air hung heavy with the scent of sweet-peas. It was an atmosphere of sportive gaiety and good health where, for a few hours each day, he could forget the show at the Palace. Martin told him how serious he had become. This was because, within the little house lost amongst all its greenery, he was dreaming of how good it would be living in some cottage – just the two of them, drinking ginger-beer and eating lamb and mint sauce!

In Paris Mistinguett had reproached Maurice for drinking so much wine – often as much as two litres a day without any apparent ill-effects. While in London, and in order to impress Elsie Janis, he had consumed only soft drinks, apart from the odd bottle of champagne when she had been paying. His fondness for ginger beer left him wide open for comment in some London circles; he probably never recognized the Cockney rhyming-slang implications, or that they might be aimed at him.

Maurice was in fact attracted to both Martin and his sister May, and part of his stay was spent rowing with them on the river, taking advantage of the warm spring weather. The talk was always very 'macho' . . . boxing matches, and of the good old days at Alten Grabow. The Kennys were also great admirers of poetry, particularly that of Byron and Shelley, who themselves had rowed along this stretch of water with the latter's sister Mary. Indeed, the irony went further than this, for in a moment's bravado and to make Maurice 'prove' himself, Martin fell head-first into the water and would have drowned, had Maurice not stripped off and dived in after him. It seems likely that the relationship would have continued had it not been for the powerful pull of the stage. *Hello, America!* closed after its twice-extended season, and Léon Volterra summoned Maurice back to Paris. Elsie Janis and Martin Kenny, now on friendly terms, accompanied him to the station, the latter helping to carry his suitcases. One of these was full of hats, in every style imaginable, which he had purchased from the hatters Lock & Co., a favourite of Harry Pilcer and Gaby Deslys; hidden among the hats was a straw boater.

Maurice was met at the Gare Saint-Lazare in Paris by a delegation headed by Léon Volterra and Jacques-Charles. As the latter wrote in his memoirs. 'In Paris, Mistinguett made him a *monsieur*, but in London, elsie Janis turned him into a *gentleman*!' Mistinguett herself was conspicuous by her absence. Harry Pilcer, still grieving over the death of Gaby Deslys – as he would for another forty years – had swallowed an overdose of sleeping pills and Mistinguett had taken him to Villerville, where over the next few weeks she nursed him back to health.

What she was saying about him, however, made it clear that though he would always remain her friend, Momo was no longer regarded as her lover – if he had *ever* been such a thing!

> Chevalier's presence never brought me anything special, but his absence dominated the rest of my life . . . I alone am living proof of his success. He wouldn't have got anywhere without me . . . In our oasis of happiness the grass was artificial and the water always unfit to drink. I never found a single reason to justify loving the man.

Maurice's publicly voiced hatred of Harry Pilcer for having taken his place in Mistinguett's affections was uncalled for. When he told a journalist that the dancer was 'immoral' for kissing another woman on stage so soon after Gaby Deslys' death, Pilcer hit back by threatening to expose Maurice's relationships with Paul Ardot and Joë Bridge, unless he apologised. Needless to say the apology was not long in coming, though the word 'forgiveness' had never figured in Mistinguett's vocabulary. Not only was Maurice's photograph replaced by Pilcer's on the soon to be printed sheet-music for 'Mon homme' – she told the journalist used by Maurice to attack her new lover, 'I wouldn't empty my piss-pot on that man if he were on fire under my bedroom window. I'll *never* set foot on the same stage as Maurice Chevalier again!'

All I Want is Just One Girl

In December 1920 Maurice opened in a loose French adaptation of *Hello, America!* It was staged at the Gaité-Rochechouart, one of Léon Volterra's less touristic establishments and, the entrepreneur decided, more appropriate for an 'experimental' project than the larger Casino. From Maurice's point of view it was not a good move. The Parisian public, then as now one of the most discriminating in the world, did not take kindly to change and Maurice's *'petit peuple'* did not approve of his 'English' image. This attitude was also reflected by the critics, and the revue closed after just two weeks. Volterra, who against everyone's advice nurtured hopes of a strictly professional reconciliation between Maurice and Mistinguett – convinced that there would be fewer backstage hassles now that she was in love with someone else – was now compelled to change his mind. Instead of putting Maurice into his latest Casino revue, he elected to send him on a 'warm-up' tour of the provinces, as he had after his return from the prison camp. This was thankfully brief. At the Bordeaux Trianon, one of the most testing music-halls on the circuit, Maurice stubbornly refused to compromise over his new image and for his pains was given a ten-minute standing ovation. Volterra at once recalled him to Paris, apologized and offered him a contract with the Casino.

Volterra's timing was perfect. Although Mistinguett had sworn never to work with Maurice again, she had also tried to put a damper on Volterra's efforts to find him another suitable female partner. In March 1921, when Maurice opened in *Avec le sourire*, Mistinguett was playing in *Madame Sans-Gêne* at the Théâtre de la Porte-Saint-Martin. This famous straight play, written by Victorien Sardou at the turn of the century for the dramatic classical actress Réjane – who had helped to put Mistinguett through her paces, only to die on the eve of its première – had taken Paris by storm. Volterra decided to play safe, and instead of offering Maurice top billing he asked him to share the programme with an immensely popular comic *fantaisiste* called Louis Boucot. One sketch saw the pair playing stagehands who put on drag in order to 'seduce' a couple of rich old men into becoming season-ticket holders of the Paris Opera. Maurice put on an old bag-lady's skirt, and Boucot wore a pink tutu! In another scene, still wearing his English clothes and a melon-shaped hat, Maurice sang 'Faut jamais dire ça aux femmes' to a bevy of bare-breasted lovelies. Incredibly, the same critics who had reviled him in the Gaité-Rochechouart revue now sang his praises to such an extent that even Mistinguett went to see the show, clinging to the arm of a yellow-suited Harry Pilcer.

What Maurice did not suspect when he met the couple after his show – with everyone trying their best to appear civilized – was that the Mistinguett–Pilcer relationship was heading towards disaster. This had nothing to do with Mistinguett's tantrums and jealousy, but with her inadvertent neglect of the dancer during the run-up to *Madame Sans-Gêne*. Still suffering badly with his nerves, and terrified of going out of Mistinguett's apartment, Pilcer had been left to his own devices and had ultimately been cheered up by the designer Gesmar, who had begun holding tea dances and inviting his friends. One of these was the singer Marie Dubas, perhaps the only female entertainer Mistinguett ever admitted to liking, who would soon enter Maurice's realm of close friends. Another was a young dancer called Jenny Golder, an up-and-coming force who had more than a little in common with Pilcer. Although even more highly strung than Gaby Deslys had been, she was a fellow American and nearer to his age than Mistinguett. What Pilcer did *not* know, however, was that Jenny Golder was two-timing him with Maurice. He had fallen for her when she auditioned for a part in the chorus of *Avec le sourire*.

There was also a somewhat humiliating incident at the Ritz Hotel during the spring of 1921, when the immensely wealthy socialite-author Princess Bibesco was asked to organize a soirée for the visit of Queen Marie of Romania. When asked to choose her entertainment for the evening, Marie replied, 'Miss and Che-

valier. Who else?' According to one contemporary report, the
couple arrived in Mistinguett's roadster, with Maurice in a smart
suit and Miss wearing every jewel she possessed. 'With a big smile
spread across her face, she stepped over the carpet of peony petals,
pausing every now and then to mutter under her breath some of
the filthiest epiphets imaginable to her escort.' Neither did it help
when, at a strategic point in the proceedings, Jenny Golder arrived
on the arm of Harry Pilcer. 'To take everyone's mind off what
might have been a terrible fuss, Queen Marie walked among her
guests brandishing a huge white lily, dubbing shoulders here and
there.'

Maurice's biggest revue thus far in his career, *Dans un fauteuil*,
opened at the Casino on 7 July 1921. Scripted and co-produced
by the singer-impressionist Saint-Grainier, who shared top billing
with Maurice, it also starred Jenny Golder, 'borrowed' by Léon
Volterra from Harry Pilcer, who is alleged to have retorted,
'You've got her, buster. You go ahead and keep her!' Jenny's big
number in the revue was 'Alors je lui ai fait de l'oeil', and though
she was successful enough to be given a small part in Mistinguett's
next Casino revue, and an actual revue of her own a few years
later at the Folies-Bergère, she did not have staying power. After
a disastrous series of relationships, beginning and ending with
Pilcer, she picked up a whole catalogue of home truths and insults
and in July 1928, in front of Pilcer, ended her life with a bullet.
Mistinguett said, 'It was the best performance she ever gave!'

Dans un fauteuil was of immense importance as far as the Chevalier property department was concerned, because in it he sported
his celebrated straw hat for the very first time. It also gave France
one of her greatest stars in Marie Dubas, who in less than a decade
would be hailed as '*La Fantaisiste des Années Folles*', a lady who
in many ways was not unlike Britain's own Gracie Fields. She sang
an 'utterly feminine' version of Maurice's 'Faut jamais dire ça . . .
aux hommes', which had everyone in the theatre weeping with
laughter. However, just like Gracie Fields, Marie had an uncanny
talent for switching from buffoonery to intense drama, and ten
years later she would make Maurice cry with 'La prière de la
Charlotte', a passionately moving song which tells the story of a
pregnant girl who begs the Virgin Mary to let her die so that her
child might not suffer the way she has. The closing weeks of the

revue also introduced the paying public of Paris to the American dancer Earl Leslie, whom Mistinguett and Jacques-Charles had brought over from London after seeing him in a Cochran revue with the Dolly Sisters. Leslie was good news for Maurice, who, now that Harry Pilcer had gone from Mistinguett's life, had become increasingly worried that she might attempt to 'reclaim' him. Not so! Mistinguett's revue, *Paris en l'air*, followed *Dans un fauteuil* at the Casino with Earl Leslie as her co-star, and by this time the American was her lover.

Immediately after the Casino, Maurice was approached by Gustave Quinson, known as 'the tsar of the operetta', to appear in a new production of *Dédé* at the Bouffes-Parisiens. Although way out of his league, the offer was tempting and Maurice knew that if he made a success of it he would gain access to the world of the legitimate stage which would present him to an entirely new public. The piece had been written by his friends Henri Christiné and Albert Willemetz as a successor to their tremendously popular *Phi-phi*, which had opened to coincide with the Armistice of 1918, and had made a star of the now-forgotten Alice Cocéa. Maurice was given several days to decide whether or not to do the operetta, but he accepted immediately once he knew that his co-star was to be Alice Cocéa.

The storyline of *Dédé* may be trite – a rich layabout buys a shoeshop which he turns into a bachelor pad so that he can seduce the girl of his dreams – but the music and spectacle were anything but. Wearing his straw hat and twirling a cane – setting another precedent – Maurice sang 'Dans la vie faut pas s'en faire', a standard which would accompany him around the world and whose sentiments fitted his casual, *boulevardier* style like a second skin.

> *Dans la vie faut pas s'en faire,*
> *Moi je n'm'en fais pas . . .*
> *Ces petites misères seront passagères,*
> *Tout ça s'arrangera!*
>
> (In life one shouldn't worry,
> And me, I never do . . .
> These little troubles will be momentary,
> All will turn out fine!)

With Mistinguett and Earl Leslie's *Paris en l'air* offering power-ful competition at the Casino, *Dédé* was hailed by the critics and the public alike as the show of the year. *Le Figaro*, not always kind to Maurice in the past, called him a 'peripatetic firework and an abracadabrant *fantaisiste*'. Even Colette said that he was 'the best hypnotist of them all'. Such praise, however, worried him, because it came so unexpectedly. 'I don't understand big words,' he confessed. 'I've never professed to being an intellectual!' Even so, anyone who was anyone in Paris, whether resident or just passing through, found themselves drawn to the Bouffes-Parisiens as though it were a magnet. Douglas Fairbanks and Mary Pick-ford, in Europe to publicize *The Mask of Zorro*, saw the show twice, the second time with Irving Berlin, George Gershwin and their former protégé Harry Pilcer, whom they had helped to dis-cover in New York. Pilcer, who hated Maurice enough to wish to see him leave Paris for ever, had 'put in a good word' with Berlin, who was searching for a French star to put in a Broadway revue. The moment he saw Maurice, he knew that he had found his man. Within the week an offer arrived from the great American showman Charles B Dillingham, offering Maurice an undisclosed salary to appear in an English-language version of *Dédé* at the New York Globe. Maurice promised that he would think about it. But he was in love again.

The lady in question was the Comtesse de Noailles, who had been born Anna Brancovan in Romania. Famed as a poet as well as a socialite, she was, at forty-five, twelve years Maurice's senior. She was also extremely difficult to get along with and, it was said, overtly fond of sado-masochism. Thankfully, her affair with Maurice lasted only a few weeks before the Bouffes-Parisiens closed for its summer break. He then decided to get away from Paris for a while, and booked himself a passage to New York. 'I wanted to find out for myself why everyone was so wrapped up in the place,' he said.

It was a brief visit, but Maurice took in as many shows as he could. He saw Charles B Dillingham and accepted his offer to star on Broadway, provided the showman was willing to put the revue on ice. This was because he was still contracted to the Bouffes-Parisiens for the continuation of *Dédé*. Dillingham agreed. He also introduced Maurice to the American step-dancer Harland Dixon, who was only too willing to put him through his paces in anticipation of his American début. In his memoirs, Maurice wrote that while in New York he was taken to see Sissle and Blake's scintillating all-black revue *Shuffle Along*, and that one young dancer in particular caught his attention. 'Her body was splendid, her face expressive, and she had the most brilliant smile. So I searched in the programme for her name: Josephine Baker.'

Exactly why Maurice suffered a nervous breakdown upon his return from the United States is not known although his extremely busy work schedule cannot have helped. His self-financed trip to New York had depleted his savings considerably, and of course he would never have asked La Louque to break into their 'emergency' cache. Therefore he felt his only option was to work twice as hard to make up for his 'loss'. Confident that he would still be able to remember his part in *Dédé*, he skipped rehearsals with the rest of the cast and elected to make a series of films for Henri Diamant-Berger.

The first of these was *Le mauvais garçon*, with Florelle and Albert Préjean, and Diamant-Berger was so confident about his team of actors that he retained them for another three features: *Gonzague, L'affaire de la rue de Lourcines*, and *Jim Bouge, boxeur*. All three were shot at the same time, between six in the morning and noon each day, regardless of the weather. Only the latter, because of Maurice's famous sketch, made any impact at the box office.

There was also a new lover in the shape of Jane Myro, the in-house singer from the Casino, who had a volcanic temperament which would have put Mistinguett to shame. Little wonder, then, that he had suddenly been reduced to a bag of nerves. Jane loved nothing more than to go out on the town, straight from the theatre, and live it up until dawn. She also had a reputation for being a nymphomaniac, which initially may have pleased Maurice but which very quickly wore him down. The crisis came soon after their first row. One evening, in front of a packed house, he fluffed his lines. This had happened so many times in the past that Maurice had lost count, and he had always remedied or even bettered the situation by ad-libbing, usually with hilarious results. This time, he simply walked off the stage and the scene had to be completed by an understudy. The next evening the same thing happened again and Gustave Quinson rushed backstage to find Maurice 'having a fit' in his dressing room. The director called a doctor. Maurice was examined and found to be suffering from exhaustion, but when Quinson urged him to take time off for a rest – without pay – he refused.

During the next few weeks, Maurice's condition deteriorated so rapidly that Quinson considered closing the revue prematurely, just to avoid the possibility of one of his artistes dying on him. At this stage, Maurice took steps to 'cure' himself. He immediately cut down on his daily litre of wine and forty cigarettes, and went to see a specialist, who diagnosed a grumbling appendix. By this time *Dédé* had closed and Maurice Yvain, who does not seem to have known about Maurice's illness, offered him another operetta, *Là-haut*, which he had co-written with Albert Willemetz after reading the libretto by Yves Mirande. Convincing his entourage that he was suffering from no more than a bad attack of 'butterflies', Maurice accepted his new role, but insisted that the show should be directed by Gustave Quinson. After some deliberation, it was agreed that *Là-haut* should be staged at the Bouffes-Parisiens, but with Dranem acting as 'safety factor-cum-co-star' – in other words, should Maurice find the show too exhausting, or should Quinson decide to fire him, the production would not have to fold. The director also sent his star to see a psychiatrist, who advised plenty of good food, and above all plenty of rest, between rehearsals. No one thought of taking Maurice to the hospital to have his appendix removed!

The Breton-born librettist Yves Mirande's methods of working were, to say the least, bizarre. His first great success at the Théâtre des Variétés had been *Un homme en habit*. Half-way through penning the script he had developed writer's block. Obsessed by the fact that his deceased wife and mother might not have approved of his work, he paid to have their bodies exhumed and their coffins cleaned and strategically placed in his study; all had turned out well in the end. For *Là-haut*, he worked mostly in the back of his car, often asking his chauffeur to drive long distances because a particular street or town did not agree with him. Once, when he thought that he might have been suffering from writer's block again, he actually set off on a cod-fishing expedition to Newfoundland, but returned after travelling just 20 miles from the Breton coast because a bout of seasickness brought him back to his senses and enabled him to find the phrase he had been looking for!

For Maurice, sharing the stage with Dranem was a costly mistake. The newspapers had carried stories of his indisposition during *Dédé*, and many people turned up at the première of *Là-haut* hoping to see him make a fool of himself while working alongside France's greatest comedian. This did not happen. Indeed, during one singing-dancing sketch with a newcomer called Yvonne Vallée, the couple were given a standing ovation and made to sing their number again.

At first Maurice found Yvonne mysterious and brooding. She was not as pretty as his other partners had been, and because she was so quiet and reserved he assumed that there must have been something wrong with her. Each evening while waiting for her cue, she would sit on a stool behind the curtain, calmly knitting while his nerves were in shreds. Eventually he plucked up the courage to ask her out, but instead of going to one of his regular haunts – no doubt because he was afraid of bumping into Jane Myro and having another row – they went for a walk along the Seine and called in at a bar on the Left Bank. These promenades became a regular feature and gradually Maurice found himself opening up to Yvonne, who told him about her own relatively uncomplicated life. After leaving her home in Bordeaux, she had travelled to Paris to live with an elder sister, and that was about it. She knew all there was to know about him, or so she thought, from listening to backstage gossip and reading newspapers. Then one evening Maurice confided to her that during the run of *Dédé* he had come very close to ending it all and she was so shocked that she swore never to leave his side until satisfied that he was completely cured.

The crunch came just a few days later when Maurice collapsed in his dressing room and had to be rushed to hospital. The surgeons decided to remove his appendix at once, but when they opened him up they found nothing wrong with it. Rather, the root of his problem was irritable-bowel syndrome, brought on by nervous exhaustion. Even so, he was very ill and La Louque, thinking he was about to die, became so inconsolable that Yvonne had her taken to Charles Chevalier's house at Esbly, in the Seine-et-Marne district. Only then was Maurice transferred to a clinic at Saujon which specialized in nervous disorders. Yvonne stayed with him for a few days before returning to her commitments in Paris. However, because Maurice's understudy was hopeless, the sketch with Yvonne had to be taken out of the show. Pleased to be free to look after him, she returned at once to Saujon to find Maurice depressed and worrying, not about himself but about what would happen to his mother should he die.

Maurice was visited at Saujon by Anna de Noailles. It is impossible to say if their clandestine meetings, always very late at night, did him any good. The comtesse had a flare for drama which would have inspired any *grande tragédienne*, always arriving in great style wearing an immense ball gown and picture hat, and with her latest tome tucked under her arm. Maurice's friend André Rivollet, who seems to have known her but was not allowed to mention her name in his script, said:

She conjured up all the suffering in the world, long dark nights and obsessive cruelty. Hers should have been the noble task of appeasement, but she brought only chronic distress, and in doing so transformed his smiles into the bitterest of tears.

Inspired by Maurice's illness, the Comtesse de Noailles did write one of her most beautiful and lyrical poems.

Je sens, ce soir, qu'on peut mourir de poésie,
Le coucher du soleil s'élargit, s'extasie . . .
Quel rêve brûle en moi!
Comme on est triste et seul
Sous ce voile odorant, sous cet ardent linceul . . .

(Tonight, I sense that one may die of poetry,
The setting of the sun sets free and enraptures . . .
What dream burns within me!
How one is sad and lonely
Under this sweet-smelling veil, under this scorching
    shroud . . .)

Little wonder then, that, during his moments of solitude after this extremely gifted but nevertheless horrendous woman had left his bedside, Maurice felt that he was going completely mad. Little wonder, too, that as soon as Yvonne discovered what had been going on behind her back, the Comtesse de Noailles was barred from ever seeing Maurice again.

With Yvonne Vallée watching over him like a guardian angel, and telling him of the latest music-hall happenings in Paris, Maurice slowly recovered, but showed no interest whatsoever in returning to the stage. When one of the doctors asked him to participate briefly in a holiday show put on by the clinic staff for the patients, he refused to have anything to do with the idea unless Yvonne agreed to appear with him. It took him more than a week to get out of his bed and sing a note, yet by the time of the concert Yvonne had helped him to perfect six songs, and a toned-down version of their sketch at the Bouffes-Parisiens. Once his doctor had given him something to combat his stage fright, he walked on to the makeshift stage and 'gave his best' – a mediocre performance but one which at least gave him a taste for the real thing.

Three months later, Maurice made his 'comeback' – not at a major Parisian music-hall but at a small cinema in Melun, singing four songs between features. This went well, and after several more such engagements he decided to take the plunge and attempt the dreaded Alcazar Theatre in Marseilles. This went down so well that in December 1923 he made up his mind to return to Paris. Throughout all this, Yvonne had stood by him, encouraging and caring as only she could. Of all the women he knew, she was probably the kindest; she was certainly the least self-centred.

Refusing to work anywhere without Yvonne, with whom he was by now desperately in love, Maurice spent a week with La Louque at the apartment on the boulevard de Strasbourg. Here they received a visit from the entrepreneurs Henri Varna and Oscar Dufrenne, who had just acquired the recently rebuilt Empire Theatre on the avenue Wagram. This was the year of the Olympics, and as Léon Volterra of the Casino had already put on *La revue olympique* with tremendous success, Varna and Dufrenne – with their new theatre seating more than 3,000 people and boasting a stage 100 feet wide and 75 deep – were confident that anything Volterra could do, they could do better. They had already engaged

Little Tich for what would be one of his last appearances in France, the Fratellinis, Sophie Tucker, the great clown Grock, Barbette, Layton and Johnston, and Jenny Golder. And sharing top billing they had been promised Damia and Yvette Guilbert! Needless to say, Maurice did not take much persuading to join such a staggering line-up, the likes of which has never since been seen on any French stage. The curtain rose on 29 February 1924 – an extremely 'unlucky' day, and a leap year to boot! Maurice and Yvonne walked on to the stage to a riotous welcome. It took him all his time to stay on his feet, but he managed it simply because the woman he loved was holding his hand. The show had been given the title *Une fête à la Malmaison*, and was loosely based on the love affair of Napoleon and Josephine. The Parisian public, of course, were only really interested in what was going on between the couple on the stage. Maurice was given a free hand over his choice of material. In a tightly packed bill which exceeded four hours, he was allowed forty minutes. Most of the songs, unfortunately, have not survived the passage of time. They included 'Je glisse, quand on est deux' and Maurice's own French arrangement of a song popular in America at the time, 'Mr Gallagher and Mr Sheen', which included an exchange with Yvonne Vallée, and which stopped the show.

> *Dîtes-moi, M'sieur Chevalier!*
> *Quoi donc, Mam'zelle Vallée?*
> *Savez-vous planter les choux?*

> (Tell me, M'sieur Chevalier!
> What now, Mam'zelle Vallée?
> Do you know how to plant cabbages?)

In spite of the triumph of *Une fête à la Malmaison*, Maurice was not in any particular hurry to work for Varna and Dufrenne, whose reputation for quarrelling was worse than his had been during his years with Mistinguett. He therefore elected to sign a three-year triple-revue deal with Léon Volterra, thus becoming perhaps the only male *meneur de revue* in the history of the music-hall.

The first of these extravaganzas was *Paris en fleurs*, which

opened in a blaze of publicity on 28 November 1925. Again, the
script and the songs were by Willemetz and Christiné, and the
glamour was provided by the Dolly Sisters, whom Jacques-Charles
had seen first of all in New York during his visit with Mistinguett,
and again in London. The posters for the revue were by a twenty-
three-year-old artist named Charles Kiffer, who some years later
would achieve lasting fame with his brilliant but sometimes dis-
turbing portraits of Edith Piaf. What is remarkable about Kiffer
is that most of his work was done from memory – his later poster
of Chevalier, comprising 'four leaves, a stalk and a straw hat' was
a revelation. So too was Maurice's big song from the revue, for it
patented and embodied the very spirit of the café-concert and the
cheeky *mec* from Ménilmontant.

> *Elle avait de tout petits petons,*
> *Valentine, Valentine!*
> *Elle avait de tout petits tétons,*
> *Que je tâtais à tâtons . . .*

This comic masterpiece, about the seemingly innocent youngster
who learns his first lesson in love by 'touching up' a lady of 'hippo-
potamic' proportions practically defies translation into English,
which is a great pity. Even so, it was always demanded whenever
Maurice sang overseas and rivalled even his mammoth hits of the
1940s and 1950s.

A tremendous influence on Maurice at this stage of his career
was *Blackbirds*, which he saw at Les Ambassadeurs. It was headed
by the singing and dancing sensation Florence Mills, who would
die tragically two years later, aged just thirty-five. This was followed by *La revue nègre*, the controversial show which made an
even bigger star of Josephine Baker, on 2 October 1925 at André
Daven's recently converted variety music-hall, the Théâtre des
Champs-Elysées.

Daven's was a concept that did not catch on, for in presenting
acts such as Anna Pavlova and the Swedish ballet he was not
catering for the general public, and these acts did not come cheap,
as was reflected in ticket prices. Many biographers have also erred
when writing about *La revue nègre*. To begin with, it occupied
only the second half of the bill – the line-up for the first half

changed over the weeks and included recitals by Damia and Saint-Granier. Neither was it inordinately long, lasting just sixty minutes. More importantly, and perhaps from Maurice's point of view somewhat disappointing, Josephine Baker was *not* the *meneuse de revue*; this honour went to Maud de Forest, an immensely fat gospel singer of whom nothing more is known. The setting of cargo ships against a backdrop illuminated by the moon was unfamiliar to Parisian audiences, and many people were as shocked by this as they were by the semi-naked girl carried upside-down on to stage on the back of a huge Negro. Paul Colin, who had designed the posters and augmented the backdrops of many revues, later dismissed *La revue nègre* as 'a flock of shaking back-sides, breasts and woolly wigs', and Maud de Forest as 'resembling an elderly oriental carpet-seller'.

Even so, the show was the biggest thing to hit Paris since the original *Laissez-les tomber*, and it inadvertently paved the way for Maurice's second professional visit to Britain. Lew Leslie, the American producer of *Blackbirds*, had seen Maurice's revue at the Casino, and when the two met backstage at the Théâtre des Champs-Elysées, Leslie remarked that he was planning a new revue which would be something of a cross between *Blackbirds* and *La revue nègre*, but with an all-white cast, headed by Maurice and Yvonne Vallée. Terms were discussed and found to be accept-able on all sides, and shortly afterwards the contract was signed. Meanwhile, *Paris en fleurs* closed and Maurice and Yvonne spent a little time resting at 'Quand on est deux', their villa near Vau-cresson, just a short drive from the Bois de Boulogne.

Morally, this was a difficult period for Maurice. He adored his mother, and would have done absolutely anything to please her. He did, however, have certain reservations when she began insisting that he and Yvonne should marry, probably because he was not sure that the relationship would last. He was also con-cerned about his image and the attitude of his female admirers should he settle down – a problem suffered by 'heart-throb' enter-tainers before and since. La Louque was fond of Yvonne, and obviously thought that her son should take whatever steps were necessary to ensure his future comfort. So he proposed to her before they left for London, insisting that from now on *he* would

be responsible for looking after *her*. What Yvonne did not realize
was that he was also expecting her to give up her career.

Whitebirds opened at His Majesty's Theatre on 30 May 1927.
It was a long show, with a large cast which included Maisy Gay,
Helen O'Shea, Carl Randall and Anton Dolin. In a skit on Oliver
Twist, the Artful Dodger was played by Billy Milton, who a few
years later would join Mistinguett's chorus. Even so, with the
exception of Maurice and his two partners (the other was Celia
Glynn), the revue was practically slaughtered by the critics.

> One got the impression that the object of this entertainment
> was to test the limits of human patience. The whole of the
> first part of this 'revue', not excluding a single item, was
> irremediably bad. The songs and sketches of the first two
> hours were tenth-rate entertainment ... the simple and
> oppressive fact was that we were dreadfully bored! The
> change after the interval was, however, miraculous. We were
> saved by the liveliness and by the intelligence of Maurice
> Chevalier, who sang an absurd little song called 'Je ne peux
> pas vivre sans amour' with adroit wit. It looked as if all the
> amusing and delightful things had been saved for the end,
> and it was almost midnight before Monsieur Chevalier was
> able to leave the stage.

Returning to France, Maurice and Yvonne were married on 10
October 1927 at Vaucresson. The union, however, would not be
a happy one. Many years later, Yvonne confessed that she had
married a child, not a man – unfair perhaps, for he was still
suffering with his nerves and in need of love and affection. She
also said that Maurice erected an invisible but solid wall between
himself and other people and it was one which only his public,
and not her, could penetrate. This of course was absolutely true,
for in keeping with the music-hall tradition, the only successful
marriages were those between artistes and their ever-faithful
audiences.

Paris–Hollywood–Paris:
The Poor Apache

In the autumn of 1928 Irving Thalberg, known by his Hollywood contemporaries as the Boy Wonder, arrived in Europe on the lookout for new talent now that the 'talkies' had begun taking over. Al Jolson's *The Jazz Singer* had received its world première in New York on 6 October 1927, and in spite of the success of this particular star, many others from the silent era – John Gilbert was the most notorious – had fallen by the wayside. Thalberg's task was to find good replacements, and fast. When he arrived in Paris with his wife, the actress Norma Shearer, it seemed only natural that his first calls should be made upon the city's two national monuments, Mistinguett and Chevalier, who were of course playing in separate revues.

Mistinguett had visited the United States for the second time in 1924. After being turned down by Florenz Ziegfeld, she worked for the Shubert Brothers in *Innocent Eyes*. The production was fraught with difficulties. During one sketch, Mistinguett had to be flung head-first off the stage into a river and return dripping wet. In effect, the river was a sheet of glass and the droplets of water, beads of glass which had been sewn on to a 'wet-look' replica of her dress. The first time this had happened, the public had booed her, and Lee Shubert had given her notice. The Queen of the Music Hall, however, had never taken kindly to being told what to do. Unable to pronounce the word 'eyes' – it always came out as 'arse' – she unofficially changed the revue's name to *Innocent Arse* and added a touch of reality to the river-scene by diving into a bath filled with water and drenching the men in the orchestra pit!

Mistinguett's enormous potential for a Hollywood film – in spite of her 'dreadful' singing voice – was at the back of Irving Thalberg's mind when he met her in her dressing room after watching her revue, *Paris qui tourne*. Miss, however, told him in no uncertain terms that she was not interested in going to Hollywood. She declared, 'I haven't forgiven Fanny Brice for pinching "Mon homme". If I met her over there I'd probably scratch her eyes out!'

Maurice, on the other hand, was an obvious candidate for Hollywood. Although forty he did not look it, and he was as handsome as most of the other male stars in Hollywood. Moreover, his was a natural charm, with a ready, off-the-peg sense of humour. Thalberg's cameraman tested him on Henri Diamant-Berger's old film lot at Vincennes, and he was found to be so photogenic that there was very little rehearsal and absolutely no need for the make-up girl. Two weeks later the test was seen by Jesse Lasky of Paramount Pictures, who at once cabled Maurice to offer him and Yvonne Vallée a single-film, six-week contract. On the face of it, the (undisclosed) fee was not as high as the ones being proposed by Paramount and other American companies to other stage-to-screen stars – for example, the Marx Brothers, Sophie Tucker, Jeanette MacDonald and Helen Morgan – and Maurice was also more or less reminded that as a foreign star he was privileged to have been considered by Hollywood in the first place. Even so, despite having been made to feel grossly inadequate, and unsure of what his reception would be, he settled La Louque with his brother Paul, and on 9 October 1928 he and Yvonne left Le Havre on the *Ile-de-France*. Tragically, he would never see his beloved mother again.

In his memoirs, Maurice described the welcome he received at New York's harbour as, 'like a cyclone, where everything seemed false and out of proportion'. About fifty journalists and photographers boarded the ship, greeting him as though they had known him for years. Their interest, or at least much of it, lay not so much in interviewing the star, who had already been 'introduced' to New York via Mistinguett, but in the fact that while America was in the throes of Prohibition and alcohol was forbidden inland, the law did not apply to ships arriving from foreign destinations. Thus some of the questions bordered on the absurd because so few of these journalists knew anything about the entertainment world, least of all in Europe, and were more interested in drinking.

Maurice must have found it exceedingly difficult to hide his contempt when one young woman, referring to the war, asked, 'Monsieur Chevalier, do you think that France will ever pay her war debts to America?' Maurice, never short of a ready response, simply shrugged his shoulders and replied, 'I don't know, madame. Perhaps you ought to go over there and ask her.' In his own, inimitably jovial style – and never less than impeccably polite – he also managed to convince his inquisitors that Paris was not a 'little town from across the pond', that the staple diet of his countrymen was not snails and frogs' legs, and that *some* French men did wear suits and not striped sweaters and berets. In short, he opened the gates to practically every other foreign entertainer who followed in his footsteps, by teaching some of the more ebullient American entrepreneurs that there were artistes in France who were as good as, if not better than, their American counterparts. All this he did not by being brash and showy, but simply by being himself.

Once they had settled in at their hotel, the executives from Paramount drove Maurice and Yvonne to a reception dinner at the Waldorf Astoria. Some 200 celebrities, producers, journalists and other members of the media had gathered to listen to him speak about his life – or so they had anticipated. 'They turned up out of curiosity, not because they knew me,' he later said. 'The speech was peremptory, and I sang instead. I rather think they liked me.'

Nothing, however, quite compared with Maurice and Yvonne's entry into Hollywood. In those days, travelling across the country took five days by train, and this gave the film world ample time to arrange a reception once Irving Thalberg had cabled to say that the couple were on their way. As they stepped on to the platform a massive brass band struck up 'La Marseillaise' and eighty uniformed dancers rushed towards the train, their arms filled with red, white and blue flowers. Above the platform fluttered a banner: WELCOME TO MAURICE CHEVALIER FROM FRANCE. Maurice is said to have felt humiliated. In France, such blatant displays of hero-worship were practically unheard of, and would never have been tolerated by the '*petit peuple*'. The official delegation sent by Jesse Lasky, one of the leading Paramount executives, comprised ten

actors and actresses headed by Adolph Menjou and Lily Damita.
The latter had recently sung and danced at the Casino, though not
in the same revue as Maurice, and Lasky assumed that they must
have known each other. They did not. He was, however, impressed
by the drive from the railway station to the hotel in Beverly Hills.
En route the chauffeur pointed out the luxury homes of Mary
Pickford and Douglas Fairbanks, Greta Garbo, Emil Jannings and
Charlie Chaplin.

The latter was, of course, the idol of every would-be comedian
on both sides of the Atlantic. When asked by Jesse Lasky who he
would like to meet more than anyone, Maurice unhesitatingly
replied, 'Charlot!' This was arranged. Unable to help himself,
Maurice was overcome by the sheer emotion of this meeting and
burst into tears. Maurice's statement, 'When the rest of us have
faded into oblivion, Charlot will keep shining like the great star
he is!' also made Chaplin cry. The tears were wept privately within
Chaplin's garden. As for the rest of the Hollywood 'glitter set',
they saw the two great men meet at a huge bash organized by
Douglas Fairbanks.

Maurice's first American film, *Hello, New York!*, was finished
in November 1928, and also starred Yvonne Vallée. No complete
print of it seems to have survived, although it is believed to have
been a poor film – through no fault of the two stars, but because
of inadequate direction by Robert Florey, who two years later
would be hired to direct the original version of *Frankenstein* and
then dropped at the last moment. Much better, though no better
received by the critics, was the film directed by Richard Wallace
during the winter of 1928–9, *Innocents of Paris*. This was pre-
mièred at the New York Criterion, and if the *New York Times*
found the plot feeble and the dialogue mediocre, at least they
praised Maurice for having 'a sense of humor, powerful magnet-
ism, and above all charm'. In Paris, of course, the film's reception
was entirely different. Released as *La chanson de Paris*, it took the
French capital by storm, and this tidal wave of adulation quickly
spread across the country. Thousands of people, female admirers
in particular, flocked to provincial cinemas, as one newspaper
observed, 'to share their most intimate feelings with a man some
of them had never seen before'.

In Hollywood, Maurice signed a contract with Paramount, this time for twelve months. Little by little, he and Yvonne had begun to 'fumble' their way around the new world which neither of them really liked – except for the money. Gary Cooper, in the middle of his stormy relationship with 'Mexican Spitfire' Lupe Velez, became a cherished friend, as did Ernst Lubitsch. Arriving from Berlin in 1918, this astonishing man with a panache for satire and directing frivolous sexual comedies the 'European' way – in the manner he wanted, and with the stars of his choice, or not at all – had ruffled many feathers in the film world before proving himself immensely successful with silent vehicles such as *The Student Prince* and *Forbidden Paradise*. Lubitsch had been given virtual *carte blanche* to direct Paramount's first talkie, *The Love Parade* and had already signed up a female lead, a pretty young singer named Jeanette MacDonald whom he had discovered in a Chicago revue.

The idea for *The Love Parade* came from Léon Xanrof and Jules Chancel's play *Le prince consort*, which Lubitsch had seen some years before in Paris. Maurice, however, with his staunch working-class roots, was not impressed with the idea of playing a prince, and he turned the part down. It has to be remembered that, like Mistinguett, he never allowed himself to be 'bossed around' when out of France because he knew that, whatever happened, his French public would always be back there waiting for him. Lubitsch knew this, and he did not press the point. However, he did ask Maurice to try on a few of the costumes that had been made for the film. Maurice did, and needless to say he changed his mind! Then, while awaiting his studio call, he travelled to New York, where he had a four-week engagement at Florenz Ziegfeld's opulent New Amsterdam Roof Garden as guest artiste in a series of variety shows headed by Paul Whiteman's orchestra, Helen Morgan, and a young singer called Bing Crosby. Maurice, still feeling unsure of himself, strode boldly on to the stage and, with his hat over one eye, sang his version of 'How Yer Gonna Keep 'em Down on the Farm Now That They've Seen Paris?' The applause which followed this was deafening, particularly as the Ziegfeld Room was a haven for snobs and social climbers who went there not to see the show, but to look at one another. He followed this with several numbers that he had sung at the Casino, and also his songs from *Innocents of Paris* – 'Valentine', 'Wait till

You See Ma Chérie', and 'Louise' – and a new number by the Hollywood team of Leo Robin and Dick Whiting, who would later write some of Marlene Dietrich's early film songs. Although he did not know it at the time, 'Louise' would very quickly become Maurice's signature tune – not just in England and America, but also in France.

> Every little breeze seems to whisper Louise,
> Birds in the trees seem to twitter Louise,
> Each little rose tells me it knows
> I love you, Louise . . .

Love Parade was filmed in California and Long Island, and took three months to complete. On the set, Maurice was often visited by Charles Boyer, a good friend but, Maurice said, something of a nuisance because at that time he was smoking eighty cigarettes a day. Gary Cooper was an enormous help, for the pair exchanged anecdotes about the women in their lives: Lupe Velez, who hurled abuse at everyone and threw tantrums every time she walked on to a film lot, and Yvonne Vallée, suffering the first pangs of the intense jealousy which would eventually end their marriage. Maurice was not seeing anyone else, but his wife was finding it increasingly difficult to take a back seat while he was receiving one accolade after another. And then, when he really was 'up on top of the rainbow' a telegram came from his brother Paul to say that La Louque had passed away on 18 May 1929, aged seventy-seven.

Maurice returned home at once, but even there his more ardent fans would not allow him to mourn. At the fashionable Hôtel Crillon in Paris, where he was compelled to stop off for a press conference, he was mobbed by hundreds of screaming women and had to escape via the back entrance. His brother then drove him down to the Riviera. They stayed quietly there for a few weeks before returning to Paris, where Maurice had a two-week season at the Empire. Here he received another cable, this time from Ernst Lubitsch in Los Angeles. *The Love Parade* had proved to be one of the biggest box-office draws of the year, and the executives at Paramount had decided to extend his contract by another year. For a few days, Maurice thought the proposition through. The

'What a stroke of luck – me at 13, no kidding!' (*André Bernard*)

The Smiling Lieutenant, 1931. (*René & Lucette Chevalier*)

November 1919, with Mistinguett in *Paris qui danse* – 'Au fond de tes yeux'. (*André Bernard*)

Relaxing on the set of *The Beloved Vagabond*, London, 1935. (*René & Lucette Chevalier*)

In 1927 with his mother, affectionately known as La Louque. (*René & Lucette Chevalier*)

In 1943, at La Bocca, Cannes, before being arrested by the Périgueux maquis. (*André Bernard*)

Compiégne, 1942, welcoming home repatriated prisoners of war. (*André Bernard*)

A 'friendly' bout with the World Champion boxer, Marcel Cerdan, in 1947. (*André Bernard*)

Escorting Barbra Streisand to the première of *Funny Girl*, 1967. (*André Bernard*)

1965, with Maria Callas. (*André Bernard*)

With Patachou and Gracie Fields, 1956. (*André Bernard*)

(*Below, left*) In 1956, during the shooting of *Love in the Afternoon* in which he played a bowler-hatted private detective, Chevalier and Audrey Hepburn got together to mark 'the end' of the straw-hat with which his name was always synonymous. (*André Bernard*) (*Below, right*) With his faithful secretary, François Vals. (*François Vals*)

'You must have been a beautiful baby!' With HM The Queen Mother and Shirley Bassey at the 1960 Royal Variety Performance. (*François Vals*)

Celebrating his seventy-fifth birthday with the Duke and Duchess of Windsor. (*François Vals*)

La Louque, Chevalier's home at Marnes la Coquette, just outside Paris, named after his mother. (*François Vals*)

On 21 October 1968 Chevalier sang for the last time at the Théâtre des Champs-Elysées, Paris. In the audience, third from the left, is his former lover, the chanteuse-réaliste Damia. (*François Vals*)

'We remember him well . . .' (*André Bernard*)

American adventure had worked exceedingly well and paid off handsomely. Paris, however, was where his roots were and he could not ignore some of his critics who were accusing him of putting his love of '*le fric*' before that of his country. Maurice did nothing to dispel this impression when, many years later, he said, 'I adored America and its people. But more especially I adored all the moh-nee!' What could not be ignored, on the other hand, was that his supreme talent had earned him a cult following in America, and that he considered it his duty to return there. The money was important, but so was the adulation, and without one there would have been very little of the other.

Maurice returned to Hollywood in October 1929, ostensibly to make two films, *Paramount on Parade* and *The Smiling Lieutenant*, for Ernst Lubitsch. The first, consisting of an assortment of music-halls stars and actors all 'doing their own thing', with no storyline to speak of, had Maurice singing 'All I Want is Just One Girl' and 'Personne ne s'en sert maint'nant' – the French version of 'Everybody's Doing It Now'. For *The Smiling Lieutenant*, made in the summer of 1930 and released the following year, Maurice's co-star was Claudette Colbert. Wedged in between these were two more 'extra' features: *The Big Pond*, directed by Hobart Henley and also starring Colbert, and Ludwig Berger's rarely seen *Playboy of Paris*, which was released in France as *Le petit café*. Maurice was also 'collared' by Charles B Dillingham, who had never really got over his disappointment at not having him in a Broadway production of *Dédé*. Dillingham asked him if he would reconsider his own American revue, for which he would be given *carte blanche*. Maurice's answer was still the same, only this time his decision was helped along by Ernst Lubitsch, who would not release him from his contract for more than a few days at a time. He did tell Dillingham, however, that he would like to sing with the Harlem Cotton Club Orchestra. This was not an easy thing to organize, considering some of the racial tensions in New York, but sing he did, on 30 March 1930 at the Fulton Theater in New York's Times Square, in the very first of his one-man shows.

> *Paris, je t'aime avec ivresse,*
> *Comme une maîtresse!*
> *Tu m'oublieras bien vite et pourtant*

Mon cœur est tout chaviré
En te quittant . . .

(Paris, I love you with rapture,
Like a mistress!
You'll forget me soon enough,
But all the same my heart turns upside-down
On leaving you . . .)

Towards the end of the November, Maurice and Yvonne, having
spent a few days in Paris attempting to mend their marriage,
arrived in London. At Victoria Station they were mobbed by hysterical fans and the police were brought in to restore some sort of
order. For Yvonne, this was almost the last straw. She knew that
Maurice's public would always have to come first, and in her heart
of hearts she also knew that very soon she would have to let him
go. His two-week season at the Dominion Theatre had sold out
in just days; the management had raised its prices, it said, to
compensate for Maurice's demand that he be allowed to retain 50
per cent of the box-office takings. His opening, on 1 December
1930, came shortly after that of his most recent film to be released
in Britain, *The Big Pond*, which was still showing at the Carlton
Cinema.

Once again, the audience had to suffer a mediocre first half,
lasting almost two hours. However, as Alan Parsons recorded for
the *Daily Mail*, the 3,000 or so people in the audience loved him.

It is all done by charm – but it is a very special kind, a subtle,
compelling, infectious charm which puts the audience in a
happy, eager and receptive mood. The moment he appeared
I felt, 'What a nice fellow this must be!' The winning run
across the stage, the French accent, the exact angle of the
straw hat to the head all contribute to help this feeling of
good will. But there is more to the man than this! The man
is a real artist! There is no fumbling or fluking – he knows
exactly what he *can* do, and that he does to perfection.

Maurice's new songs included 'You Brought a New Kind of
Love to Me' and the fascinating 'Ma regulière'. There was also a

novelty number called 'Mon p'tit Tom', which told the story of an elephant who becomes heartbroken when her 'husband' absconds to Paris to join the circus. Maurice performed it so convincingly that many people were reduced to tears! And when asked by a pretty female reporter if he could define his popularity as 'a matinée idol', he retorted, 'I do *not* like the words "matinée idol". A matinée idol is the kind of artiste I have *never* tried to be. I am *not* a ladies' man!'

Maurice's stay in London was not without its share of sniping from that section of the press which seemed to be jealous of his success. In one publication, directly under the review praising Maurice's show, the Dean of Chichester had persuaded the editor to print a piece 'appealing for £4,500 for repairs to the cathedral' – almost what Maurice was being paid for a week's stint at the Dominion. He was also criticized for demanding extra money for 'incidental expenses', which he later attributed to his 'ignorance' of the British tax system.

M Maurice Chevalier, the French actor and film star, who for appearing at the Dominion during the last fortnight was guaranteed £4,000 a week, was paid a cheque last night for £8,800. This is £400 a week more than the guarantee. He afterwards wrote a cheque for £1,800 on account to the Inland Revenue for income tax and super tax on his fortnight's earnings in London.

With his customary good humour, Maurice laughed off this slur on his character and, before leaving for Paris, took Yvonne on a sightseeing tour of London – no easy task, considering that he was now public property in Britain as well as in France and the United States. When he was 'summoned' to an audience with George Bernard Shaw he politely declined, professing that he had never been an intellectual. When informed that to refuse a man of Shaw's status would be tantamount to 'slapping London in the face' he went along with the idea. Shaw told him that he had never heard any of his records, and that he had never been witness to any of his stage and screen performances. When asked why he had bothered asking to see Maurice in the first place, he replied, 'To see what all the fuss is about.' Maurice then retorted that in this respect they were equal: he had read none of Shaw's works, he had seen none of his plays, and neither did he want to!

Maurice's reputation for avarice followed him from London to Paris. After his show at the New York Fulton Theater one columnist had labelled him 'the world's highest-paid star', not knowing whether this was true or not, and the phrase quickly caught on. What was without doubt the case was that Maurice was earning more in America than he would have done in Europe – particularly for films; but he believed he deserved the extra money, because of the pressures and what he considered the unnecessary 'kowtowing' to executives and producers that did not always apply in France. He did worry, however, about what effect such a statement would have on his French admirers, and he was not helped along by a handful of media and music-hall *aficionados* who accused him of 'deserting everything he had formerly stood for because of his greed for money – money which he spends hours counting, each morning'. Such was the power of these foolish, irresponsible people that they actually succeeded in blocking his opening night at the Théâtre de Châtelet in May 1931. When he walked on to the stage, to his dismay he observed that the house was less than half-full. In spite of this he gave his usual spirited performance, and when his admirers realized that his American adventure had not turned him into a '*grosse tête*' they cheered him all the way and he was forced to take several curtain-calls. He was further defended by Philippe Soupault, a reporter with *L'Europe Nouvelle*, who said, 'It's pathetic to think that since his return to Paris, this man has been forsaken and scoffed at by the people he loves.' After this, the press gave him only good reviews, and the rest of his Châtelet season was a sell-out!

Unfortunately, Maurice's reputation for meanness would dog him for the rest of his life, thanks to the media, most of whom had no idea that as a member of the '*petit peuple*' from the poor district of Ménilmontant, he had been taught the value of money from an early age. He knew that it made sense to look after what he had, for even in the heady world of success, there were such things as rainy days. Not a great deal of publicity was given, however, to his generosity at this time – the fact that he regularly sent cheques to an old café-concert entertainer named Blon-Dhin to help found a dispensary for sick artistes on the rue de Réamur.

At least one of these payments is known to have been in excess of 200,000 francs.

Maurice made two Hollywood films in 1932, both with Jeanette MacDonald. The first of these, *One Hour with You*, was assigned two directors, Ernst Lubitsch and George Cukor. The plot and the songs, with the exception of Leo Robin's 'Oh! Cette Mitzi!', did not do great justice to the stars, though the film was successful at the box office. The next film, however, was a masterpiece of wit, realism and photographic genius, and is regarded by even the sourest of critics as one of Maurice's best films. *Love Me Tonight* was directed by Rouben Mamoulian, who one year later would triumphantly bring together Greta Garbo and the failing silent-screen idol John Gilbert for *Queen Christina*. It captured the very essence of Paris in the 1930s, with its inevitable class wars. Maurice plays the hard-working tailor who, in the feeble disguise of a baron, goes to the local castle to reclaim his debts and inevitably falls in love with the beautiful princess, only to be temporarily rejected when his true identity is revealed.

The opening shots in the film, displaying a grimy Parisian dawn complete with backdrops of Notre-Dame and the Eiffel Tower, old washerwomen, cobblers, baguettes and bicycles, klaxons and all – with the sounds of these forming the introduction to Maurice's first song – gave cinema-goers a clear indication that they were in for a rare treat. Maurice's chirpy sense of humour during 'How Are You?' – a plum line was, 'Hello, Mrs Bendix. How's your appendix?' – was spot-on. So was Mamoulian's devilishly clever 'Isn't It Romantic?' scene, introducing each of the film's characters, for it was reminiscent of René Clair's enigmatic film of 1930, *Sous les toits de Paris*, but without the slightest hint of duplication. Here, his reworking of Rodgers and Hart's song was particularly biting, especially from Maurice.

> Isn't it romantic?
> While I sit around my love can scrub the floor,
> She'll teach me by the hour,
> Or she'll get the sack . . .
> And, when I take a shower she can scrub my back . . .

The *pièce de résistance* of the film, during the denouement, was

'The Poor Apache', which, incredibly, was also written by Rodgers and Hart – incredibly because as one of Maurice's few recorded *chansons-réalistes*, and a work which could not have been bettered by the poets who were writing for Damia and Fréhel back in Paris, he performed it so well in the film, in an atmosphere of shadows and dramatic intensity. Indeed, it would seem grossly inappropriate not to present the lyrics in their entirety, taking into consideration the far-reaching consequences of the song once the recording reached Mistinguett's gramophone.

Wear a muffler when you wear a collar and tie?
Why not? I'm an apache!
A thing that makes me happy is to make a woman cry!
Why not? I'm an apache!
My sweetheart's a shop girl, she's a treasure,
I am a gentleman of leisure,
When I grab her wrist and twist it,
No woman can resist it! I'm an apache!
I'd love to treat her pretty and take her round the city,
But what's a poor apache got to do?
With one big sigh I must black her eye . . .
I'd love to buy things for her,
And tell her I adore her,
But what's a poor apache got to do?
With one good kick I make her pay me quick . . .
While all the men are dancing, tenderly romancing,
I've got to throw her body around,
The spot that no one dares touch,
The spot that only chairs touch
Is frequently touching the ground!
She comes and whispers sweetly:
'I love you so completely!'
And then I gently whisper to her:
'Nuts to you!' That's how I say 'I love you, too!'
That's the truth, what a poor apache must do!
I was found in a basket in front of a church
But my childhood was not very sainted,
I didn't know my mother . . . who didn't know my father,
My parents were not well acquainted!

I soon joined a gang who taught me their plan,
To pick pockets and rob girls of lockets,
I learned how to slouch in doorways, and crouch,
To master a wench with a hammer and wrench!
It's the game I could blame . . .
Maybe some day I'll be caught at some dirty work,
Maybe that day the police will lead me away . . .
Maybe I will be seen by Madame Guillotine!
And when at last I'm led off
To have them chop my head off,
I'll tell the executioner this:
'Nuts to you!'
And then I'll close my eyes of blue,
That's what a poor apache must do.

Rouben Mamoulian became a life-long friend, and never stopped singing Maurice's praises. During the making of *Love Me Tonight*, however, he did consider Maurice's 'behaviour' a little strange.

I had never worked with anyone quite like him before. He strode on to the set, with that heavy walk of his, looked about him, and sat in his corner with the unhappy expression of a homeless orphan. I called him for his opening number. He said it would be a disaster, and looked beaten before he started. Then the camera started rolling and he underwent a complete transformation. He became happy and jovial, full of life. The take was perfect! Then I shouted 'Cut!' and he went back to his corner, looking just as lost and miserable as before.

Someone else who was also feeling 'lost' was Mistinguett, who from afar had been monitoring not just Maurice's career but his private life as well. She had heard that he was friendly with Myrna Loy and Marlene Dietrich and was naturally jealous that there might have been more to them than met the eye. This was not true. Marlene would remain one of Maurice's closest friends for another forty years and one only has to read the Preface to this book to observe their deep respect for each other. Myrna Loy, on the other hand, was not a name familiar to Mistinguett, though she soon would be thanks to *The Great Ziegfeld*, the bio-pic of the showman's life. In this film, MGM's costliest since Ramon Novarro's *Ben Hur*, Robert L Leonard would copy a tableau from one of Mistinguett's Casino revues – a staircase sequence with Myrna Loy and a somewhat over-made-up Virginia Bruce descending under a huge mushroom of flowers, while a chorus of lovelies crooned 'A Pretty Girl is Like a Melody'.

Maurice's renewed problems with the woman he always referred to as 'the greatest love of my life' seemed to recommence during the summer of 1932, when he returned to France. No sooner had he unpacked his suitcases than a missive arrived from Bougival – the former seat of the ill-fated Madame Dubarry, which Mistinguett had bought some years before – inviting him to dinner. She was feeling particularly low because she had just returned from an unsuccessful German tour – unsuccessful in that, like Maurice at the London Dominion, she had asked for 50 per cent of the box office, but had received next to nothing because most of the tickets had been sold cheaply to government workers and their families. On top of this, there were problems with her partner Earl Leslie, no doubt because she had found herself another lover in the form of the Italian dancer Lino Carenzio. During the years since their split, Mistinguett and Maurice had written to each other occasionally, as most friends do. Between June 1932 and the end of 1934, however, these exchanges took on a noticeably more serious tone, hers increasingly demanding, his patient and gently rebuffing.

Aware of what the tension at Bougival must be like – the guests included Carenzio, Leslie, Harry Pilcer, Jean Gabin and the American dancer Lad, all of whom had slept with their hostess at some time or other – Maurice declined the dinner invitation. A letter was sent to the effect that while he wished to remain Mistinguett's 'best mate', he did not want to spoil their friendship by letting her feelings run amok. Obviously, he was thinking back to the joke played on him at the time of her 'marriage' to Mayol. There was also an air of intrigue about the letter which she wrote him on 7 October 1932. It was headed 'Geneva' and was indeed posted there, even though Mistinguett is known to have been in North Africa at the time. Geneva, of course, would have been a perfect setting for her *cri de cœur*, which is probably why she went to the trouble of getting one of her friends there to mail it, almost sixteen years to the day since Maurice's release from Alten Grabow.

> My little Maurice, these are sad days for me, grieved as I am that you refused to come and see me. All forlorn, I have left for Juan-les-Pins. But you should have ignored the gossips who are jealous of others being happy. Nothing could have been more natural than our meeting. It was the most exciting moment of my life, and something I think of every day. Now I am burned out by this murderous tour. I wanted to see you in Paris before you left – to kiss you with all my tenderness. Believe me, my little Maurice, if I say that my thoughts never leave you, no matter how far away you may be, on land or sea. No one can prevent *that*! So, with my unhappy heart I wish you bon voyage, that you may be happy, and that your success may continue. You are a great artiste and I love you. Write to me every now and then. Just a little piece of paper, so that no one need ever know. I love you. I love you.
> Mist.

Maurice did not take Mistinguett's letter too seriously – he had known her for a long time. He did, however, send her a curt reply, shortly before sailing for New York on 2 November, promising that he would see her upon his return. This moved her so much that she sent him a telegram, which he received on board the *Paris* twenty-four hours after setting sail from Le Havre. It read, 'Your last letter brought me a ray of sunshine.'

For several months, Mistinguett's letters continued, though she did tone down their amorous content. There was a good reason for this. While appearing in Vienna she had met a dancer named Fritz Rey, who had been engaged for the chorus of her revue at the Theater Ronach. Fritz was, she said, the most beautiful man she had ever seen in her life. He was only seventeen – more than forty years her junior. Unable to speak any German, Mistinguett had enlisted the services of the American dancer Ben Tyber, at that time the lover of Lino Carenzio, and it had henceforth been plain-sailing. Mistinguett had then set about getting Fritz out of the country and back to France. This was achieved by hiding him in the bottom of a wicker basket 'under a heap of feathers and dirty underwear'. Many years later, as Frédéric Rey, he would become world-famous – he was certainly the best nude adagio-dancer the Folies-Bergère ever had. Mistinguett did not hang on to him for long, however. Less than a year later he left her for the actor Ramon Novarro.

Greatly relieved that Mistinguett was out of his hair for the time being, Maurice concentrated on his Hollywood career. However, his next two films, *A Bedtime Story* and *The Way to Love*, both directed by Norman Taurog, were not very successful. In February 1934 he attended the wedding of his friend Charles Boyer to the Bradford-born actress Pat Paterson – the couple had met at a Hollywood party just two weeks before. A bigger name in those days than Boyer, she had starred in Herbert Wilcox's production of *Bitter Sweet* alongside Anna Neagle, and had been noticed by Robert Kane of Twentieth Century-Fox. At the time of her meeting with Boyer she was filming *Bottoms Up*! with Spencer Tracy. Their marriage was not given much press coverage, primarily because neither were major stars, otherwise Maurice's critics who had accused him of parsimony would have discovered that he had paid for the reception banquet.

Towards the end of 1933 Maurice was often seen in the company of the actress Kay Francis, who earlier that year had appeared in *Storm at Daybreak*, a successful film which had opened with the assassination at Sarajevo. They spent a lot of time together on the set of Ernst Lubitsch's *The Merry Widow*, sometimes lunching with Marlene Dietrich, who was filming *The Scarlet Empress* in a nearby studio. Léhar's operetta had first been filmed in 1925, directed by the tempestuous Erich von Stroheim and starring Mae Murray and John Gilbert. Maurice's choice of co-star was the opera singer Grace Moore, who had moved him to tears with her portrayal of Jenny Lind in *A Lady's Morals*. Maurice told his friend Irving Thalberg, then recovering from a serious heart attack, 'Either I have Grace, or I don't do the film!' Still ignoring the Hollywood 'law' that only the executives made such decisions, Maurice was prepared to sacrifice what was to be one of the greatest successes of his career. However, in this case, events were out of his control. Columbia Pictures, who effectively held Grace Moore under contract, told MGM that they could borrow the singer, but only if MGM put her name above Maurice's in the

credits. Maurice, considering that he had had enough of that sort of
thing in the early days with Mistinguett, refused, and Irving Thalberg brought in Jeanette MacDonald. He and Lubitsch then
engaged Ernst Vajda and Samson Raphaelson to write the script,
and Oliver Marsh for the photography, which was, to say the least,
sumptuous. Among the other stars were Una Merkel, who five years
later would engage herself in one of the most famous cat fights in
movie history, with Marlene Dietrich in *Destry Rides Again*.

The story and the acting in *The Merry Widow* were wittily
summed up by Maurice's friend the director Billy Wilder in 1979.

> It starts off with the king and queen in bed one morning,
> just before they get up. The king was George Barbier, an
> extremely large actor. The queen was Una Merkel. There was
> a lot of kissing, then the king gets dressed, kisses his wife
> goodbye and leaves the chamber. Standing outside the door
> is a lieutenant [Chevalier], wearing a sword which he raises
> in salute as the king goes by. The king salutes him back, and
> laughing, starts down the steps. Chevalier puts the sword
> away, and enters the chamber. Then the king stops and
> realizes that he has forgotten his sword and belt. He goes
> back up the steps – the suspense! The door closes, but still
> we don't see inside. Then he comes out again with the belt
> and the sword, still smiling. He tries to put the belt on but
> it's too small, so he goes back inside the chamber. We go
> with him and see that he finds Chevalier is under the bed.

In 1935, Maurice made *Folies-Bergère*, which was directed by
none other than Jerome Kern. Again, there were problems when
he asked to choose his own star – this time, Charles Boyer – and
he had to 'make do' with Ann Sothern and Merle Oberon. The
songs included 'La romance de la pluie' and 'Singing a Happy
Song', but the film was not over-praised by the critics, who had
been expecting something along the lines of *The Merry Widow*.
Furthermore, after finishing the film Maurice announced his
decision to leave Hollywood, probably for good. The immense
popularity of his recitals – the fact that he could determine whether
he had been a success or not there and then in the theatre, as
opposed to having to wait six months for a film to be released –

reminded him that the music-hall had perhaps always been his true vocation. This was misinterpreted by Mistinguett, who for some reason believed that 'The Poor Apache' had been recorded with her in mind. Indeed, she also assumed that on his return to Paris Maurice would be willing to resume their 'partnership'.

All the time Maurice had been working in America, there had been a steady stream of letters from Mistinguett, most of them written with sufficient passion to suggest that they were still lovers – replied to by Maurice very much in the same vein. What the pair were saying about each other privately to friends was of course another matter.

Two aspects of the last two years had fuelled Mistinguett's anger and jealousy: Maurice's success in Hollywood and the unheard of earnings which this had brought, and the reports of his love affair with Marlene Dietrich. It mattered little that she herself had had countless lovers since his departure: that Maurice could cheat on *her* was another matter!

Hoping to woo Maurice away from Marlene – though by this time their initial ardour had cooled and they were just good friends – Mistinguett had taken steps to resurrect their partnership by approaching the directors of the Folies-Bergère, the Casino and the Moulin Rouge along with any other 'secondary interested parties' – had had already taken the liberty of commissioning Jacques-Charles to write *La Revue des Revues* which, she claimed, with herself and Chevalier sharing the bill, would become the biggest show-business event to hit Paris since Joséphine Baker's *Revue Nègre*. It was simply a matter of agreeing the highest fee possible!

Considering her reaction to Maurice's press-attack on Harry Pilcer, Mistinguett, two-faced as ever, should not really have been surprised by his response to her impassioned letter all but begging him to work with her now. 'He sent me a telegram,' she wrote in her memoirs. 'It said only one word – IMPOSSIBLE!' Can you imagine how absolutely mortified I felt? How could my beloved Momo treat me so *shamefully*?'

Quelle Pagaille!

Although he did not know it at the time, Maurice would not make another American film for twenty-one years. On 6 June 1935 he opened at the Adelphi Theatre in London, supplementing the revue *Stop Press!* As with his previous London shows, the critics praised only him, some even going so far as to dismiss the rest of the programme as rubbish. Maurice's act had become noticeably more polished. The Mayol impersonations raised loud guffaws of laughter, even though most people did not even know who Mayol was, and there were also impressions of other artistes impersonating him. His opening song was 'Rhythm of the Rain', which was followed by half a dozen numbers from his films. Incredibly, he was told not to sing 'The Poor Apache', because the Adelphi management thought some members of the audience might be offended at its 'suggestion of prostitution'. Maurice explained to everyone that this was precisely its subject matter, sang the song, and received a standing ovation! One critic wrote, 'Never before has his mastery and subtlety been so definitively apparent.'

Maurice made it clear that he did not wish to answer any questions about Yvonne Vallée. For some time the French had been expecting him to divorce her. There had been many stories in the press about Maurice's 'involvements' with other women – most of them invented by journalists – and Yvonne Vallée had also seen the photograph of Maurice and Marlene Dietrich, sitting on the steps of his dressing room in bathrobes. In fact, Marlene told me that whilst in America, Yvonne Vallée had kept so much in the background, meeting almost no one outside her hotel, that few people had had any idea that Chevalier had been married at all. Gradually, Maurice had wearied of his wife's not to be unexpected jealousy, and the last straw had come when she lost the child she had been expecting. Maurice had filed for divorce, and in doing so had ended an unnecessarily unhappy phase of his life with as little fuss as possible. Yvonne Vallée did, however, later say some pretty unforgivable things to the French press about Marlene Dietrich and Elsie Janis.

Between performances at the Adelphi, Maurice made his first British film, *The Beloved Vagabond*. He had been introduced to its director, Kurtis Bernhardt, by Marlene Dietrich, for whom he had directed *Die Frau, nach der Man sich sehnt* (released in Britain and the United States as *Three Loves*) in 1929. Like many Germans who fled when the political climate in their country became far from healthy, Bernhardt Americanized his first name, changing it to Curtis. The film co-starred Fernand Ledoux and Margaret Lockwood, but it was a costly and disappointing flop. So too would be Bernhardt's 1952 remake of Maurice's *The Merry Widow*, with the unlikely pairing of Lana Turner and Fernando Lamas.

Maurice returned to France, where he entered into negotiations for his first major Parisian revue in seven years. Léon Volterra had left the Casino in 1929, but as Maurice was on amicable terms with the new director, Henri Varna, he had no difficulty getting accepted for *Parade du monde*, which had been scheduled to open on 30 September 1935.

During Maurice's absence, the concept of the French revue had changed. *Cocottes* and *horizontalistes* were out of fashion. More popular, particularly after the 1934 boom in 78 rpm records in France, were variety spots or 'mini-recitals' which had nothing whatsoever to do with the story line. The most popular artistes of this genre were Lucienne Boyer, whose 'Parlez-moi d'amour' had sold several million recordings worldwide since its release early in 1930, Jean Sablon, Marie Dubas and Damia. In the big Casino revue of 1934, *Parade de France*, the Corsican ballad-singer Tino Rossi had scored a tremendous success with 'O Corse, île d'amour' and 'Vieni-vieni-vieni'. Maurice therefore decided to follow suit, though he was not over-interested in singing too many of his film songs to French audiences. In fact, from now on songwriters would be falling over themselves to get him to perform their material. The first was Mireille Hartuch, a twenty-nine-year-old phenomenon who a few years before had teamed up with Jean Nohain to write a string of hits for herself and others – 'Couchés dans le foin', for example, had been recorded by Bing Crosby and the Andrews Sisters. Maurice and Mireille met while holidaying at La Bocca, near Cannes, and he was given the song 'Quand un vicomte', which was subsequently added to the footage of *The Beloved Vagabond*, not that it improved the film a great deal. A little later, Albert Willemetz and Charles Borel-Clerc gave him 'Ah! Si vous connaissiez ma poule', and from the pen of Géo Koger and Vincent Scotto – a true genius who in a sixty-year career composed more than 4,000 songs and has been interpreted by just about every French singer since the turn of the century – there came the sublime 'Ma pomme'.

> *Ma pomme, c'est moi-â-â-â!*
> *J'suis plus heureux qu'un roi!*
> *Je n'me fais jamais d'mousse,*
> *Sans s'cousse,*
> *J'me pousse . . .*

> (My apple, it's me-e-e-e!
> I'm happier than a king!
> I never get myself into a lather,
> Without shaking,
> I shove myself to the front . . .)

Maurice sang 'Ma pomme' in the film *L'homme du jour*, directed by Julien Duvivier in 1935. Surprisingly, the film was not as great a success as he had anticipated. Then this and his other new numbers and routines were tested on a provincial tour which took in many of the country's more opulent theatres. Maurice assumed, and wrongly so, that his American success would enable him to ask for much higher fees and that the public would be willing 'to pay a few extra francs' for the privilege of seeing him. This was not so. At the Eldorado in Nice hardly any tickets were sold at all, and there was a very real danger that his recitals in Cannes and Biarritz would have to be cancelled. Fortunately, Maurice came to his senses and reminded himself that even if he had tried hard to change his *'petit peuple'* image, his public were determined that he never should. The rest of the tour was a sell-out!

It was around this time that Maurice met Charles Trenet, who would very soon become one of the greatest singer-songwriters in Europe, though never the most sociable or easiest of men to get along with. Trenet had been born in Narbonne in 1913, and while in his teens had teamed up with Johnny Hess to form the duo Charlie et Johnny. In 1933 they had been booked by Henri Varna to open a new revue at the Palace, but Trenet had stormed out of the theatre less than a week later, accusing Varna of putting him on while latecomers were finding their seats. Soon afterwards he had been engaged by the Folies-Bergère, where Maurice saw him for the first time, though he soon fell out with the usually genial Paul Derval over the costume for his sketch.

On the night of the première Trenet refused to wear his costume, claiming it didn't fit. Then he appeared at the top of the staircase, among the glitter and spangles, in sweater and flannels, and wearing yellow shoes. His get-up was preposterous, but the shoes outraged me the most. 'They match the colour of my hair,' he said. Mercifully, his stay at the Folies was brief, and he was very pained when I deducted the cost of his costume from his salary.

Even so, Trenet's distinguished, almost surreal style quickly revolutionized the French *chanson*. One particularly remembers with great fondness such masterpieces as 'Douce France', 'L'âme des poètes', and of course 'La mer'. After Maurice's immense success in *Parade du monde*, followed by the film *Avec le sourire* in which he sang Borel-Clerc's amusing 'Le chapeau de Zozo', he was offered another revue at the Casino – *Paris en joie*. He began rehearsals in December 1936. A Casino tradition was that every revue staged there should have thirteen letters in its title and, if possible, a major song based on the keyword. Charles Trenet's 'Y'a d'la joie' was therefore accepted by Henri Varna at once, though not by Maurice, who accused Trenet of 'taking the piss' with the absurd lyrics.

Le garçon-boucher qui va sur ses quinze ans,
Est fou d'amour fou pour une femme agent,
Et la femme agent qui va sur ses cent ans,
Est folle de bonheur pour cet amour d'enfant . . .

(The butcher's boy, going on fifteen,
Is madly in love with a female agent,
And the female agent, going on a hundred,
Is mad with happiness over her child-lover . . .)

It may well be that Maurice had suspected Trenet of getting at him over his affair with Mistinguett, which some believed was still going strong. In fact, Maurice had a new love in his life in the shapely form of nineteen-year-old Nita Raya, a very pretty Jewish singer-dancer who had appeared in the revue *Broadway* both in New York and in London. Even so, when Trenet was asked to write new words to 'Y'a d'la joie' he did so without hesitation, and liked them so well that he recorded the new song himself. But in spite of posing for photographs with the great troubadour and publicly acknowledging his formidable talent, Maurice is thought to have disliked Trenet. Even so, it was probably Maurice's interpretation of one of his songs that persuaded Trenet to split from Johnny Hess – this, and the fact that he was called up for military service – which resulted in him reaching cult status.

Maurice was happier working in *Paris en joie* than he had been for some time, no doubt because Nita Raya had been given a part in the production. Although he did not look forty-eight, he was sufficiently concerned about the difference in their ages to make sure that he lived as long as possible – pressures of work while in America, followed by his divorce, had affected his nerves to such an extent that he was back on sixty cigarettes a day. Nita, he declared, had been sent to him by the gods. Thus, by way of a 'sacrifice', he destroyed every cigarette he could lay his hands on, and never smoked again. He said of his latest love, 'In the artistic world there could not have been such a blending of beauty, spirit and modesty, and such a work of art!'

His joy was shattered, however, by the death of his great friend Dranem, at the age of sixty-six. The tragedy did, however, pay him an unexpected dividend, as of the so-called 'Four Aces' of the music-hall – Fragson, Polin, Dranem and Mayol – only the last-named remained, and his career was virtually over. Maurice's music-hall colleagues and admirers therefore bestowed upon him the title 'showman' – a title he would carry well for more than thirty years, and one that he of course richly deserved. On top of this he was asked to take over the presidency of Ris-Orangis, the actors' retirement home which Dranem had founded a quarter of a century before. It was an appointment he took very seriously. Not content to be just another figurehead, he visited the home regularly, handing out gifts and writing cheques, and putting on impromptu recitals for the residents, some of whom he recognized from his café-concert days.

During the summer of 1937 there were further problems between Maurice and Mistinguett, this time of an artistic nature. One of the toughest entrepreneurs in Paris at the time was Mitty Goldin, the Hungarian-born director of the ABC music-hall on the boulevard Poissonnière. Goldin was not a popular man with some of his artistes on account of his tendency to pay badly, but this was more than compensated for by the fact that, until the reopening of the Olympia by Bruno Coquatrix in 1954, the ABC was the very pinnacle of French entertainment. In March 1937 Goldin had, under some considerable pressure, engaged a young artiste named La Môme Piaf to top the bill in a programme of songs mostly by Raymond Asso. Half-way through the run she had changed her name to Edith Piaf, and the rest is, of course, history. Mistinguett and Maurice had attended Piaf's début performance at Gerny's some eighteen months before with the aviator Jean Mermoz, but if Maurice never stopped adoring Piaf, Mistinguett always pretended to dislike 'the funny little bugger in black', even though she once admitted that 'Mon légionnaire' made her cry. She went with Maurice to see her at the ABC only because, she declared, she was 'casing the joint' for her next revue. She could have added that in spite of Nita Raya – whom she referred to as 'The Jew', but only when she was feeling particularly kind – she had every intention of winning back Maurice's affection. One of Piaf's big hits at the time was a song called 'Reste', written not by Asso but by Jacques Simonot and Pierre Bayle, who had also worked for Mistinguett. The words would, she hoped, get her ex-lover to see sense.

Maintenant que tout est bien fini,
Et que nos cœurs se sont repris,
Reste, que nous parlions un peu
Du temps où nous étions heureux . . .

(Now that it's over,
And our hearts are recovered,
Stay, let us talk a while
Of the time when we were happy . . .)

Needless to say, the ruse failed, although Mistinguett did make a point of inviting Maurice to the première of *Chansons de Paris* in June – Nita was also asked along, but told to pay for her own ticket. Mistinguett then flaunted her new co-stars, Léo Kok and Carlos Machado, in their faces. There was also a young singer-dancer named Georges Lambros, who some time later would achieve considerable fame as Georges Guétary, one of the stars of *An American in Paris*, and a duo named Kramer and Zibral whom Léo Kok had picked up in a bar. Zibral, it would appear, was not a very good dancer, but Mistinguett engaged him just the same because of his slight resemblance to Maurice. The sketch in which he appeared was entitled 'Ma pomme', after the now-legendary song, and the young man strode on to the stage, 'almost giving Momo a turn', sporting a straw hat. Mistinguett appeared as Marie, an old bag-lady with worn-down shoes and a tattered straw hat decorated with thistles. While Zibral was dancing around her, she opened an umbrella which was full of holes and leaves, and crooned a ballad which recounted the tawdry story of her hapless youth. The sketch was the biggest success in the revue, but it only infuriated Maurice, who marched round to her dressing room to give her a piece of his mind. Under normal circumstances Mistinguett would have enjoyed a brawl, but she knew that doing this in front of Nita Raya would only result in her running the risk of losing Maurice's friendship for ever. Thus she apologized and promised to remove the offending routine from the revue. She also retitled it 'Titine', and it became the most famous of her latter roles. After she had played it for the first time, Chevalier himself walked on to the stage and shook her by the hand.

During the autumn of 1937 Maurice visited Britain, where he had been contracted to make a film with René Clair. The director, until that time one of the most popular in France, had recently fallen foul of the media there with *Le dernier milliardaire* – it ridiculed various right-wing organizations, and had caused fights to break out in some Paris cinemas. Clair had therefore moved to Alexander Korda's studio to director Robert Donat in *The Ghost Goes West*. *Break the News*, which starred Maurice and the British star Jack Buchanan as a pair of down-and-out music-hall veterans, was by Clair's own admission 'silly and uninspired'. It was in effect a loose remake of *La mort en fuite*, which had starred Michel Simon and Jules Berry, and it was not that bad. (Neither was Clair's next film, his first for Hollywood, *The Flame of New Orleans*, with Marlene Dietrich.)

Maurice returned to France, where in October 1938 the French government decorated him with the Légion d'Honneur 'for signal services to French propaganda in all countries'. He also gave a special performance at the Quai d'Orsay before a select audience headed by King George VI and Queen Elizabeth. Afterwards, he was photographed with the royal couple and said that it had been one of the proudest moments of his life. A few weeks later, however, another handshake would cause him problems with his admirers. It occurred during the première of *Amours de Paris*, which opened at the Casino with Nita Raya as Maurice's co-star. American columnist Janet Flanner was present at the première, when Maurice came very close to being booed off the stage.

The current offering features forty-five tableaux illustrating everything from the love life of the rose to the parlour existence of the famous courtesan Cora Pearl. It offers two imported dancing troupes, 'The Eight Exciting Skibine Ladies' and 'The Sixteen Red and Blonde Greasely Girls', and Maurice Chevalier. The German love ballad which he renders in the voice of Hitler hating democracies is the hit of his act. Chevalier still has more *métier* in his lower lip than any newcomer can offer. Unfortunately, he still has the knack of offending his Paris devotees. When, after having kissed Marlene Dietrich and Grace Moore, he only shook hands with Mistinguett, his devotees, by their devoted booing, made him kiss her too.

Prior to this, on 29 September 1938, Hitler, Mussolini, Chamberlain and Edouard Daladier had signed the Munich Agreement, and though war clouds had been dissipated for the time being, everyone knew what would happen.

A few days after attending Maurice's première, Mistinguett and her company had sailed for Argentina. The tour of South America was fraught with difficulties. Two of her male dancers were arrested and imprisoned for importuning young boys, and most of the others were laid low with dysentery. The star herself admitted that she had not given her best performances because, she said, she was worried about her Jewish friends in France. These included Marie Dubas, Mitty Goldin and Harry Pilcer, who were worried at what might happen should war be declared and Germany be successful. In April 1939 Marie Dubas had opened at the ABC in *La revue déchaînée*, and although most of the seats for this had sold out weeks in advance, Maurice advised her to cancel and leave the country while she still could. Mistinguett sent a telegram to the same effect, but Marie waited as long as she could before leaving the revue, when her place was taken by Charles Trenet. Accompanying her on her journey across the Atlantic was the American jazz-singer Lena Horne. By this time, Mistinguett had already left Rio on the *Campana*, and it was while the ship was heading for France, on 3 September, that the news was transmitted that Britain and France had declared war on Germany. A few days later, the *Campana* docked at Casablanca, where two of Mistinguett's dancers were arrested by the Moroccan police and sent to a surveillance camp. Mistinguett immediately tried to get in touch with Maurice, only to be told that no one knew where he was. For several days she worried herself ill, thinking that something dreadful might have happened to him. Finally, Lino Carenzio drove her to the airport and she caught the plane back to Paris. Maurice telephoned her there to say that he and Nita had been staying with the Duke and Duchess of Windsor at Cagnes-sur-Mer when Chamberlain had delivered his speech. Although very relieved that he was safe and well – and at this stage in the war there was no reason for him to have been otherwise –

Mistinguett is said to have been 'peeved' to discover that he and Nita were still together.

Early in 1939, Maurice made one of his best films in the French language, *Pièges*, directed by Robert Siodmak. His co-star was Maria Déa, who played a 'taxi-girl' dancer engaged by the police to track down the murderer of a number of young women who have replied to his advertisement in a lonely-hearts column. In order to do this, she herself places an advertisement and meets Robert (Chevalier), a tough but smiling variety agent who, it turns out, has been set up by a colleague. His final scenes, as a condemned man, were nothing short of excellent and so were the cameo performances from Mady Berry, Pierre Renoir and Erich von Stroheim. And of course there were a number of songs, the best of which was 'Il pleurait', for which Maurice stuck out his lip rather a lot and acted gormlessly in a chauffeur's uniform.

In France, with Hitler making no attempt to cross the Maginot Line, the autumn and winter of 1939 were known as *La drôle de guerre*, or the phoney war. Paris was little affected by the political maelstrom, so long as the curfew and lights-out were observed. Initially there had been panic, resulting in some music-halls and theatres pulling down their shutters, but as this passed a few of the braver directors, fearing financial ruin, had begun offering their services again. Mistinguett was among the first to take advantage of the situation. Always the realist, she had a 'gut feeling' that things could only get worse. Josephine Baker, her greatest enemy apart from Damia, had already begun reporting daily to the Red Cross Relief Centre on the rue de Châteaudun, where much of her time was spent cooking and comforting homeless families. Although Mistinguett would have loved to help she had not forgiven Josephine her latest 'indiscretion' – a brief affair with the dancer Frédéric Rey. From now on Josephine would be referred to only as 'Old Banana-Tits' or 'Black Pearl'. Rey, on the other hand, received but a mild ticking-off when summoned to Bougival to explain himself, especially when he told Mistinguett that making love to Josephine had been 'just like screwing another boy'. Moreover, Mistinguett asked him to be her *vedette-américain* in a new recital-revue which she was planning to put on at the Empire-Palace. Remembering the last war, she declared, 'I'm too old to be engaged as a spy, so when the Germans come, I'll fight them from the stage!' Frédéric Rey was also worried about his own security, and because he had made plans to visit his parents in Vienna he turned the offer down. Mistinguett replaced him with a twenty-seven-year-old *chanteuse* named Léo Marjane, a decision which was backed firmly by Maurice, who had seen her at Lucienne Boyer's nightclub. Had they been able to look into the near future, they would have steered clear of this pretty but frowning blonde. It was Léo Marjane who introduced 'Septembre sous la pluie' and 'The Chapel in the Moonlight' – two very popular songs on both sides of the Channel. When engaged by Mistinguett, her big song was 'J'ai donné mon âme au diable', which is precisely what she *would* do during the German Occupation. As for Maurice, he again raised Mistinguett's hackles by opting to work with Josephine Baker at the Casino.

Paris–Londres opened in October 1939 and, as before, Nita Raya was given an important part in the revue. She was hardly noticed. Josephine, amazed that she had been given equal billing with someone as great as Chevalier, pulled out all the stops and went on to steal the show. During the tableau entitled 'L'île heureuse' she danced the samba and sang 'Mon cœur est un oiseau des îles', and from then on it was plain-sailing. A tireless self-publicist, she announced that in order to ensure the soldiers fighting at the front a happy Christmas, she had organized 1,500 'gift parcels', each containing a signed photograph. 'Josephine is not a real star,' Maurice told the press. 'She just gets up there and shows her arse!' To which Mistinguett is alleged to have retorted, 'And so she should. The sound that comes out of there is far better than that which comes out of her throat!' Even so, Josephine's intense bravery and her tireless work for the French Resistance throughout the war would speak volumes for the fact that her character had been grossly misinterpreted. Very soon even Mistinguett would be praising her and inviting her to Bougival, although she never stopped calling her 'Banana-Tits'.

On 30 April 1940 Maurice flew to London to appear in the Anglo-French Matinée at the Drury Lane Theatre, aimed at raising money for the British services. His performance was given a mixed reception, the major problem being his insistence before going on stage that a no-smoking call be given out on the Tannoy – a move supported by his co-star for the afternoon, Gracie Fields. Maurice was also criticized for 'rushing off' after the show in order to catch his plane back to Paris. 'He stopped for just one moment to give autographs to two soldiers outside the theatre,' commented the London *Evening Standard*.

On 7 June 1940 the war took a serious turn when the Germans took the Seine at Rouen. The Parisian exodus south began in earnest – police estimates suggest that as many as 4 million people left the city in one week. Mistinguett and her fleet of five cars headed for St Jean-de-Luz near Biarritz. Her convoy included those chorus boys whom she deemed worthy of transportation, her son Léopold, Paul Derval, and as many of her animals as she could pack into her cars. Josephine left in similar style, driving her expensive Packard, which contained several dogs, her maid, two refugee dancers and a large crate of champagne bottles – the champagne had been emptied out and replaced with petrol for the long journey to Les Milandes, her castle near Sarlat in the Dordogne. Maurice travelled in the same direction. Unable to take up residence at La Bocca, which had been requisitioned by the French Air Force, he accepted an invitation to stay with two dancers from the Folies-Bergère, the now-forgotten Myrio and Desha, at their house near Mauzac, 545 kilometres south of Paris, and about an hour's drive from Les Milandes. With him were Nita Raya and her parents, a young comic named Félix Paquet and his wife Maryse, and Maurice's old army pal Joë Bridge, now in his mid-fifties. A few days later, on 13 June, the Germans entered Paris and the swastika was unfurled from the top of the Arc de Triomphe.

During the next few weeks Maurice received innumerable calls begging him to return to Paris. His public needed him. Nita and her parents, on the other hand, needed him more and he refused even to think of leaving them behind when it was rumoured that very soon the whole of France would be occupied by the Germans. This precipitated a series of cables from his friend Charles Boyer, who had been 'bought out' of the French army by the executives at Paramount. Boyer urged him to bring his 'family' to Hollywood, but Maurice rejected the idea of turning his back on France. He said, 'The Mother is ill, so it's up to her sons to stay put and look after her!' On 14 July Maurice received word that the Air Force had relinquished La Bocca, and he and his company left for the Riviera without further ado. So did everyone else in the showbusiness world, it seems. Mistinguett's fleet drove across the Pyrenees towards Antibes, picking up long-lost members of her entourage en route. In Toulouse she collected Georges Guétary, who had spent some time in prison for deserting the army. Harry Pilcer was already in Cannes, and Lino Carenzio had taken up the position of artiste-in-residence at the Kan-Kan Club in Nice. Both Tino Rossi and Charles Trenet were in the area, along with half the French film industry.

For several weeks Maurice toured the Riviera, trying to boost his own morale as much as the morale of those who flocked to see him at local galas, cinemas and clubs. He was approached by a twenty-three-year-old classical pianist, Henri Betti, who told him that he had written him a song. Maurice listened to the young man's hard-luck story, of how he was responsible for looking after his mother and his seven brothers and sisters. He turned the song down, but he took Henri on as his accompanist. The partnership would last the rest of the war, and their friendship the rest of Maurice's life. One evening, possibly during a long, lonely pause for thought at Mauzac, he had written a poem capturing perfectly the spirit of the moment. He had called it 'Notre espoir'.

> *Désormais quels seront les pauvres mots,*
> *Sur les chansons que pour nous on invente,*
> *Qu'on osera placer vraiment sans risquer trop?*
> *Pour n'pas m'tromper voilà c'que je chante:*
> *Tra la la la la, zim ba boum ba la,*
> *En chantant comme ça, c'est notr'espoir . . .*

> (From now on, how poor the words will be,
> Of the songs they devise for us.
> Dare to be honest without risking too much?
> So as not to slip up, I sing thus:
> Tra la la la la, zim ba boum ba la,
> Singing like that, it's our hope . . .)

Maurice's friends expressed their admiration for his poem, particularly Henri Betti, who was asked to add a suitable melody, even though he had never composed before. The result was a tremendous success and set the precedent for Maurice's first songwriting 'boom'. Collaborating almost non-stop with Betti, the pair produced around fifty songs, at the rate of three or four a month. Some of them were mediocre, but most were first-rate and at least ten – labelled 'straw hats' – would remain in his repertoire until the end of his career.

During his two months in the Free Zone, as it was now called, Maurice saw a lot of Mistinguett. It was at her villa in Antibes that Maurice received an urgent appeal from Henri Varna, begging him to return to the Casino. A few weeks before, the Gestapo had appointed a specialist committee to inquire into the directorships of every theatre in Paris, assuming – and rightly so in many cases – that the French showbusiness scene was being run by Jews. The Théâtre Sarah Bernhardt had already been rechristened, and one of the first stars to suffer at the hands of the Nazis had been Maurice's friend Marie Dubas. Although she herself was safe in South America, Marie's apartment had been seized, a large number of her records burned, and her very name was forbidden by the Propagandastaffel. The Casino, singled out by Hitler as a symbol of decadence, headed the list of 'suspicious' establishments, and it was taken for granted that its director could only have been a Jew. In fact, Varna had been raised as a Jesuit, but he was told that unless he opened the Casino's doors immediately with pro-German material he would be replaced by a German. Maurice, although desperately missing the revue stage, told Varna that he would never work under such conditions, even if he *could* be guaranteed safe passage back to the Free Zone afterwards. Varna then contacted Mistinguett, only to be told exactly where to go!

On 16 September 1940 the Casino opened with its first revue of the Occupation. The tableaux were few and uninspired, many of the costumes had been revamped, and, horror of horrors, there was no *meneuse de revue*. Otto Abetz of the Propagandastaffel, who had personally vetted the libretto, was so incensed that he subsequently took over the revue and brought in his own leading lady, a young singer-dancer who at that time was enjoying a tremendous success by imitating Mistinguett and Josephine Baker in Berlin. Her name was Marika Rökk. Mistinguett and Maurice were both back in Paris in time for the German star's launch, but only Mistinguett actually attended the première. She said, 'When

I saw that Nazi whore descending the staircase, *my* staircase, I wanted to get up there and throttle her. It was as though Hitler had spat in my face.'

The love-hate relationship between Maurice and Mistinguett took a savage turn – though as usual they would soon make up – in October 1940 when he turned up unannounced at her villa in Antibes. Firstly, she bawled him out for not publicly attacking the Nazis the way she had – all very well for her to criticize, from the comparative safety of the Free Zone, what anyone should have been doing in Occupied France when the repercussions for anyone vociferously insulting the Germans, particularly an entertainer of Chevalier's status, would have been severe. Next, she tore a strip off him for his 'abysmal treatment of that poor Joséphine' her former enemy who had suddenly earned her admiration by joining the Résistance. Maurice and Joséphine had recently entertained troops at the Maginot Line, and he denounced her as a 'scene-stealing whore' for baring her breasts during her final number – resulting in so many encores that, with curfew about to be called, Maurice had been left with just ten minutes of bill-topping performance time instead of forty!

Mistinguett was, however, supportive of Maurice's condemnation of Ben Tyber and Charles Trenet, two of the many hangers-on in Antibes. Tyber, aware of Maurice's affair with Joë Bridge, had scrawled in English under a poster of the pair, 'What is the difference between the Seine and Chevalier? – Twenty bridges lie under the Seine, but only one Bridge lies under Maurice!' Maurice sorted the American dancer out by socking him in the jaw – Tyber, big and butch despite being a cross-dresser, gave as good as he got and the two became friends. Trenet was not so lucky. Maurice and Mistinguett reported him to the authorities for having sex with under-age boys. After the war he was committed to prison, though with France's draconian privacy laws this was not made public knowledge until after Trenet's death in 2001. And the composer of immortal *chansons* such as 'La mer' and 'I wish you love' went to his grave never knowing who had shopped him.

The Bricklayer's Song

It took Paris less than a month to settle down, commercially at least, under the jackboot. Although cafés and bars displayed the 'Jews Forbidden' signs, it was to a certain extent business as usual. Gradually, most of the theatres and music-halls followed the example set by the Casino, and if a greater part of the clientele happened to be German this was, by and large, taken to be irrelevant. Thus began the question of who was, and who was not, a collaborator.

Mistinguett was the first to arrive in Paris, driving a white Chrysler along the boulevard des Capucines and sneering at a group of young German officers who were waiting, with hundreds of curious but genuine admirers, on the pavement outside her apartment. When asked by a reporter what she thought about Marshal Pétain, the hero of Verdun, who had been returned to power at the age of eighty-four, she replied, wisely under the circumstances, 'No comment!' Her true feelings were expressed only some years later, when it was safe to do so. 'Pétain?' she quizzed. 'He was an old wanker, an old fart who blew no good!' The general attitude towards Pétain was, however, for the time being, expressed by André Dassary, the twenty-eight-year-old lead singer with the Ray Ventura Orchestra. Known as '*l'hymne du régime*', André Montagnard and Charles Courtioux's 'Maréchal, nous voilà,' was positively played to death on Radio-Paris.

> *Maréchal, nous voilà!*
> *Devant toi, le sauveur de la France,*
> *Nous jurons nous tes gars*
> *De servir et de suivre tes pas . . .*

(Marshal, here we are!
Before thee, France's saviour,
We, your boys, swear
To serve and follow your steps . . .)

Many people believed, of course, that from its inception Pétain's regime was never too far-removed from Hitler's – a fact which time ultimately proved. Maurice, on the other hand, might have acted more circumspectly on arriving at the Gare de Lyon had he known exactly who was who. His big mistake was to take a drink from a bottle of Vichy water, and to chat to one of the reporters working for Radio-Paris, now under German control. He was unaware of this because the station's transmissions had never reached as far as the Riviera. Later that evening, on one of the news bulletins reporting his arrival in Paris, he was referred to as *le cabotin*, the 'ham' actor. Also, the mere fact that he had spoken to an 'enemy' reporter made many listeners suspect him of 'suspicious' activities.

The day after his return to the capital, Maurice was again met by a number of journalists, who began by discussing his Hollywood film career. He made it perfectly clear that while he was willing to talk about his work, he was completely apolitical and did not therefore wish to speak about the war. This only made everyone more suspicious, and eventually the very same reporter from *Le Petit Parisien* who had questioned Mistinguett asked, 'Well, Monsieur Chevalier, and what do *you* think of Le Maréchal?' Maurice's reply, though he had been forced into a very tight corner, was nevertheless an honest one. 'Like everyone else I myself am against the war. What I think is that there should be more understanding between the peoples of the world.' In replying to the question in a roundabout manner, Maurice had unwittingly flung himself into a trap from which he would find it increasingly difficult to extricate himself. As the German-controlled newspaper, in its edition of 15 September 1941, reported:

The popular Maurice Chevalier, who is going to sing for us in Occupied France, tells us that he welcomes collaboration between the French people and the Germans. And the journalist reports what Chevalier is ascribed to have said. 'You must understand, I have never been interested in politics. An artiste's mission is to distract his public from these things. The *chanson* is an admirable instrument for drawing people together. While I was in America I did my utmost to love France. Staying in France, coming back to Paris, I'm blindly following Le Maréchal, and I believe that everything which may be induced by a collaboration between the French and German people should be undertaken. It was in this sense that I spoke yesterday on the radio.'

Stunned by the way in which his comments had been 'distorted and twisted', Maurice went to see the editor of *Le Petit Parisien*, demanding an apology. The offending journalist was actually told to print a retraction, although it was too late now for the damage had been done. Subsequently, when he opened in *Bonjour Paris* at the Casino on 30 September his reception was decidedly lukewarm and the house less than half-full. It was a repeat, of course, of his potentially disastrous season at the Théâtre Châtelet some years before, and once again he was going to have to untangle himself from a tricky situation. This he did, little by little each night, again by being himself and showing, some thought, considerable humility – alone on the huge Casino stage, accompanied only by Henri Betti at the piano, and with a minimum of props. Some of his new numbers were funny, such as 'La polka des barbus', in which his artificial beard and moustache dropped off at an inopportune moment, and 'Le régiment des jambes Louis XV' was typically risqué. The one song which told everyone that Maurice was just as patriotic as the next man, and more so than most, was Henri Betti's stirring 'Ça sent si bon la France'. The sentiments of this alone endeared him to many people who at that very moment had been about to boo him off the stage.

> *Ce vieux clocher dans le soleil couchant,*
> *Ces grands blés mûrs emplis de fleurs des champs,*
> *Ces jardinets où l'on voit 'chiens méchants',*
> *Ça sent si bon la France . . .*

(That old steeple in the setting sun,
The great ripening cornfields of wild-flowers,
Little gardens where one sees 'Beware the dog',
Oh, how good France smells . . .)

Like everyone else in the music-hall, Maurice's material and songs had to be vetted by the Propagandastaffel. Though willing to allow most artistes to sing 'patriotic ' songs, based on the Nazi theory that the French would never get the better of the so-called Master Race, the Germans did clamp down on anything remotely smacking of propaganda. Edith Piaf had been ordered not to sing 'Il n'est pas distingué', a song which was a direct attack on Hitler, and later during the war Fréhel would be attacked by an incendiary device for singing the same song in Hamburg. Mistinguett got over her particular ban by singing a song with a line referring to Hitler having just one testicle in a heavy English accent. Maurice was instructed to remove 'C'est notre espoir' from his repertoire; either that or substitute the line 'Tra la la la la, zim ba boum ba la' for real words instead of 'sounds which could have amounted to a secret code'. One song which caused him a great deal of trouble at the time, however, was Henri Betti and Maurice Vandair's 'La chanson du maçon', an inspired work which Maurice sang in a paint-spattered shirt and with a bricklayer's trowel in his hand.

La maison du Bon Dieu,
Et quand viendrait la belle saison,
Nous serions des millions de maçons,
A chanter sur les toits de nos maisons!

(The Good Lord's house,
And when the fine weather comes,
We'll be the millions of bricklayers,
Singing on the rooftops!)

The idea that the honest men of France would rebuild what the Germans had tried their utmost to destroy was too much for the Propagandastaffel. The news of 'La chanson du maçon' spread around Paris like the proverbial wildfire. Mistinguett listened to the song and wept. The Casino box office, which had considered

lowering its prices in an attempt to encourage people to come and
see the revue, now found itself turning customers away. The song
was, of course, blatant propaganda, and Maurice was ordered to
remove it from his act or else. Fortunately for posterity, he did
record it for Pathé, and not all the copies were destroyed, for it is
the original pressing of 1941 which stirs the blood, and not the
post-war recording which is often heard.

One man who was unafraid of expressing his opinion about
anything during the sombre years of the Occupation was Jean
Cocteau, who regularly penned articles for *Comedia*. Cocteau
went to see Maurice at the Casino, and wrote about the event in
his own bizarre but inimitable way.

> Monsieur Chevalier enters suddenly, stage-left. I call him 'Le
> Grand Sympathique'. He is possessed of mentality, mystery
> and emotional radiance. If 'Le Grand Sympathique' breaks
> down, then everyone will break down. That is why I desire
> for this fruitful epoch to reproach itself for the insults it has
> bestowed upon him.

Cocteau's comments were noted by the Vichy government, and
soon afterwards Maurice was invited to sing on Radio-Paris. At
first he refused, as Edith Piaf and a number of others had done.
On a much more serious note, he was asked to sing at the Scala
in Berlin. Again, he refused. He was then reminded of Edith Piaf's
own frequent trips into Germany, where she had been unofficially
made *marraine* or godmother to the French prisoners of war in
Stalag III. One can never be sure whether Piaf got around to
confiding in Maurice, or if indeed she actually trusted him after
some of the lies she had been told. Thus he may not have known
that she was liaising with the Resistance. Posing for photographs
with the prisoners, she would have these enlarged and mounted
on to forged identity papers. Thus, each time she entered a camp
with eleven musicians, she always left with seventeen, and incredibly she was never caught. Maurice's approach was slightly different, once he had made up his mind to travel to Germany. One
evening after his show at the Casino he met several Vichy representatives and told them that he would be willing to perform in
Germany, but only on certain conditions. The visit would last no

more than twenty-four hours, there would be a single engagement at Alten Grabow, and instead of receiving his usual fee Maurice wanted the kommandant to free ten prisoners with addresses in Ménilmontant. To have demanded such a favour from a man like Otto Abetz must have taken quite a lot of nerve, and to cover himself Maurice agreed that he would do a series of broadcasts for Radio-Paris upon his return, although this was to be 'for the people of Paris who want to listen to me, not for the Nazis'. Astonishingly, Abetz gave him the go-ahead and in November 1941 he and Henri Betti boarded the train for Berlin. After spending the night here, they were escorted by a delegation to Alten Grabow, arriving at noon. The camp had changed little over the years; conditions for prisoners were still grim, though bearable. As soon as the men saw Maurice they began chanting 'La chanson du maçon'. After his performance, during which many tears were shed, Maurice told the prisoners of his own experiences in the same camp, twenty-seven years before. Then, shortly before dusk, he returned to Berlin.

Back in the German capital a number of Nazi-favoured artistes, including Emil Jannings, who had starred opposite Marlene Dietrich in *The Blue Angel*, met him at the railway station with news that a reception had been laid on in his honour in a government building. Maurice was afraid of flinging Jannings's hospitality in his face for fear of repercussions if the Germans should ever get hold of Nita Raya and her parents. But neither did he wish to stay on Nazi soil one moment longer than necessary. In order to get away he joked, 'I'm sorry, but I've got to get back home. Can't I take the piss out of the English in my songs instead, or Churchill?' Such a comment, though light-hearted, might not have been taken with a pinch of salt back in France, where the ex-prime minister, Pierre Laval, had issued a proclamation that if need be he himself would collaborate with the Master Race if it meant helping them towards a speedy victory over the British. Fortunately, Maurice's 'jest' did not become public knowledge for many years.

Returning to Paris, Maurice was upset to find himself at the centre of yet another smear campaign. Naturally, he had spoken to reporters about his proposed trip to Alten Grabow, but their articles, or at least the scurrilous ones, had been published during his absence. *Paris-Soir*, dated 26 November, repeated his alleged statement, 'My week-long tour of Germany will be the finest of my career. I'm going to sing "Notre espoir" for the German people. My hope is that I will soon see them taking their place among us, and that they will help the Marshal to build a new France.' Similarly *Le Petit Parisien* of 1 December reported him as having said of his reception in Berlin, 'I was officially received by Oberleutnant Bentmann, who is Monsieur Abetz's father-in-law, and by Monsieur Liencathal, who is a representative of Monsieur von Ribbentrop. As you can see, I am very well in with the German authorities!' And even in London, where the servicemen had always held him in high esteem, one newspaper branded him 'pro-Nazi'.

A further insult awaited him from Josephine Baker, who in spite of her spitfire temperament had always been regarded by Maurice as a reliable and understanding friend. While working for the Free French with Frédéric Rey, from a base in Casablanca, she had met and started an affair with the lecherous Pasha of Marrakesh, El Glaoui. When Maurice flew to Casablanca to begin a brief tour during April 1942 he naturally paid his respects. The event was described by the American author Lynn Haney in her biography of Josephine Baker.

> For Chevalier, Josephine made no attempt to primp. Of all the French who had played hanky-panky with the Germans, none was more the target of her wrath than 'the man in the straw hat', France's goodwill ambassador around the world. Josephine considered Chevalier a shallow opportunist . . . she greeted him with a barrage of insults, calling him coward and traitor. Her vehemence reached the point of hysteria. She later told an Associated Press reporter, 'Chevalier is to the stage what Laval is to diplomacy. His type of propaganda, trying to put Nazism over to the French people, is worse than a speech by Hitler.'

Under different circumstances, Josephine might have found herself facing a law-suit. In spite of the suffering she had been forced to undergo because of the colour of her skin, and in spite of her own undisputed heroics during the war, she did have something of a sizeable chip on her shoulder. When faced with what she had said, Maurice simply shrugged his shoulders and told a reporter, 'She's just a wasting has-been who doesn't know what she's saying.'

During the autumn of 1942 Maurice returned to the Casino with *Pour toi, Paris!* The revue titles now had only twelve letters because, Henri Varna declared, while the Germans were in power no show could ever be complete. Maurice found each performance a trial of mind over matter. For every genuine admirer there were often two of the other kind, and there would always be a reporter hanging around the stage-door waiting for a new 'exclusive' to add fuel to the fire which had already begun to consume him. Suffice to say, when the Casino revue closed in the December Maurice announced that he had had enough – until the 'climate' in Paris changed, there would be no more shows, and definitely no further radio broadcasts. As for his new apartment on the boulevard de Courcelles, this was left in the capable hands of the concierge, whom Maurice referred to in his memoirs as Mama Delpierre.

Sojourning briefly at La Bocca, Maurice was afforded relative peace of mind with Nita Raya and her parents, and Henri Betti. Because there was little else to do, he began writing the lengthy series of memoirs which would be published intermittently over the next twenty-five years under the heading *Ma route et mes chansons*. The first of the ten volumes, *La Louque*, was published by Julliard in 1946. The first draft kept him busy until July 1943, when news came that the Allies had landed in southern Italy and Sicily. Thinking that they were done for, this triggered panic among the Germans, and all over France people were terrified that if the enemy began to retreat, reprisals would be inevitable. Maurice therefore sent Nita's parents to a place of safety in a suburb of Nice; Nita should have gone too, but she flatly refused to leave his side and, although he might not have admitted it, Maurice needed her more than ever. Once again he had begun having problems with his stomach, and his difficulties with the media and with Josephine Baker had almost pushed him over the brink. He was also finding it hard to get work, or at least work from sources which he believed were not connected in some way with the Vichy government. He told one reporter residing on the Riviera, 'I would rather *die* first!'

On 1 February 1944, in the Criterion Gramophone Room at the headquarters of the BBC in London, the Dance Music Policy Committee held an important meeting as to what should or should not be broadcast on the radio. No one, it seemed, was spared. Even recordings by Frank Sinatra, whose standard was described as 'variable', were ordered to be controlled, as was the broadcasting of a seemingly innocent number called 'Paper Doll'. More damning, however, was the list headed 'Collaborationist Artists and Their Material'. This contained seven names – Mistinguett, Maurice Chevalier, Doctor W Mengelberg, the pianist Alfred Cortot, Sacha Guitry, Charles Trenet and Lucienne Boyer, in that order – and was followed by the titles of eight Trenet songs.

Soon afterwards, Lucienne Boyer's name was 'cleared', when the news was leaked that her 'secret activities' had involved helping British parachutists land in the French countryside. For her pains, the singer known affectionately as 'La Dame en Bleu' spent several days being interrogated in a Gestapo prison. Maurice and Mistinguett were also exonerated eventually, and praised for their intense patriotism. Others were not. Léo Marjane was seen often riding through the streets of Paris in an open-topped carriage, flaunting her affair with von Stuchnabel; each night on Radio-Paris she would sing 'their' song, 'Je suis seule ce soir'. Another famous singer, Suzy Solidor, whose dashing Aryan looks made her a clear favourite with the Germans, transformed her nightclub into an establishment which many regarded as a miniature Berlin. Tino Rossi, of whom Mistinguett said, 'That man would collaborate with his embalmer for a song!', played Don Juan in the German-backed film of that name. Marcel Carné accepted German patronage, as did his most famous star, Arletty. Several of his contemporaries, among them Robert Bresson, Henri Decoin and Jean Delannoy, followed suit, taking the actresses Danielle Darrieux and Suzy Delair with them. Sacha Guitry was reported to have dined with Hermann Goering. Jean Marais, Fernandel, Vivianne Romance and Jean-Louis Barrault all worked for the other side, whether through fear or through sympathy.

A few evenings after the publication of the Dance Music Policy list, Maurice was adding a few paragraphs to his memoirs at La Bocca while listening to the BBC's broadcast to Europe. One of its most popular programmes during the German Occupation was

Les Français parlent aux Français, which was presented by Pierre Dac, known to the French as '*le comique absurde*'. Dac himself had devised the catchy but apt introduction to the series, which very nearly became as famous as that of Lord Haw-Haw.

> *Radio-Paris ment, Radio-Paris ment,*
> *Radio-Paris est allemand . . .*

> (Radio-Paris lies, Radio-Paris lies,
> Radio-Paris is German . . .)

Dac's 'speciality' was to take the songs of those artistes whose work was featured regularly on the German-controlled radio and add biting lyrics of his own. This was one of his ways of working with the Free French, and he was often fed biased information by otherwise reliable contacts such as Josephine Baker. Maurice had a few months before recorded a song called 'Et tout ça fait d'excellents Français' – loosely translated as 'That's what makes a good Frenchman'. The Pierre Dac 'version' ended,

> *Et tout ça, ça fait d'mauvais Français,*
> *Les colloborateurs doivent payer . . .*

> (And all *that*, that's what makes the worst Frenchman,
> The collaborators must pay . . .)

In the occupied part of France, few people were distressed by Dac's diatribe. Along the Riviera, however, where he had come to be regarded as 'Our Maurice', things were very different. Many of the listeners to Dac's radio programme felt not just shocked and offended, but cheated. He was defended, vehemently and probably in the nick of time, by the actor René Lefèvre, who had made a name for himself in the films of René Clair but who was now actively engaged with the Resistance. Lefèvre sent a secret message to Pierre Dac, at his London headquarters.

MISTAKE ABOUT MAURICE STOP CAMPAIGN ILL-TIMED STOP
MAURICE HAS GIVEN EVIDENCE STOP WILL GIVE SAME TO
OTHERS.

This vital telegram was delivered by a young Resistance worker named Lionel, at considerable risk to himself. Twenty-five years later Lionel would contact Maurice again. His real name was Francis Leenhardt, and he was a native of Marseilles. He had been decorated with the Légion d'Honneur, the Croix de Guerre and the Rosette de la Résistance. In 1969, he invited Maurice to help at the inauguration of the Marseilles Palais des Congrès. In 1944, however, he was just another remarkably brave '*inconnu*'.

Pierre Dac acknowledged the message, and gave his word that he would not play another Chevalier record in his programme, or so much as mention his name. The promise was kept, but this did not mean that Maurice had been 'forgiven' by the British. Far from it. His name was kept on the BBC blacklist until after the war, and even then he was not told what had happened. For another twenty-seven years the secret of how his name had continued to be held on a 'list of collaborators' would be kept from him and his many thousands of British fans. And again, as with the damning articles in *Le Petit Parisien*, René Lefèvre's 'apology' went out *after* the damage had been done.

Maurice's predicament was now more perilous than ever. He was kept under surveillance by the Périgueux *maquis*, and at the same time watched by Gestapo agents working in the region. Terrified that the former might take their revenge because of Pierre Dac's statement, and the latter because he was sheltering Jews, he at once transferred Nita's parents to a hidden location near Saint-Meyme in the Dordogne, and a few days later he, Nita and Henri Betti joined them. Here, dangerously close to Les Milandes – although Josephine Baker and Frédéric Rey were entertaining the American troops in Corsica – he found out that he had been followed all the way from Cannes and that the Périgueux *maquis*, led by a man named Soleil, were out to track him down. At this stage, still pestered by various organizations to perform, and confused as to who was who in the maelstrom of events, Maurice decided to return to Paris to consult a specialist in internal disorders, confident that his assailants would not find Nita and her parents. In his memoirs he admitted that he was only feigning illness, though with his history of bad nerves it was quite plausible that the events of the last few weeks had taken their toll and that he was genuinely unwell. In any case, his doctors in Paris issued

him with the medical certificate which would be essential to prevent him from working and thus making more 'mistakes'. The
Germans, of course, refused to believe that there was anything
wrong with him and he was asked to participate in the annual,
now enemy-sponsored '*La nuit du cinéma*'. The fee for this –
200,000 francs for a fifteen-minute spot – would have tempted
many artistes, but not Maurice. He set off on his return journey
to the Dordogne, accompanied by Félix Paquet.

On 6 June 1944 Maurice, in common with everyone else,
thrilled to the tidings that the Allies had landed in Normandy,
heralding the beginning of the end for Nazi oppression. The news,
as it came in, was relayed to the people of Mauzac by loud-
speakers set up outside the post office, and Maurice was one of
the first to toss his cap into the air. His joy, however, was short-
lived when he was warned not to return to Saint-Meyme because
a group of *maquisards* were waiting there to arrest him. For the
first time since the outbreak of the war, Maurice panicked. Fleeing
across the open countryside, he and Félix Paquet ended up in the
village of Cadouin, some 5 miles away, where they flung themselves upon the mercy of a music-hall couple named Delemarre.
At this stage Maurice, the eternal gallant, urged Félix Paquet to
leave him and make his way back to Bergerac, insisting that he
was the party being hunted, and no one else. Paquet refused, which
was just as well, for a few days later the avenging Nazis bombed
and burned the village of Molières, just 2 miles from where the
friends were hiding. For several weeks, while the Périgueux and
Bergerac regions were being liberated by fighting forces from the
Resistance, the pair lay low, though there was some consolation
when they were joined by Nita Raya and Maryse Paquet. There
was, however, worse to come.

On Tuesday, 29 August 1944, the Belgian newspaper *La Prov-
ince de Namur* carried the following headline: THE TRAGIC END
OF A GREAT ARTISTE – MAURICE CHEVALIER IS NO MORE.

In our edition yesterday we announced the news sent to us
by the British Reuter Agency, to the effect that the celebrated
comedian Maurice Chevalier had been killed by a hail of
terrorists' bullets in a Paris street. There is still no confir-
mation of this, although Maurice Chevalier did bring this

action upon himself by collaborating along with such artistes as Raimu and Albert Préjean.

The statement was brief enough, but it was the most damning attack on Maurice so far because the actual word 'collaboration' was used to describe him for the first time. His name was also on the 'Dead Traitors' list pinned to the noticeboard in the town hall at Périgueux a few days later. The news of his 'elimination' was also announced by the Reichstag on 10 September. In retrospect, of course, it is difficult to ascertain whether Maurice was genuinely thought to be dead or the rumour was circulated by intimate friends trying to get the Resistance off his back until he himself had cleared his name. There again, the Germans may have wished to lull him into a false sense of security, into believing that he was no longer being pursued; they may have been hoping thus to flush him out and hand him over to the Gestapo. If so, this did not work, for during the morning of Sunday, 14 September, three men armed with machine-guns barged into the Delemarres' house and apprehended Maurice. Because he gave himself up without making too much of a fuss, his hosts and Félix Paquet were allowed to stay put, although they were warned not to leave the house. Maurice was driven into Périgueux, where his interrogation took place on the third floor of a building not far from the town hall. Because of his status, a large crowd of onlookers had gathered outside, and these were allowed inside the room a few at a time in order to observe that the proceedings were being conducted legitimately.

Maurice recorded in his memoirs that during his ordeal, one of the few lighter moments was when a female admirer walked up to him and asked for his autograph. He was made to stand with his back to the wall between portraits of Stalin and de Gaulle while his inquisitors grilled him. He did not fare badly during the preliminary interview, for the *maquisard* was from Ménilmontant and knew him. He was, however, obliged to hand Maurice over to his immediate superior, an apparently horrendous individual who, because of his great height, was known as Double-Mètre. This man read out the charge: that Maurice had fraternized with the Nazis, and that he had also entertained in Germany. Maurice denied the former, and explained that the latter had been for the benefit of the inmates of Alten Grabow. The fact that he had enabled ten prisoners to be set free was not mentioned, as it had been similarly 'overlooked' by the media. According to Manouche, the friend and unofficial god-daughter of Mistinguett, 'Not content with beating him up, they were about to shoot him when Maurice, his sang-froid totally abandoned, offered them a large sum of money, which of course they accepted.' This may have been true, and indeed who would have blamed him for wishing to purchase not just his freedom but his life? He was certainly sentenced to be 'eliminated', though Double-Mètre informed him with sardonic satisfaction that the actual execution would not take place until he had received orders from *his* superiors. He was also told that the original orders to arrest him had come from Algiers, which had, of course, been one of the venues of Josephine Baker's North African tour – a coincidence, perhaps. Thus, still under threat of death, Maurice listened while his 'confession' was read back to him.

I returned to Paris only in September 1941. During my brief stay in the capital I was asked to go and perform in Berlin. I refused. Afterwards I was asked to sing for voluntary workers in Germany. I refused. Then they insisted that I accept a tour of the prison camps. I refused also, although I did agree to sing one afternoon in *one* camp. I insisted this would have to be Alten Grabow, where I myself had been held prisoner for twenty-six months after being wounded in the war of 1914–18. I accepted no fee for this, but demanded the liberation of ten French prisoners from Belleville and Ménilmontant. This was granted.

I can now say that my gesture was twisted by Nazi propaganda, aided by way of the 'French' and International press. They turned *one* performance into an entire tour. This I find impossible to deny. It seems to me, on reflection, that my urge to help others has been a mistake, for it has given rise only to scandal.

I have also been criticized for several broadcasts that I made for Radio-Paris which, at the time, it was impossible for me *not* to make – not without endangering my freedom and the freedom of those whom I held dear. I made just eleven of these broadcasts, in spite of the great number demanded.

Therefore, in accordance with the Intellectual Resistance, I decided to cease all professional activities in order to avoid the pitfalls and ambushes which certain journalists and collaborators were setting constantly about me. I completely abandoned my career from the beginning of 1943, on the pretext that I was too ill to work.

Since August 1942 I have been in contact with Cannes, and the notaries of the Resistance, in particular the writers Louis Aragon, René Laporte and René Lefèvre, to whom I have proved myself, and the *chansonnier* Pierre Dac, who early in 1944 broadcast my name on Radio-London. René Lefèvre sent him a message, since when he has refrained from mentioning me.

In spite of incalculable pressures to do so, during the Occupation I have refused the following:

a) to appear in any politically motivated gala.

b) to have anything to do with foreign intellectuals.

c) to sing for German relief, or to offer my services in galas organized by Germans residing in France for their families and workers.

d) to help at any reception for German artists in Paris.

e) to make any film for 'Continentale' [a German-backed film company].

f) to sign the 'statement of fidelity' which the government required from all holders of the Légion d'Honneur.

On the other hand, I donated millions of francs, earned by me in other galas, to prisoners and ex-music-hall stars. Thus, in my soul and my conscience, I consider that I have done all that I could to behave as an honest man.

After signing this document, Maurice was given permission to leave the interrogation room. He had no money, and no means of getting back to Cadouin – a distance of some 35 miles – and Double-Mètre of course did not care if he reached his destination or not; in all probability he had arranged a *maquis* hit-squad to complete the job which they had allegedly already done. In the event, Maurice was driven back to the Delemarres' house by friends of the Ménilmontant *maquisard*, who had never considered him guilty in the first place.

Maurice's situation was greatly helped by Nita Raya. A few days after his 'trial' she drove to Toulouse, where she had arranged a meeting with the writer René Laporte, one of the chief members of a Resistance group known as 'Les Etoiles', an organization which had been co-founded by the poet Louis Aragon and his companion Elsa Triolet. Laporte was also director of Radio-Toulouse, 'The Voice of the Liberation', and an extremely important man to have as a friend. He listened to Nita's story, believed it, and decided to help. The following day two armed bodyguards were sent to escort him to Toulouse. They are supposed not to have known his identity, but even with the heaviest of disguises it is almost certain that they recognized him. Again, Manouche has alleged that Maurice handed out more 'safety' money at this stage, a story which came from Mistinguett, who may have been taken into his confidence at some time or other. In any case, he was treated kindly and hidden in a backstreet bedsit while all around him the *maquisards* continued to round up and question suspected traitors.

For several days Maurice practically lived on his nerves. He was still unsure of his safety and knew only too well that Double-Mètre could have spies in Toulouse. Then he was joined by Nita and her parents, and he sensed that he was over the worst. Further aid came from his secretary, Max Ruppa, who had persuaded a young reporter from the British *Daily Express* to hear Maurice's side of the story. The article did him much good, and other publications soon followed suit.

Maurice was not the only entertainer in France to be rigorously interrogated. The actress Arletty, in particular, was given a very hard time and forced to have her head shaved. The actor Pierre Fresnay, then married to Maurice's friend Yvonne Printemps, was also charged with collaboration. Even Mistinguett was suspected for a time. Before going on stage, she would make a point of putting an announcement over the theatre Tannoy for anyone with any meat, coal or vegetables to spare to leave these on the steps of her boulevard des Capucines apartment. Manouche, who admitted to loving her more than anyone but who nevertheless reviled her in her own memoirs, said that the cash raised from selling these on the black market was used to swell Mistinguett's own coffers, coffers so full that she had begun buying gold ingots and burying them in the garden at Bougival. The money had in fact been donated to the war effort. Maurice's meeting with Double-Mètre did, however, come to an unexpected climax some two years later when, while signing copies of his memoirs at a Paris bookstore, the big man himself appeared. He introduced himself as André Urbanovitch, the wealthy patron of one of the city's largest art galleries. 'I just signed the book, and that was that,' Maurice said.

Because he was never called upon to face the same scrutiny as many of his music-hall and film colleagues – officially, he was never condemned, but neither was he totally vindicated – Maurice had to suffer the indignity, for several weeks, of not knowing if the general public had actually forgiven him. Then he received a second visit from Max Ruppa, this time accompanied by two British aviators and a cameraman from Paramount News. Maurice was filmed in the Toulouse bedsit, looking glum and forlorn, and the next day he, Nita Raya and Max Ruppa set off for Paris by plane. Half an hour into the journey, they ran into a storm and the aviator was forced to return to Toulouse. Maurice was terrified of being murdered, should any of his persecutors have followed him to the airfield and be waiting for him to land. However, all went well. The next morning the company set off again, and if Nita suffered from air-sickness, Maurice was overjoyed when the pilot gave him an aerial tour of Paris before going on to Le Bourget. A few hours later, looking remarkably refreshed and invigorated, Maurice was filmed delivering a speech in his Paris apartment. This was added to the footage taken in Toulouse and in the plane, and shown in cinemas all over England, France and America. The song in the background was Maurice's old American hit, 'Up on Top of a Rainbow', which he and his Resistance friends had considered appropriate. Many critics found it contrived and insincere, and one wrote, 'The entertainer has tried to exonerate himself in a cowardly manner behind closed doors, rather than face the people like a man.' This was untrue. Maurice's seclusion had been forced upon him by the *maquis* death-threat, and anyone else would have done the same.

Maurice's best and ultimate defence came from Louis Aragon, at that time a literary contributor to *Le Soir*, the controversial Communist newspaper which he had co-founded in 1937 and which had been banned two years later by the French premier. With the Liberation of Paris in 1944, *Le Soir* had gone back into circulation with daily sales in excess of half a million copies, and the edition dated 9 October contained an article which, having been 'blessed' by the intellectuals, gave Maurice's constant proclamations of innocence absolute credence.

> Maurice Chevalier was a victim of circumstance, singled out as a collaborator when one knew only too well that he had been assisting the intellectuals of the Resistance, and since 1942. I for one can vouch for the service that he has offered to our friends. It suited some people to have the Parisians believe that the great artiste had something in common with our enemies, so much so that even our readers began doubting him.

The day after this article was published, the French Communist Party arranged a parade through the streets of Paris, ending up at the Mur des Fédérés in the Père Lachaise cemetery, on the very spot where, in 1871, the Communards had faced the firing squad. Marching alongside Maurice, Aragon and Elsa Triolet were Paul Eluard and the painter Picasso. Maurice was terrified, of course, that something would go wrong, but when the crowds began chanting his name, he knew that he had almost won his battle – almost, for in seeing him publicly with key members of the Communist Party, many of his admirers believed that he had joined them. It is also a fact that the Party gained many new recruits who simply 'wanted to follow Chevalier's example'.

Impressed by Louis Aragon's article in *Le Soir*, and Maurice's reception in Paris, back in Toulouse René Laporte contacted the troublesome Pierre Dac and informed him that an apology was now in order. Their meeting was arranged for 13 October, but Maurice proved understandably reticent in the face of the man who had inadvertently almost cost him his life. In his memoirs he recorded, 'He stood before me, his blue eyes looking into mine. Then he grasped my hand very strongly. I felt ashamed of him.' Dac's actual words to Maurice were, 'Give me a full account of your activities and I'll see what I can do higher up.' He was referring to the Haute Comité de la Résistance, in Paris, but Maurice refused to be intimidated any further; his public had accepted him, and this was all that mattered.

A few days later, Maurice received a visit from his great friend Marlene Dietrich, whose own plight during the last year of the war had moved him to tears. Marlene, an honorary lieutenant with the American army, and under the direct command of General Patton, had found herself trapped with the division in the Ardennes, in some of the worst weather the region had ever known. She had come dangerously close to being captured by the Germans, yet she had never once given up hope, and was rescued only in the nick of time by the Allies.

> Marlene Dietrich – and she should be blessed for being my friend – had read the article in *Le Soir*. She asked for my address, and arrived with open arms and open heart. We embraced affectionately, and she informed me that everyone who knew me personally in Hollywood and New York refused to believe the persistent stories that had been circulated about me. She was wearing her army uniform and had just returned from entertaining American troops in Europe. We had tears in our eyes, although we were soon laughing. And God, how good *that* made me feel.

One of Maurice's first important engagements as a 'free' man took place in Melun, in the barracks of the 31st Infantry, his old regiment. There was no fee, and the show was attended by more than 200 *maquisards* who had more or less adopted the newly resurrected 'La chanson du maçon' as their anthem. Soon afterwards he gave two charity concerts for the Resistance at his former stamping ground, the Folies-Belleville in the heart of Ménilmontant. During the second show, he was heckled by a young woman who 'reminded' him of all the Resistance workers who had been killed during the Liberation. Maurice was defended by a youth who stood in front of the stage and yelled, 'So what? He didn't do it!' And the evening ended on a hysterical note.

Shortly afterwards he gave an open-air concert at the Palais de Chaillot on behalf of the Fête des Midinettes, followed by another at Luna Park – both on the same day – to a capacity crowd of 15,000, a figure in those days exceedingly rare for a music-hall artiste. He also had a brilliant new song – Maurice Vandair and Henri Bourtayre's stirringly patriotic 'Fleur de Paris'.

> *C'est une fleur de Paris,*
> *Du vieux Paris qui sourit,*
> *Car c'est la fleur du retour*
> *Du retour des beaux jours . . .*

> (It's a flower of Paris,
> From old Paris who smiles,
> For it's the flower of homecoming
> A homecoming to fine days . . .)

Although Maurice loved the song dearly, 'Fleur de Paris' did not belong to him or any of the other artistes who sang it – ranging from Mistinguett to the orchestra-leader Jacques Hélian, whose 1945 recording was one of the first to sell over a million copies in France. It belonged to the men and women in the street, the ones who nominated it 'the hymn of the Liberation'. Maurice also gave a number of concerts for the Allies, although he appeared only once in Paris, in a star-studded gala at the Casino. He was well received, but not enthusiastically so, and ultimately decided that perhaps he had given a bad performance on account of his nerves. For this reason he returned to the Riviera, where over the Christmas period he sang in Nice, Cannes and Antibes. Here he visited Mistinguett, who was living with the cycling champion Toto Gérardin, a young man some forty years her junior.

In January 1945 Maurice accepted an engagement in Marseilles, at the Variétés-Casino, and proved so popular that the management kept him on for several weeks. His audiences comprised mostly American marines, not renowned for paying attention while an artiste was on stage. Each night he was given a standing ovation and took several curtain-calls. From Marseilles he travelled to Lyons to give a two-hour recital at the Théâtre des Célestins. There was no orchestra; just Henri Betti at the piano. His repertoire had also been slightly modified. Apart from 'Fleur de Paris', there were no songs appertaining to the war; instead he had resurrected and rearranged several of the 'forgotten' songs from his films. One of these was Révil and Vandair's 'Il pleurait'.

Il pleurait comm'une Mad'leine,
Il pleurait, pleurait, pleurait!
Il pleurait comme une fontaine,
Tout' les larmes d'son corps y passaient!
Oh, la la la la! Quel cafard!

(He cried like a Mad'leine,
He cried, cried, cried!
He cried like a fountain,
All the tears passed from out of his body!
Every tear in his body! What blues!)

Maurice's devilishly funny song may have raised loud guffaws of laughter among his public, but outside the theatre his tears were very real. After almost a decade, he and Nita Raya had decided to go their separate ways. Maurice blamed the split on the wide difference in their ages – he was coming up to fifty-seven, and she was still only twenty-nine. He also confessed to his friends that their affair had lasted far longer than either party had expected, simply because Nita had not wished to leave him in the midst of his troubles. Fifteen years later she would write a number of successful songs, including two for Edith Piaf. The words to 'Toujours aimer' echoed her earlier feelings for Maurice exactly.

On croit avoir trouvé le seul être sur terre
Qu'on ne peut remplacer . . .

(I thought I had found the only being on earth
Who was irreplaceable . . .)

As for Maurice, he wrote in his journal, 'Nita was young, and full of dash. Physically and morally, I had come to the end of my tether. We had become strangers; our love had become tinged with latent irritation.'

On Top of the World – Alone

Throughout the German Occupation, the ABC music-hall on the boulevard Poissonnière had more or less thrived under what the Jewish director Mitty Goldin had scathingly called 'Aryan control'. In January 1945, when he returned to the helm of his ship, Goldin at once thought of Maurice and might even have been willing to 'up' his salary in order to lure him away from Marseilles, had not his conscience told him that the first artiste on the new ABC bill should be Jewish. He plumped for Marie Dubas, who had returned to Paris on 9 January after an absence of more than five years. The great *fantaisiste* had, like Maurice, changed a great deal during her exile, though to a certain extent her suffering had been compensated for by a new husband and a young son. Her talents, though, had not diminished, even if some critics did find her act a little old-fashioned now that Paris was into the 'swing' era. Maurice did not attend her 19 January première, but he did send a telegram, and towards the end of her short season he went to see her. In March 1944, from her base in the Swiss town of Lausanne, Marie had given a concert which had been broadcast not just to France but to England as well, and sitting in front of his wireless Maurice had clung to every word. One song in particular had offered him hope: 'Ce soir je pense à mon pays'.

> *Quand la nuit tombe sur la ville,*
> *Quand l'ombre descend sur la rue,*
> *Je suis dans ma chambre, tranquille,*
> *Si seule, et si perdue...*

(When night is falling on the town,
When shadows descend on the street,
I'm in my peaceful room,
So alone, and so lost . . .)

Maurice told Mitty Goldin that, in his opinion, his Paris 'début' should be at the ABC, away from the glitter, the nudes, and the general hype of establishments like the Casino. This was arranged and he opened on 4 May 1945. His popularity stunned even him. Within hours of the box office opening all tickets for the first two weeks had been sold on the black market for many times their face value. Maurice was not paid for his opening night; instead, all the proceeds were given to his old friend Gardel, now down on his luck and very ill. Three days later, the unconditional surrender of all German forces occurred, and this was ratified in Berlin on 9 May. The ecstasy of the Parisians in particular was indescribable – the dancing and singing in the streets continued throughout the day. Mistinguett, who on 25 August the year before had cycled into Paris and all the way up the Champs-Elysées – at sixty-nine years old – to join thousands of cheering Parisians in welcoming General Leclerc and his army, now drove into the city and gave an impromptu recital in a shoe factory! Edith Piaf, who had used most of her money from a series of recitals at the ABC to charter a ship in Marseilles for the transfer to Dover of 100 prisoners of war, sang 'Les gars qui marchaient' outside her apartment. A few years earlier she had been severely rebuked by the Propaganda-staffel for performing 'Où sont mes petits copains?' before a tri-colour backdrop; the song, like Maurice's 'La chanson du maçon', had been deemed 'an insult to the dignity of the Third Reich'. Now Piaf quickly asked her songwriting team of Marguerite Monnot and Henri Contet to supply her with a suitable song with which to welcome the boys home. Similarly, Maurice co-wrote 'La marche de Ménilmontant' with Maurice Vandair and Charles Borel-Clerc, and the song raised the roof the first time he sang it at the ABC.

Les gars de Ménilmontant,
Ils ont le cœur ardent,

Tant qu'ils s'en vont chantant:
'Mé-nil-mon-tant!'

(The boys from Ménilmontant,
They have eager hearts,
So long as they can go away singing:
'Mé-nil-mon-tant!')

'La marche de Ménilmontant' was one of the twenty or so numbers which Maurice included in his recital at the Théâtre Municipal de Bergerac on 16 June. His fee was waived, and all proceeds from the evening went to the local day nursery. What made this engagement extremely important, however, was that it took place in the very locality within which the horrendously fierce Soleil *maquis* had reigned supreme. It was also very much of a 'family' affair. The orchestra-leader was Emile Barouk, Maurice's old pal from Bordeaux. The show was opened by Myrio and Desha, the dancing couple who had hidden Maurice when he had first arrived in the Dordogne, and he himself was introduced to the people of Bergerac by Monsieur Delemarre, with whom he had been staying at the time of his arrest. His pianist was Henri Betti. After his performance the Mayor of Bergerac stepped on to the stage, shook him by the hand and called him 'the undisputed prince of the music-hall'. Moreover, printed on the programme was the statement,

Maurice Chevalier is more than an inspired actor. He is a good Frenchman who, in a critical hour of the Resistance, took refuge among us. Therefore tonight we are gathered here to thank him for his most magnificent gesture towards the victims of the war and towards our little babies.

If this was not incontrovertible proof of Maurice's innocence, coming from the very heart of the locality which had, less than a year before, accused him of treason, then nothing was!

During the autumn of 1945 Maurice spent as much time as he could afford writing his memoirs, but he was back at the ABC in December, this time for a three-month stint. This was a new concept as far as Mitty Goldin was concerned, for even great stars

like Piaf and Damia stayed only for two-week runs. Neither did
he have many new songs to offer his public. With the exception
of 'La chanson populaire' and 'La fête à Neuneu', the audience
had to be happy with the songs they had listened to hundreds of
times before; and in any case, the ambience and the sheer personality of the man more than compensated for the mediocre quality
of some of his lyrics. Like Mistinguett and to a certain extent
Josephine Baker, Maurice was primarily a visual artiste.

Maurice spent much of the early part of 1946 completing the
first volume of his memoirs, *La Louque*, and even found time to
map out the next one: *Londres–Hollywood–Paris*. The book
appeared in the June, and was well received by both critics and
public, who were of course expecting some in-depth 'confession'
about the war years. Unlike most showbusiness autobiographies,
it was a literary work. An important critic of the day, Robert
Kanters, described Maurice's style as 'wildly Dickensıan'. In an
interview Maurice confessed that his favourite writer was the
sixteenth-century essayist Montaigne, but that he also admired
Henri de Montherlant and André Gide. Of Simone de Beauvoir he
said, 'She opened up a part of my brain that I didn't know I had.'
He was also able to quote a passage from Marcus Aurelius: 'One
must excavate from within, for on the inside one may find the
gushing, ceaseless spring of wellbeing.' Maurice repeated the
phrase on stage during his subsequent recital at Scheveningen in
Holland, and again in Stockholm on 12 September 1946 – his
fifty-eighth birthday – when he sang for more than two hours at
the Bersbee, the country's most prestigious music-hall, in front of
5,000 hysterical fans. The great film-director Marcel Pagnol wrote,

> Maurice Chevalier is the master of *'le spectacle'*. He is a flesh
> and blood puppet who manipulates his own strings. What he
> does on the stage is neither a turn nor a recital; it is a master-
> piece of dramatic art.

It was another maestro of the cinema, however, who persuaded
Maurice to step in front of the cameras towards the end of 1946.
René Clair, with whom he had made *Break the News* in 1937,
and who had just scored a great success in the United States with a
film adaptation of Agatha Christie's *And Then There Were None*,

asked him to play the lead in *Le silence est d'or* (English title, *Man About Town*). Maurice was unsure of this. The part called for him to seduce a much younger woman (Marcelle Derrien) and eventually lose her, when she realizes the mistake she is making, to a man nearer her own age (François Périer). Obviously, he must have been thinking about his own relationship with Nita Raya, which had more or less ended the same way. In the end he agreed to do the film because Clair convinced him, by showing him the results of his private 'poll', that he was still considered by many women to be a heart-throb, and the film was a good one. It won first prize at the Brussels Film Festival, and again at the Locarno Festival in 1947, where Maurice was nominated Actor of the Year. Even so, it was not appreciated by everyone, as Clair explained.

It was not a great success in the Anglo-Saxon countries. I analysed this and decided it was because the film was only about love. Even in the English-speaking theatre there has been almost no treatment of love as a subject, whereas in French literature and theatre, love is so often treated as the main subject.

René Clair's views would be echoed by every one of the French *réaliste* singers, and most of the romantic ones. Asked why she had never sung in Britain. Edith Piaf retorted, 'Because they know nothing about love!' For this reason, Maurice was able to reign supreme as the most popular foreign entertainer outside of France, as most of his songs were *not* about love, and audiences did not have to get emotionally involved when he was on the stage.

Towards the end of 1946 Maurice also became aware of the new word which had entered the French language: Existentialism. He began taking an active interest in the goings-on around the Saint-Germain-des-Prés area of Paris. He was often seen drinking coffee with Jean-Paul Sartre in the Café de Flore, or enjoying an enlightening conversation with Juliette Gréco, Léo Ferré or Anne-Marie Cazalis in the Rose Rouge, the movement's cabaret on the rue de Rennes. He met Boris Vian, the singer Mouloudji, Raymond Queneau and other members of *la jeunesse de la Libéra-tion*, whose unkempt hairstyles and then bizarre beatnik-like mode of dress must have seemed strange to him. He loved Sartre's *Les chemins de la liberté* (English title, *The Roads to Freedom*), with its central character Lola said to be based on Damia, and read the first volume twice. 'It helps me to understand life, and all that's happened to me in my past,' he said.

In March 1947 Maurice travelled to England, not to sing but to board the *Queen Elizabeth* at Southampton for his first trip to America in twelve years. With him were his secretary Max and Yvonne Ruppa. Throughout the long sea voyage he worried almost constantly that the Americans would have forgotten him and that he would have to 'start over' at an age when many entertainers were thinking of calling it a day. In fact, his welcome was the same as it had been in 1928: tumultuous. Waiting there to meet him in New York was his old friend Charles Boyer, whom he had not seen for eight years, and who had made the gruelling five-day train journey from Hollywood especially.

A few days later Maurice opened a four-week season on Broadway at the Henry Miller Theater; the stint was eventually extended twice. A few people may have remembered his very first one-man show at the Fulton Theater in 1930, though most of his audiences were now seeing 'the new Chevalier' for the first time. Not only this; the great stars flocked to see him. He was photographed backstage or in his dressing room with Barbara Stanwyck, Robert Taylor and Mary Pickford. Greta Garbo went to see him, but dashed off just after the show. It is alleged that they had met at a Hollywood party some years before, after which Garbo had suggested that he join her in a midnight dip. Maurice's response, that the Pacific was too cold, is said to have outraged her. Though she often went to see his shows, she never spoke to him again. His reunion with Marlene Dietrich, on the other hand, was a pleasant one – though his decision to take her to a screening of *The Blue Angel* was hardly inspired! Maurice also met the boxer Marcel Cerdan, then at the height of his love affair with Edith Piaf (the following year he would beat Tony Zale to become World Middleweight Champion, and then, the year after that, he would be killed in a plane crash over the Azores). On the radio, he appeared with Lucienne Boyer, singing her theme song, 'Parlez-moi d'amour', and he guested several times with Bing Crosby.

Maurice's success on Broadway was followed by a lightning tour of Canada, and two shows in Boston and Philadelphia. He then signed another American contract for the autumn, and returned to France in July. Much of the summer was spent at La Bocca, receiving friends and finishing the second volume of his memoirs, again published by Julliard. There was no love in his life, and his loneliness added a definite edge, an almost heartfelt quality to his writing. He also spent some time with Mistinguett, at her villa in Antibes. The great star, not in the best of health after falling through a staircase at the ABC – she had tripped over the microphone wire – needed both cheering up and to be given sound advice, because at the age of seventy-two she was about to make her London début. It is also interesting to note that when Harry Pilcer turned up unannounced at one of her gatherings, he and Maurice were reported to have got on 'like a house on fire'. This was, of course, untrue. Pilcer had never tried to hide the fact that he had always despised Chevalier because of the way he had treated Mistinguett in 1916.

Maurice arrived in New York on 2 October 1947 after spending nine days on the *De Grasse*, the first Transatlantic liner to leave Le Havre after the Liberation. One of his first engagements was a repeat appearance on *The Bing Crosby Show*, during which he and Bing duetted wonderfully on 'You Brought a New Kind of Love To Me', 'My Love Parade', 'Mimi' and 'Louise'. A few weeks later he went to see Edith Piaf at The Playhouse on New York's 48th Street, and encouraged her as best he could. Piaf was not the average American's idea of what a French *chanteuse* should have been; they had expected another Mistinguett or Josephine Baker, decked out in expensive gowns and jewels, and instead they saw a dour little woman in a black dress, dishevelled and wearing no make-up, singing songs about sadness and death in a language they could not understand. Maurice advised Piaf to introduce each song in English, the way he did, and explain what it was about. This did not work, either, for speaking in between dramatic songs only robbed the *chanteuse-réaliste*'s act of its essential continuity. Thus, Piaf's season at the Playhouse was a disappointing failure and she told Maurice that it might be for the best if she booked herself a passage on the first boat home. In the end, she was saved by the theatre critic Virgil Thompson, who devoted several columns to her on the front page of the *New York Times*. Moreover, and it would appear via Maurice, she was introduced to

Marlene Dietrich, beginning a close friendship which would last for the rest of her life. Maurice also sang Piaf's new song while in America: 'La vie en rose'.

Maurice's visit to the United States lasted almost eight months, and must have made him very homesick for France. He broke all the house records with his season at the Golden Theater, which opened in February 1948. Although he had by this time recorded almost as many songs in English as in French, his most popular numbers were 'Valentine' and 'La marche de Ménilmontant'. There was one song, however, which went down especially well, proving without a doubt that, regarding Maurice's 'activities' during the war, the Americans were that much more forgiving than the French.

> I've learned life's lesson!
> Fighters who always win
> Are those who can take it on the chin!
> Let the whole world sigh and cry,
> I'll be high in the sky,
> Up on top of a rainbow,
> Sweeping the clouds away!

Maurice's *au revoir* to America took place on the same stage the following May, in a special benefit concert for the American Heart Foundation. Prior to this, the Mayor of New York had, in an official ceremony, presented him with the keys to the city, and this had been followed by a luncheon at the Waldorf Astoria. He joked with reporters, 'Now I can go back to France with my famous American diploma. That should give them something to talk about, back home!' There was an element of truth in this, of course, for it is no exaggeration to say that the American media had mentioned more about the ten freed prisoners of Alten Grabow than their French counterparts *ever* would.

Eager to get back to France as quickly as he could, Maurice decided to take a plane – his first flight across the Atlantic, and almost his last. Half-way through the journey the aircraft ran into the tail-end of a hurricane and he spent six hours in the cabin with the pilot, having a severe attack of nerves and yet still seeing the funny side of the situation. 'That's what you get for trespassing on the birds' territory,' he joked with reporters at Le Bourget.

Maurice spent the summer of 1948 at La Bocca, resting initially, until urged by Mistinguett to take a more active interest in the Tour de France. Her reasons for this are obscure, though she is said to have been distressed to learn that her 'opposite' in the music-hall was thinking of retiring – something he mentioned in his memoirs, and which almost came about.

People didn't wish to believe me when I assured them that I would soon give up the stage, having clocked up fifty years on the boards. A singing recital requires a physical strength which, at the age of sixty, one no longer has – and oh, what it would be like *not* to have butterflies in one's stomach at four in the afternoon! No, I will retire while my heart is still in my work. A film every now and then, radio and television, books, songs, journalism – an entirely different life!

In spite of her 'bad' leg and the fact that her doctor son had advised her to refrain from driving her cars, Mistinguett was at seventy-three still incredibly fit. She had recently told a British reporter, 'I've never smoked, or drunk anything other than watered-down wine. As for the other? Sex is the only bad habit I never wanted to give up. *That's* what keeps me fit!' Thus the mere idea that Maurice was about to give up the stage simply because he did not consider himself up to it physically appalled her, and she made him aware of her own strict morning routine: up at six, a 2-kilometre jog followed by a rigorous work-out, several laps around the swimming pool, and a massage. She also accused Maurice of ruining his health by having smoked heavily in his younger days, although he then riposted that the greatest *chanteuse-réaliste* of her day, Damia, had 'maintained' her fitness and her famous gravelly voice by smoking seventy untipped Gitanes daily! Maurice also watched Mistinguett in rehearsal for her new revue at the ABC – her last – and was stunned to see that she was able to dance the be-bop for twenty minutes without even pausing for breath. He admitted defeat, and never spoke of retirement again. As for his 'active' interest in the Tour de France, he announced that this would involve no more exertion than picking up a pen!

In fact, on 15 July he covered the Cannes–Briançon stage of
the race for the newspaper *Paris-Presse*, arriving on location at
five in the morning and eagerly supporting the people's favourite,
Louison Bobet. Many journalists were astonished at the quality of
the subsequent article: it was lyrical, detailed and accurate.
Maurice knew his subject exactly. The next day he covered the
Besançon–Aix-les-Bains stage, an arduous one over the moun-
tains. The event took up thirteen pages of his memoirs, and
Maurice said that he would like nothing more than to cover the
entire event, from start to finish, the following year.

Early in November 1948, Maurice arrived in Britain to play a
season at the London Hippodrome. On 14 November, not content
to listen to the BBC for news of the Princess Elizabeth's confinement, he joined the crowds outside the gates of Buckingham Palace
and began signing autographs the moment Prince Charles's birth
was announced. His première, a few days later, was regarded by
many as his best ever. Though he sang only eighteen songs, he
managed to notch up his usual two hours on a bare stage – save
for Fred Freed, the pianist who had replaced Henri Betti, who
'merged' into the backdrop – by adding many amusing and sometimes saucy anecdotes. Earlier, there had been a slight hitch with
the management when he had refused to use the now mandatory
microphone. Standing behind it, he declared, prevented the public
from concentrating on the facial expressions essential to his act.
At the same time, artistes in Paris were waging a similar war.
Damia was contemplating retirement, even though her vocal
powers were still tremendous. 'That horrible lump of metal has
finally taken over!' she growled. Marie Dubas flatly refused to
work in any theatre with a sound-system. Mistinguett also dismissed the microphone. Maurice's ultimatum that he would sing
at the Hippodrome without a microphone or not at all – though
one wonders if things would have been allowed to go that far,
considering he had signed a contract – was much appreciated by
the critics, and in particular by the great Harold Hobson.

> There is an exuberance about Chevalier that prevents his
> being still for a single moment. In the great swift circles in
> which he endlessly promenades round the stage he will, with-
> out for an instant disturbing the rhythm of his progression,

lift up his knee with the pleasure and pride of a high-stepping horse in its first run of the season. Better than the great screen lovers does Monsieur Chevalier, with apparent entire unconsciousness, express the splendid, quite harmless joy of the body. The fact that he himself is not so young as he used to be is an enormous joke to him. In his universe there is nothing for tears. He has forgotten, he does not believe, that tomorrow we die. In private life I am told that he is a good Catholic. On the stage he is the complete, happy pagan whom the shadows have never touched.

In January 1949 Maurice opened at the Alhambra in Brussels, and what ostensibly began as just another season was transformed into an 'official' visit when his première was attended by Queen Elisabeth, the mother of Léopold III. A great fan of the *chanson*, she had previously entertained Mistinguett and Damia at one of her lavish dinner parties, and now it was Maurice's turn to be invited to the Palais Royal. This was followed the next day by lunch with the country's prime minister. Much more important, however, was Maurice's invitation to spend an afternoon of private conversation with Charles, the Prince Regent, who in 1940, while his brother Léopold had been held by the Germans, had joined the Resistance. What the two men discussed is not known, although all protocol was dispensed with and the two henceforth remained on first-name terms.

Also of immense importance to Maurice was a ceremony which took place before an immense crowd one afternoon on the famous place de Brouchkère, and which had been organized by the burgermaster. That most famous of Belgian 'personalities', the Mannekin-Pis, had been given a Chevalier smoking jacket, together with the two most famous props in the music-hall. Maurice did the unveiling, and sang, perhaps a little falteringly,

> *Vieux canotier-chapeau de paille,*
> *Qui fait parti de mon métier,*
> *Toi qui livra tant de batailles,*
> *Mon compagnon et mon allié . . .*
> *Cher canotier, laisse-moi te remercier!*

(Old straw boater,
Who takes part in my act,
You who delivered me from so many battles,
My comrade and my ally . . .
Dear straw hat, let me thank you!)

Ever-smiling though he might have been, Maurice was going through a particularly bad patch: never in all his life had he felt so desperately alone and unwanted. A chance meeting with Nita Raya, in the company of her younger lover, only made him more aware of his own mortality; the fact was that at sixty he considered himself 'over the hill'. He was also troubled by the sudden rise of relatively new performers such as Yves Montand, Charles Aznavour and Gilbert Bécaud. Montand in particular worried him because his act was not that dissimilar to his own, added to the fact that the ex-docker from Marseilles was extremely handsome, and had been given the 'official' Edith Piaf seal of approval. On top of this, he was a very fine, convincing film actor, having scored a tremendous hit in Marcel Carné's *Les portes de la nuit*. No *chanteur* in France since Carlos Gardel in the 1930s and Maurice, of course, had had quite the impact on working-class audiences as Montand. Maurice went to see him several times in order to 'monitor' his performances and hopefully glean something from them. Artistes now found it considerably easier to reach the masses with the advent of the television. Another 'charm-singer' who posed a threat in a minor way, and who had competed against Maurice in New York, was Jacques Pills, who since the Liberation had separated from his partner Georges Tabet to become known as 'Monsieur Charme'. All over France, women were swooning to songs such as 'Cheveux dans le vent' and 'Une femme par jour'. It was Pills who introduced Gilbert Bécaud to Paris – until around 1950 he was his pianist – and a few years later he would marry Edith Piaf. From a comedy angle, there were also Philippe Clay and Henri Salvador, an ex-member of Ray Ventura's Collegians, though neither of these would prove a threat on the world stage. Even so, Maurice spent more time watching these new stars than paying attention to his own career, and as he slumped into the deepest depression, like so many others he attempted to find the solution to his problems in the bottle.

The next six months of Maurice's life were, in effect, a mess. Afforded temporary Dutch courage by his gradual addiction to alcohol, and in order to prove to himself as much as to others that he still possessed the experienced *boulevardier*'s ability to seduce a good-looking woman, he embarked on a humiliating affair with a twenty-three-year-old painter named Janie Michels. A vivacious redhead, Janie was a devout Christian with a four-year-old daughter from a failed marriage. She is also said to have been domineering, treating Maurice like some elderly servant, no doubt having more interest in his money and his name than in the man himself – two assets which would, of course, have endeared him to many a woman in France, hot-blooded or otherwise. Janie Michels used him, much as Fréhel had used him forty years before, but Maurice was so besotted with her that he did not realize until it was too late that he had fallen into a trap.

During the next few months, spending time with Janie Michels became such a preoccupation that he actually began neglecting his career. He wrote hardly anything in his journal, and because he genuinely believed that he was running out of steam, he reduced the length of his recitals, sometimes by as much as half. When he was with Janie, he tried not to drink and his depression did ease somewhat, only to get worse when she was not there. Being seen in public with a pretty woman, of course, boosted his morale considerably and he tried to forget that not so long ago he had criticized Mistinguett for 'socializing' with men who were young enough to be her grandsons. With Mistinguett, however, things had been different. The media, and her public, had always realized that the 'stud of the moment' was invariably homosexual and there simply for decoration. Mistinguett had never been regarded as a joke because she had always been equipped with the facility to laugh at herself. Journalists, and foreign reporters in particular, began referring to Maurice as 'just another old lecher'.

Maurice was not exactly ignorant when it came to art. He knew Maurice Utrillo, and he had visited some of the larger galleries in the company of Gisèle d'Assailly, the art-fanatic wife of his publisher, René Julliard. Janie's hero was the post-Impressionist painter Henri Matisse, and Maurice found himself being dragged around on a seemingly endless tour of museums and art galleries until one day his lover told him that she had fixed up a meeting with the great man himself at his home in Cimiez, not far from Nice. The eighty-year-old artist only made Maurice more aware of the ageing process. Sitting up in his bed, which he rarely left for more than an hour in any one day, he was surrounded by the collection of tools and gadgets that enabled him to work. More importantly, Matisse hammered home the fact that at sixty-one an entertainer such as Maurice was still in his prime, and would be for some time. A few weeks later he ended his relationship with Janie Michels, and realized that he was lonelier than ever.

There was compensation when Mistinguett summoned Maurice to the ABC, where she was adding the final touches to her come-back – a revue which had been provisionally entitled *La Revue des Revues*, in other words the be-all-and-end-all so far as her magnificent career was concerned. This was of course the title she had chosen some years ago when attempting to woo Maurice into joining her in a tour of the Free Zone. Terrified that at seventy-four she might end up being laughed off the stage, she begged Maurice even now to join her in what could well prove her final venture, telling him, 'It'll be fun, just like an old age pensioners' outing!'

In retrospect, one could not envisage anything more rewarding than a series of joint Mistinguett-Chevalier recitals of the pair performing their old hits and doing sketches. She, however, had already made up her mind not to sing any of the songs that had made her famous – even her signature-tune, 'Mon Homme', would not be included in the programme – and as Maurice did not have any new material (or so he told her) he politely turned the offer down.

Maurice's real reason for not doing the revue – which would run with phenomenal success between May 1949 and February 1950 under the title, *Paris S'Amuse!* – was on account of the cast Mitty Goldin and Mistinguett had assembled. Aside from The Peters Sisters, there was scarcely anyone in the production under the age of twenty-five.

'How's a doddery old bugger like me expected to cope with *that* sort of competition?' he asked his friend and former lover Marlene Dietrich, in Paris for a visit.

Passage Interdit

In the autumn of 1949 Maurice recorded in his journal, 'I am very tired and ashamed, but I will fight with my last ounce of strength to pull myself out of this.'

Public opinion had already condemned his shows – few of them lasting longer than an hour, and not always with a supporting act – as poor value for money, and some of his critics were even of the opinion that the time was close at hand for him to hang up his celebrated straw hat. Maurice knew that he would never retire so long as he could still stand up on his feet, and he really did make a supreme effort to assert his authority over all the comparative youngsters who were out to wrestle his crown from him. On 30 November, in Strasbourg, he was on the stage for two and a half hours. In Bordeaux a few days later he gave two two-hour recitals in the same day.

During the Christmas break, he took his mind off his own problems by inviting his recently widowed brother Paul to La Bocca, and the pair spent a great deal of time sitting in front of the fire, discussing their youth. Early in 1950 Paul accompanied Maurice to Lille, his first professional visit to the city since 1904, when his escort had been La Louque. It was a time for remembering, and cannot have done much to help the fits of depression which, in spite of his 'resurrection', appeared to be getting worse, along with his drinking.

Afterwards he embarked on a short tour of Italy, taking in Rome, Turin and Milan – on his day off he went to see a performance of *Tosca* at La Scala. Returning to Paris, he went to see Edith Piaf, in a dreadful state after Marcel Cerdan's death the previous October. To his mind, the Little Sparrow had just written the quintessential anthem of pure love, 'Hymne à l'amour', and he was present when the song was given its Paris première at the Salle Pleyel. The last few lines, he said, would always make him think of his beloved mother.

> *Si un jour la vie t'arrache à moi,*
> *Si tu meurs que tu sois loin de moi,*
> *Peu m'importe, si tu m'aimes,*
> *Car moi je mourrais aussi.*
> *Dieu réunit ceux qui s'aiment . . .*

> (If one day life snatches you from me,
> If you die while far away,
> I won't care, so long as you love me,
> For I'll die too.
> God unites those who love . . .)

One of the most important showbusiness entrepreneurs in Paris at the time of Maurice's 'slump' was the Bulgarian-born Jacques Canetti, who was still only forty yet commanded the respect and admiration of everyone who crossed his path. During the early 1930s he had launched the famous Radio-Cité – among his first protégées had been Lucienne Delyle and Edith Piaf – and he had also organized the first French tour of Louis Armstrong. Since the Liberation he had founded the Théâtre des Trois-Badets, an equally renowned institution near the boulevard de Clichy, and from here he had already or would soon help to launch the careers of a whole host of stars, including Georges Brassens, Mouloudji, Guy Béart, Félix Leclerc, Boris Vian and Jacques Brel. Another Canetti stronghold was the Club des Cinq, a small theatre in the rue du Faubourg-Saint-Martin, and it was to this establishment that Maurice was summoned one evening in February 1950 to introduce an up-and-coming young star named Patachou.

Born Henriette Ragon in 1918, this famous *chanteuse* had chosen her name because as a child her complexion had reminded everyone of a cream cake! As a teenager, she had appeared, though only in a minor role, in the film *Rigolboche* with Mistinguett, and from the moment he saw her Maurice was reminded of his former mentor. He decided at once that he would make her a big star, though she was so tremendously talented that she would have made it without anyone's help. She had what the French call *'gouaille'*, which may be loosely translated as 'the gift of the gab'; and, most important of all, she had been born in Ménilmontant. Maurice fell head-over-heels in love with her, and assured his friends that this was not just another infatuation but the real thing. Patachou was without a doubt, he declared, the most important woman in his life since Mistinguett – something which did not go down very well with the ageing siren, who was rehearsing for an American tour at her villa in Antibes when, in a blaze of publicity, Maurice arrived at La Bocca with his latest love clinging to his arm. *'Patamerde,'* she growled. 'Patashit!' And a few years later, Patachou would get her own back on Miss by recording 'Mon homme'.

Maurice decided, within weeks of meeting Patachou, that he would ask her to accompany him on a proposed trip to the United States. Billy Wilder, who two years before had directed *A Foreign Affair* for Marlene Dietrich, had hit upon the idea of making a film loosely based on Maurice's life, with Marlene as his leading lady. The film was to be called *A New Kind of Love*, after the song. Maurice, meanwhile, began filming *Ma pomme*, based on an even more famous song, at Deauville, and it was here that he was inadvertently roped into a political scandal which would almost shatter his hopes of ever working in America again.

In 1950 the entire United States was locked in the throes of the McCarthy witch-hunt. On the last day of shooting *Ma pomme* the film crew approached him with a petition, part of the vast Moscow-inspired Stockholm Peace Petition for the eradication of thermo-nuclear weapons. Maurice may not have understood some of the big words written at the head of the sheet, but when asked if he was against the atom bomb, in spite of his earlier lack of interest in politics, he signed. So did 275 million others, among them Yves Montand and Simone Signoret, Louis Aragon and a young politician named Jacques Chirac. Neither did Maurice give much thought to the document once he had signed it, for immediately after completing the film he began rehearsing for what would be the longest uninterrupted season of his career: 131 two-hour recitals at the Théâtre des Variétés. Prior to this he embarked on yet another provincial tour, and it was while he was in Bordeaux that he met an important young admirer named François Vals.

Aged twenty-three and fresh out of the army, François had been an avid collector of Chevalier memorabilia for almost a decade, and after the show he and his girlfriend, Madeleine, waited outside the stage door hoping to get an autograph, not in the usual album or across the front of a programme, but on the cover of his enormous portfolio. François recollected:

Maurice just smiled, and said that he could not sign such an important document in the street, so he arranged for us to meet in the foyer of the Hôtel Splendid the next day. He told me to drop in and see him again whenever I saw his name outside a theatre. One week later he sent me a signed photograph. I saw him again, some time later, in Paris at the Théâtre des Variétés. He told me that his secretary was ill, then asked me if I would like to replace him – not at once, but after his next visit to America. I was told to ask my parents' permission, and given six months to make up my mind. And I was stunned that I, a complete unknown, should be awarded this honour!

Max Ruppa, Maurice's secretary of twenty years, was in fact very ill indeed, suffering from leukaemia. This affected Maurice badly, and he flung himself into his work like never before. The third volume of his memoirs, *Tempes grises*, had been published at the end of 1948 and now Julliard issued *Y'a tant d'amour*. The title, though outwardly not an unusual one, had been borrowed from a Damia song which she had recorded shortly after the death of her former lover, the great Russian bass Fyodor Chaliapin. It is thought that Maurice himself sang the song during his subsequent trip to Montreal, even though it was as far removed from his own style as could be. It is a great pity that he never got around to recording it, for its poignant lyrics expressed exactly how he had felt during those long, lonely months before his meeting with the woman who was now almost always addressed as Lady Patachou.

> *Faut pas s'moquer de ces rengaines,*
> *Qui durent plus que les amours,*

À que mon cœur a de la peine . . .
Adieu musique! Adieu beaux jours!

(One must not mock these old refrains,
Which last longer than love affairs,
For which my heart pains . . .
Goodbye music! Goodbye fine days!)

At the Théâtre des Variétés between September 1950 and the end of January 1951 Maurice was riding on the crest of a wave. Jean Cocteau was so impressed, particularly when Maurice returned to the stage after his umpteenth curtain-call to sing 'Ma pomme', that he wrote, 'Under the greenish rags of a character from a Daumier lithograph, Monsieur Chevalier has once and for all sculpted his individuality on the philosopher-tramp.' Besides coping with Max Ruppa's rapidly declining health, however, he was also worried about Mistinguett, who had just suffered a mild heart attack at her villa in Antibes. Maurice rang her, but she dismissed her illness as 'just another dose of flu', adding that her son Léopold, for many years a qualified doctor, had prescribed a nightly shot of pastis which, at seventy-five, she had tasted for the very first time. Mistinguett also told him, when he explained that he had been offered a series of engagements in America, that she too was rehearsing for a tour of Canada, to be followed by a lengthy tour of the New York cabaret circuit. Maurice promised that he would try and ensure that their paths crossed. Indeed, what would the Americans have loved more than seeing Mistinguett and Chevalier, the most famous 'couple' in the French music-hall, together again on the same stage after more than thirty years?

Then a few weeks later, on 21 February, tragedy struck. Maurice received a telephone call informing him that his old flame, the great *chanteuse* Fréhel, had been found dead in her Paris apartment of a suspected heart attack. Maurice's reaction to the news is not known, though like Mistinguett, who was touring Canada when he rang her, he must have been reminded of his own vulnerability so far as his health was concerned. Fréhel had been just fifty-nine, and though, unlike Maurice, she was immensely fat, she too had been constantly warned by her doctor not to over-exert herself. Although her great years had ended with the German Occupation, Fréhel had staged an immensely successful comeback in 1949, for which she had been paid large fees. Instead of investing, however, she had frittered away her earnings on friends and leeches, so much so that her last months had been spent in abject poverty. She had received a more than modest cheque for royalties from her record company, but this had gone not on herself but on her collection of dogs, cats and exotic fish. The post-mortem reported cause of death as heart failure brought on by self-neglect. Her funeral took place at the Pantin cemetery, in sub-zero temperatures, and remains one of the biggest there has ever been in France; only Piaf's was larger. Some 30,000 people turned out to pay their last respects. Maurice thought about going, but decided against it at the last minute, probably thinking the publicity would be bad for him; many of Fréhel's adherents had never forgiven him for what he had, or had not, done to their idol. He did send a wreath, and so did Mistinguett's representative in Paris. Later, the two visited the singer's grave.

On 15 April 1951 Maurice sailed from Liverpool on the *Empress of Canada*. With him were his pianist Fred Freed and his wife, and Patachou, who had been engaged to open Maurice's shows. Ten days later, as the boat was heading up the St Lawrence River towards Quebec, he was summoned to the captain's office and given a telegram. A statement from the Washington State Department, issued a few days before, effectively banned him from performing anywhere in the United States 'until further notice'. The fact that he had signed the Stockholm Peace Petition had caused Senator McCarthy and his council to brand him as a Communist.

Maurice was knocked sideways. He tried to explain that he had never been interested in politics, and that he had signed the controversial document for reasons of humanity. He said, 'The American government may have smacked me in the jaw, but the blow hasn't affected my heart.' Even so, the McCarthy committee refused to give him a fair hearing from afar, and some newspapers carried stories of his wartime experiences, particularly his participation in the Communist march to the Père Lachaise cemetery which had been organized by Louis Aragon. Staying for a few days in Quebec, Maurice and his friends made their way to Montreal, and the first engagement in what should have been a two-month tour. By and large, his shows were well received. The Canadians loved Patachou, who had very quickly put together a repertoire of '*rétro*' songs. She also had a habit of snipping off the tie of any man sitting next to the stage who happened to be talking instead of listening to her – something which would later be repeated during her appearances in London. Maurice was heckled, however, in some theatres in French-speaking Canada, and this resulted in his abandoning the second month of the tour and leaving for South America, which he had last visited in 1924.

The first country on the agenda was Venezuela, and Maurice was delighted to learn that all the seats for his show in Caracas had been sold within one hour of the box office opening. From there the company flew to Montevideo, where they performed for the students of the university, and here Patachou did not go down too well. A few days later, after a decidedly rough flight which must have reminded Maurice of his first plane journey back from New York, he was welcomed, at two in the morning, by thousands of screaming fans who, without warning, streamed on to the tarmac as the plane was landing at Rio de Janeiro.

In Brazil, Maurice appeared in a television show for the first time. He hated the whole experience. There were problems with lighting and sound, and the technicians spoke only Portuguese. Much worse than this, though, he was asked to perform 'ambiance' songs such as 'Prosper' and 'Valentine' in a closed set without an audience. More rewarding was his public meeting with President Vargas, who, with his cabinet, unofficially welcomed Maurice as 'ambassador of the French nation'. Patachou also took Rio by storm when she occupied the entire first half of the programme at the Copacabana, and she was subsequently offered a contract, as top of the bill, at the Vogue Theatre. Maurice must have been disappointed to learn that he would be finishing the rest of his South American tour on his own. All the same, on her opening night he personally escorted her on to the stage, and the pair received a ten-minute ovation.

In August 1951 Maurice returned to France. However, as he was missing the company of Patachou, he had no particular desire to rest and he at once set off on a gruelling tour of the Middle East. This did not receive a great deal of press coverage, so hardly anything is known of his recitals in Beirut, Safar and Aley. Neither was much said of his show in Istanbul, though his arrival in Egypt did make the front pages of the newspapers there. He was received by Oum Khalsoum, the greatest singer the Middle East has ever known. Maurice told reporters, 'Listening to her gave me a little bit of God.'

On 20 December Maurice returned to La Bocca, where he chaired a conference with the cleric Père Boulogne on the importance of religion in popular song. The individual used as an example the controversial writer Jehan Rictus, whose claim to fame in Europe was his 1904 poem 'La Charlotte priant Notre-Dame', which had been adapted and recorded by Marie Dubas three decades later. Also at La Bocca was the unveiling of Henri Blattes's superb sculpture of Maurice's mother, La Louque. Maurice's brother Paul helped with the ceremony.

Two important events occurred in Maurice's life early in 1952. First of all, he officially appointed François Vals as his right-hand man and secretary (Max Ruppa was fading fast, and died in the May). Secondly, he decided to put his Cannes villa on the market and find somewhere suitable closer to Paris. The search was not a long one. The lyricist Albert Willemetz lived at Marnes-la-Coquette, near the Parc Saint-Cloud, which was not too far from Mistinguett's house at Bougival and at most was a twenty-minute drive from the city centre. One day when Maurice was visiting Willemetz his friend took him to view the Castel des Rois, in the same park. The huge twenty-room mansion had formerly been the home of Sir Richard Wallace, who had endowed Paris with her magnificent wrought-iron ornamental fountains. Maurice bought one of these, and the house to go with it. The statue of Maurice's mother was then brought up from Cannes, and he rebaptized the house La Louque in her memory. Shortly afterwards his brother Paul moved in with him, along with the household staff, but not François Vals, who, although young and about to marry Madeleine, was determined to retain his independence. He was, however, given a sumptuous office on the ground floor, close to the salon which Maurice would use for receiving guests. Much of the first floor was out of bounds, particularly Maurice's study. Here, surrounded by dozens of photographs and portraits of himself and his friends, he would write the next six volumes of his memoirs.

He said, 'I have finally found the house in which I would like to die, when the time comes.'

Early in 1952 Maurice appeared in an edition of the television programme *La joie de vivre* – almost the equivalent of Britain's *This is Your Life* – honouring Albert Willemetz. He also signed a contract with Paul-Louis Guérin of the Lido, not to work there but to appear with a part of the company in *Plein feu*, a new revue planned for the Empire. Then, on 1 January he left for Barcelona, the first stop on a massive tour, one which would wear out his entourage but not Maurice. At the Windsor Theatre, after his show, he met the great Spanish star Raquel Meller, who in the 1920s and 1930s had been one of the biggest box-office draws in Paris. Seeing her, old and no longer beautiful, affected Maurice badly for the rest of the tour, which took in Portugal, North Africa, Switzerland and Belgium. Surprisingly, he enjoyed working in Germany again, and his concerts in Hamburg, Frankfurt and Berlin all sold out weeks before his arrival. Even so, the latter must have brought back some terrible memories.

Maurice returned to Paris, and in the April *Plein feu* opened, with Colette Marchand as his partner. It is also interesting to note that one of the chorus girls, engaged by Miss Bluebell of the Lido to dance around Maurice while he was singing 'Valentine', was Odette Meslier, who would cause so many problems for Maurice's friends and family after his death. The revue did not fare well. The public were by now used to seeing their idol all alone on a bare stage. Also, the Empire was not suitably equipped for putting on Casino-style extravaganzas. On top of this, Maurice's actual performances suffered because he was grieving for Max Ruppa. The revue dragged on for four months, leaving him more depressed than he had been for some time. There were a number of '*petits amours*', all of them one-night stands, including one with his co-star which did not go unnoticed by the media.

What Maurice was pining for, though, was not a great love to sweep him off his feet but a chance to 'resolve matters' in the United States now that he had been promised a visa. First of all, however, there was the question of his new European tour.

Increasingly worried about having to use a microphone, and fearing that at sixty-four his voice would give up on him at any moment, Maurice had recently taken up *solfège* and projection lessons. In fact, he should have started using a microphone some time before, for in not forcing himself he would have prevented the tedious attacks of laryngitis which now threatened his career. In Venice he was forced to cancel a show for the very first time because he had lost his voice altogether. Returning to France, he went to see a doctor, who gave him penicillin injections. These helped a little, though his injured vocal cords had not recovered sufficiently for him to perform adequately when he reached St-Jean-de-Luz, Mistinguett's old wartime retreat, on 29 August. After some deliberation – he flatly refused to cancel a second show – he finally agreed to use a microphone for the first time ever. A few weeks before he had seen a young American singer named Eddie Constantine 'actually brushing his lips against one of these contraptions' and he decided to do the same. He discovered that he did not have to strain his voice quite so much, and what the public heard was a distinctive, mellow sound far better than the old Chevalier voice. At a time when most men of his age were getting ready to draw their pension, Maurice had begun a new career – as a *crooner*! Moreover, he was able to put his new '*idole des jeunes*' approach into practice when a few days later he topped the bill in a gala at Jonzac. His supporting artiste was Gilbert Bécaud, known to the French as 'Monsieur 100,000 volts' on account of his highly charged, frenzied, performances which often had audiences ripping up seats. Maurice won the popularity contest with comparative ease, and this made him feel much better in himself. The French tour ended with a recital in Biarritz, where François Vals asked for a day off, to get married!

From France Maurice travelled back to Berlin, where he gave a splendid account of himself at the Titania-Palast. From Germany he travelled to Scandinavia, an area that was also being toured by Louis Armstrong. The pair dined together in Copenhagen, and when Maurice explained that he was having trouble with his throat, 'Satchmo' offered him a bottle of his own 'vocal remedy' – a mixture of glycerine, honey and ipecac much used in America. Maurice found this amusing, bearing in mind that Armstrong was famous, apart from his trumpeting skills, for his 'sandpaper' voice! Even so, he swore later that the mixture had done him good, and kept the bottle as a souvenir.

When Maurice opened at the London Hippodrome on 27

October 1952, it was estimated that he had been paid £10,000 for the three-week season – a sizeable amount at the time. Half-way through the run, when 24,000 tickets had been sold, the box office announced that another 30,000 had been unsuccessfully applied for – there could be no extension because the next season had already been booked. Maurice had the solution: 'Find me another theatre!' he instructed. So it was that in the middle of November he opened in exactly the same show at the Prince's Theatre. But while the public were fighting, literally, to get seats, the critics were mixed in their opinions. While Harold Conway of the *Evening Standard* compared Maurice's rapport with his audience to 'an evening out with an old friend', and the reviewer for *Punch* remarked that he could add an air of innocence to songs which would 'make an ice-cap of an archdeacon's drawing room', practically every reporter was critical of his choice of material – or rather the lack of it. Apart from his opening number, the self-composed 'Sur l'avenue Foch', all his songs were ones he had been singing for years. This problem was rectified half-way through the season, and not even noticed by Maurice's more ardent fans, or the millions of television viewers who tuned in to see the second half of the opening night broadcast live on the BBC, without too many cuts from the censor's department. Nor were there many songs – fifteen in almost two hours, interspersed with long anecdotes or exchanges of dialogue between Maurice and his public, or more often Maurice and himself. Kenneth Tynan, who was sitting in the front row, wrote,

> His cat-footed ease, his power of suggesting a whole pirouette by a sly flick of the heel, had dimmed not at all. Nor had his wicked bountiful grin, which brings up apple-cheeks and eyes like diamonds. This tubby old schoolboy breeds happiness wherever he glances. Two hours with Chevalier would confer a happy benediction on the sharpest cynic in Soho. He belongs in the company of Rabelais and of Kenneth Grahame, between whom there is a gap which no one else can bridge. I have two complaints. I wish he had not sung Reg Dixon's 'Confidentially', and I wish he had not stopped so soon!

Jack Hylton, the British impresario responsible for Maurice's

season in London, included him in the bill for the Royal Variety
Performance which took place in November, and was also tele-
vised. Maurice sang four songs, including one which is said to
have been much appreciated by his royal hosts, the yet-to-be
crowned Queen Elizabeth, Prince Philip and Princess Margaret.

> *Un air de chanson populaire,*
> *Les cœurs sont pleins de chants nouveaux,*
> *Après le boulot*
> *C'est des chansons qu'il nous faut,*
> *Ecoutons chanter le populo!*

> (A melody of a folk-song,
> Hearts are filled with new tunes,
> After work,
> We must have songs,
> Let's listen to the 'populo'!)

After spending his first Christmas at La Louque, content maybe
though certainly not happy, because there was no woman in his
life, Maurice returned to Britain in January 1953 to begin a provincial tour – his first in the UK – and in the middle of a decidedly
cold winter. It lasted eight weeks, and he did not restrict himself
to just the stage. The perfect example of a working-class Frenchman, in spite of his mansion and his riches, he was invited to visit
hospitals and factories, and even took time out of his busy schedule
to open a distillery. The tour ended with a week-long engagement
at the Manchester Opera House, a television show, and countless
appearances on the radio. He then returned to London, where he
was photographed for *Paris-Match*, strolling around Piccadilly,
signing autographs for children, drinking a pint of beer, or trying
on hats. While in London Maurice also decided to take La Bocca
off the market and donate it to the SACEM (La Société des Aute-
urs, Compositeurs et Editeurs de Musique), of which anyone writing a song had to be a member, by way of examination. There
was just the one condition, Maurice told Albert Willemetz, the
committee president: 'One room must be kept locked and never
used by anyone, just in the event of my wishing to die in Cannes.'
His generosity was, of course, misinterpreted by the press, par-

ticularly those journalists who had attacked him during the war and were still trying to get at him whenever they could. These narrow-minded individuals decided that Maurice had been compelled to give his house away because no one was willing to live there after him. Another theory was that La Bocca had been in urgent need of repair and Maurice too stingy to foot the bill – ridiculous when one considers how much money he lavished on La Louque, stamping it with his own unmistakable identity. And SACEM were eternally grateful to Maurice for his benevolence. The two buildings and several acres of parkland comprising La Bocca are now known as Le Village Maurice Chevalier, and are approached by the avenue Maurice Chevalier.

Maurice faced two more problems upon his return to France, one minor and the other considerably more serious. Janie Michels, the young painter who had done so much for his libido but little for his morale, had moved into the park at Marnes-la-Coquette, into a bungalow with her mother and daughter, less than 50 yards from La Louque. At first, Maurice assumed that she must have done so to get back at him, but this was not the case. Once the two met for a chat they realized that they would be able to live side by side without giving each other cause for concern. Much more serious was the inexplicable rift that had suddenly developed between himself and Patachou. Since returning from South America, she had become a very big star in France and there had also been a successful season, complete with 'tie-snipping', at the Savoy in London. Charles Aznavour, Léo Ferré and a number of other up-and-coming *auteurs-compositeurs* had written for her, she had sung and recorded cover-versions of several Piaf songs, but worst of all she had committed the cardinal sin of 'poaching' 'Mon homme' from Mistinguett. Maurice might not have taken exception to such an insult, coming from a woman who in the past had always been able to get away with almost anything, had it not been for a young man named Georges Brassens.

Born in Sète in 1921, Brassens had published his first volume of poetry, *À la Venvole*, in 1942. Towards the end of 1952, by which time he had begun setting some of his more ribald poems to music, accompanying himself by guitar, he was noticed by the songwriter Jacques Grello. In Montmartre, at the same time, Patachou had opened her famous nightclub, Chez Patachou, and when Grello introduced her to Brassens, she 'flipped' – though it is not clear whether she was interested in the man or in his work. Brassens labelled himself '*Le Pornographe du Phonographe*', and one has to say that he looked the part, appearing on stage in a toreador's outfit, sporting a thick moustache, and using direct epithets as though these were going out of fashion. In time, Patachou herself would sing many of his songs, including 'Les amoureux des bancs publics', which was a tremendous commercial hit in France. Exactly why Maurice despised him so is not known, though it may have something to do with Brassen's self-confessed atheism and anarchic tendancies, and the fact that the newcomer, for all his obvious talent, really *did* look like the archetypal 'dirty old man' – something Maurice had been called only too often by his critics. Whatever the reason, François Vals was packed off to Patachou with a letter, the contents of which ensured she would never have anything to do with Maurice again. Only once did she mention his name publicly, when she snarled at a reporter, 'Chevalier? He's a great artiste, but he's also a *petit monsieur*!'

The rupture with Patachou brought a reunion of sorts with the 79-year-old Mistinguett, now in very poor health, and depressed: Lino Carensio, her lover of twenty years, had left her, callously declaring that it was no longer practical for him to live with a woman with one foot in the grave. Manouche told me:

Miss was terrified of dying alone and had only loved two men in her whole life – Pilcer and Chevalier. She asked Pilcer to move in and agreed to turn a blind eye to his screwing the young gardener. He refused, so she asked Maurice if they might take up where they'd left off thirty years ago. I'm pleased he turned her down gently. He was no longer young but the spark was still there and he needed a young woman to ignite it, not one who behaved like a bossy stepmother!

It would take several more years of soul-searching, self-loathing and abject loneliness before that special person came along.

Hello Again, America – Goodbye, Miss

The Americans had a new president, Eisenhower, and in June 1954 Maurice received word from the American ambassador to Paris that his visa had been granted. Needless to say, offers of work came flooding in from across the Atlantic, and at the age of sixty-six Maurice found himself being offered many more engagements than he could cope with. René Julliard had just published *Noces d'or*, the sixth volume of his memoirs, and the next one was well under way. In the introduction to *Artisan de France*, Maurice wrote: 'Public, my love; public, my friend, allow me to lay my work at your feet. For I have enjoyed such joy, such gratitude and honour . . .'

During August he began rehearsing in earnest for a season at the Théâtre des Champs-Elysées, on the avenue Montaigne. This, he declared, would be no ordinary recital, for he was sick and tired of being criticized for the size of his repertoire, and for the lack of 'real' lyrics in some of his songs. Marguerite Monnot and Louiguy, famed for the works they had written for Edith Piaf, were commissioned to compose for Maurice and came up with 'À Las Vegas' and 'Donnez-m'en de la chanson'. Maurice himself adapted the Sophie Tucker classic 'Some of These Days', and from the repertoire of Al Jolson there was 'There's a Rainbow Round My Shoulder'. The rehearsals were marred, however, by the death of Colette. Though they had not always seen eye to eye – particularly when the great writer referred to him as 'a human snake' – Maurice respected and admired her. He did not attend her funeral at Père Lachaise, but he did send a wreath. Another floral tribute was sent to the great clown Grock, who began a series of farewell performances in Paris on 1 October, ending in Hamburg a few months later. In his younger days, Maurice had idolized the man known as '*L'empereur des clowns*', and had often imitated him. He said, 'Now that he's gone, there won't be many more real clowns.' To a certain extent, this was true.

Maurice's season at the Théâtre des Champs-Elysées also opened on 1 October, and in all there were fifty-five shows – one for every year of his career. The première was important from a media point of view, because it was attended by Mistinguett, accompanied by Lino Carenzio. Toto Gérardin had been dispensed with and he had run straight into the arms of Edith Piaf – in anger Mistinguett had named a monkey after him. His relationship with Piaf had not lasted long – Gérardin's wife, Alice, had had the couple followed by a private detective, and a large number of stolen items, including dozens of gold ingots, had been found in Piaf's apartment, hidden there by the errant husband. Piaf threw the cyclist out into the street, and several months later she had married the singer Jacques Pills. Marlene Dietrich was a witness at the ceremony in New York. Piaf herself was rehearsing for what would be a record-breaking season at the Paris Olympia. Unable to make the opening night, she sent a telegram. As for Mistinguett, she virtually stole the show in what would be one of her last public engagements. She and Maurice were greeted with loud cheers when they posed for photographers.

Early in 1955, Maurice embarked on yet another exhausting tour. The first stop was in Berlin, where they were showing *Schlager-Parade*, a German production for which he had filmed just one song during his last visit. The film was never released anywhere else, although the French were more than compensated by *J'avais sept filles*. Directed by Jean Boyer and co-starring Louis Velle, this was Maurice's first film in Technicolor, although it would be his last in the French language. From Berlin, he travelled to Copenhagen and from there to London, where in April he began a month-long stint at the Palace Theatre. In June, after a brief rest at La Louque – spent working on his memoirs – he visited South Africa. For a man with an almost uncontrollable fear of flying, he handled himself rather well. The flight to Johannesburg dragged on for thirty bumpy hours, but according to his pianist Fred Freed,

Maurice went off and watched a film starring Fred Astaire. The next evening he imitated Astaire during his performance and when he left the theatre he was mobbed by hundreds of excited fans, many of them wearing straw hats.

On 15 September Maurice, Fred Freed and François Vals boarded the *Ile-de-France* at Le Havre, destination New York, after many months of deliberation. For François, the trip would be particularly trying as his wife, Madeleine, expecting her first baby, was left behind in France. For Maurice, it would be like a journey into the past, taking him back to October 1928, when he and Yvonne Vallée had set out as pioneers. He had no illusions about the fight he would have on his hands; and it was a fight he had every chance of losing. Since the end of the war New York was positively teeming with crooners, most of them half his age. Time and time again he asked himself the same question. How would he compete with the likes of Frank Sinatra, Sammy Davis Jnr and Danny Kaye? A few months earlier, he had been served a writ by Arthur Lesser, his American agent, who had organized the previous tour which had been cancelled by Senator McCarthy. Lesser had sued him for loss of commission, and rather than fight the case Maurice had paid up. Lesser lost out in the end, however, because Chevalier replaced him with the more amicable Gilbert Miller, though even then he had 'got one over on Chevalier' by marrying Patachou. Now this troublesome man was threatening Maurice with bad publicity – the last thing he wanted. Needless to say, his morale was at a decidedly low ebb when the captain of the *Ile-de-France* asked him to put on a show to entertain the other passengers, who included Prince Albert of Belgium, a young American senator named John Fitzgerald Kennedy, his wife, Jacqueline, and his mother, Ethel, and Antoine Pinay, the Minister for Foreign Affairs. For twenty-four hours, Maurice hesitated, probably afraid that the gesture would be interpreted as some kind of political stance – at least by the media. He relented, of course, after insisting that all the money raised from his show should be donated to charity, and the event took place on the evening of 20 September, during a terrible storm. One journalist reported, 'Chevalier's great charm stopped everyone from being seasick!'

The *Ile-de-France* docked in New York on 24 September, and before leaving the ship an ever-thoughtful Maurice dispatched a

cable to Madeleine Vals which ended, 'While we are preparing
your future over here, embellish your nest and your chick so that
François may be even more proud of you when he returns.' Only
then did he face the barrage of reporters and photographers waiting on the quayside – though it has to be said most of these were
more interested in the Kennedys than they were in him. One man
who was eager to shake his hand, however, was Gilbert Miller,
his American agent who had engaged him for forty-five performances at the New York Lyceum. The première was to be in four
days' time. This was a grave mistake on Miller's part, for publicity
had been kept to a minimum; apart from a handful of brief television appearances, spiced with clips from his old films, the
younger generation in New York had been given no clear idea of
what to expect. There was also a great deal of competition on and
off Broadway – younger entertainers, exciting musicals – and for
this reason ticket sales had been very poor. Hoping to surprise
him, the Franco-American society hostess Rosette Reine, who had
seen Maurice at the Théâtre des Champs-Elysées, had bought up
most of the seats in the stalls to dole out among her friends, but
she had unfortunately written 9 pm on the invitations instead of
8.30. The management seems to have known this, though they did
little to rectify the situation, explaining the promptness of American audiences: to delay curtain-up by thirty minutes would have
resulted in Maurice playing to an empty theatre instead of a half-
empty one. Thus, when he strode on to the stage with his usual
joie de vivre and vigour, instead of rapturous applause he was met
by a glacial silence. The songs in his first half were directed to
several rows of empty seats. During the interval, he lost his temper
with Gilbert Miller and swore that he would never complete his
contract. Then, when he returned to the stage he saw that the
empty seats had been filled, and he finished his show with several
curtain-calls and a standing ovation.

Even so, Maurice was far from satisfied, and things could only
get worse. During his second night, even the presence of Marlene
Dietrich, Edith Piaf and Danny Kaye, did little to lift his spirits.

New York had been hit by a terrific storm which had caused
widespread flooding, a great deal of damage and several deaths.
In spite of this, Maurice and Fred Freed were photographed taking
a stroll through Central Park during the afternoon of Friday, 30

September, one of the darkest days in cinema history. At 5.45 pm a young, rebellious actor named James Dean climbed into his Porsche Spyder sports car – which he had affectionately baptized 'Little Bastard' – and a few minutes later, on Route 466 in California, he had crashed into an oncoming vehicle, dying instantly. Aged just twenty-four, with only three feature films behind him, he managed to plunge the entire United States into the deepest state of mourning it had known since the death of Rudolph Valentino. All over the country theatres and cinemas dimmed their lights as a mark of respect, though many parents had accused Dean of teenage corruption. A sultry, temperamental but nevertheless enigmatic presence on and off the screen, he had influenced an entire generation during the McCarthy witch-hunt. Dean's death, if anything, jolted Maurice out of his depression and made him realize perhaps that he had every reason to count himself lucky. Then, a few days later, President Eisenhower suffered a serious heart attack, and there was talk of his having to stand down from office. This only made Maurice more aware of his own mortality – he was two years older than Dwight D Eisenhower. Thus there followed more brisk walks in the park and stringent attention to diet.

With considerable difficulty, Maurice staggered bravely on at the Lyceum. Marlene Dietrich went to see him for the second time, and told him that his recital might have sounded better had he sung with an orchestra. Danny Kaye suggested that a troupe of dancing girls might enhance his stolid presentation, adding that if he did wish to come to terms with the new generation, he would have to glamorize his act. Maurice listened, and the rest of his season was an unprecedented success. His American agent immediately negotiated with Claude Philippe, the French-born director of the Waldorf Astoria, for a season in the famous Empire Room. A date was set: 12 November, just three days after the closure of Maurice's show at the Lyceum. During the 'cooling-off' period he flew out to Dayton, Ohio, to the première of Danny Kaye's new one-man show. 'This man is the best in the business!' he enthused. Returning to New York he received a telephone call from Samuel Goldwyn, inviting him to the première of the film *Guys and Dolls*. At the supper after the screening he was introduced to the stars: Frank

Sinatra, Marlon Brando, Jean Simmons and Stubby Kaye. None of them impressed him quite so much, however, as Audrey Hepburn, whom he kissed on both cheeks as if he had known her all his life, much to the amazement of her husband.

At a time when a very young Elvis Presley was beginning to make his mark on the world entertainment scene, Claude Philippe hit on the idea of offering Maurice the maximum publicity by advertising him as 'The King'. Posters were plastered everywhere announcing 'The King is Back!' and Maurice's première at the Empire Room almost rivalled that of Edith Piaf at the Versailles. There was no getting away from the fact, of course, that most of the 800 or so diners were snobs whose Parisian counterparts would have probably thought twice about going to see a sixty-seven-year-old music-hall star with a penchant for shocking his public with songs which often ventured beyond *double entendre*. Probably for this reason, Maurice announced that the proceeds from his first show would be given to the French Hospital in New York. He was applauded by most of the stars from Samuel Goldwyn's party, and of course Marlene Dietrich and Danny Kaye were there too, along with Duke Ellington, Mary Pickford and Joan Crawford. Initially, Claude Philippe had asked him to do two shows each evening, but this had been expecting too much. So, to make good any losses, the director upped his prices, and nobody complained. But only a star like Maurice, 'heading towards seventy without so much as a care in the world', as the Americans put it, could have got away with a song like Albert Willemetz's 'C'était moi'.

> *Le joli jeune homme c'était moi!*
> *Le vrai bébé de Cadum c'était moi!*
> *Et la reine d'Angleterre,*
> *Qui passait pour toucher ses coupons,*
> *Disait à ma grandmère:*
> *'What is this poupon?'*

> (The nice young man was me!
> The real Cadum baby was me!
> And the queen of England,

Who passed by to change her coupons,
Said to my grandmother:
'What is this infant?')

Maurice's five-week season at the Empire Room broke all previous box-office records, and ten days into it he was approached to star in the *Max Liebman Spectacular*, the most popular television show of the day. Maurice was reticent at first, probably remembering his last major television appearance outside France – the one in the closed set in Brazil. He was then told that the programme would be filmed in front of a live audience, and that he would be accompanied by a young musician called Michel Legrand, then making his début in New York. Maurice accepted at once, though the title was changed to *The Maurice Chevalier Show*. And he asked Liebman if he could include a guest of his own. This was a young mime artiste named Marcel Marceau, whom he had first seen at the Rose Rouge a few years before. This was agreed upon, and the show went out live on 4 December. Within five minutes of the closing credits the television-station switchboard was jammed with calls. One was from Marlene Dietrich, and on the strength of this he was offered a season with the New Frontier, an opulent cabaret in Las Vegas, for a staggering $30,000 dollars a week.

Even Maurice had not anticipated staying in the United States for more than a few weeks, and he was just as worried about Madeleine Vals as her husband was. Then, a few days later, a telegram arrived from Paris: 'Mother and daughter doing well.'

Maurice opened in Las Vegas on 19 December 1955. This was Edith Piaf's fortieth birthday, and he cabled his wishes as did Marlene Dietrich, also in town for a show. The competition in Las Vegas was, of course, considerably stiffer than it had been in New York: Frank Sinatra, Sammy Davis Jnr, Dean Martin and the comedian Danny Thomas all had shows of their own. He was actually introduced to his first-night audience by Danny Kaye, by now a very good friend. However, Las Vegas was as far removed from his roots as any city could have been, and in spite of his tremendous success he felt out of his depths, and even more so on New Year's Eve, when he sang at the Dunes Hotel.

Then, quite suddenly, Maurice's world was turned upside-down by the news he received from France. Mistinguett was ill, dying. On Friday, 23 December, Marcel Bourgeois had dropped in to see his sister at her Paris apartment, and he had found her shivering in her chair. She had planned to spend Christmas at Bougival – she had recently signed over the big house to her brother – and she now insisted that she should be taken there, rather than to a hospital, and placed in her beautiful swan-shaped bed. Léopold, her doctor son, had examined her and diagnosed a slight stroke. For a while she had seemed on the verge of recovery. Then, on Christmas Eve, she suffered a heart attack. Early the next morning she had been placed in an oxygen tent, and her family had gathered around her, anticipating the end. That evening, the news was broken to the media after numerous unsuccessful attempts to get in touch with Maurice. For two days, news bulletins were read out every hour, on the hour. Telegrams and letters were delivered by the sackful: one was from Harry Pilcer, and another from the Queen of England, to whom Mistinguett had written at the time of her coronation in June 1953. The news finally caught up with Maurice shortly before he went on stage at the Dunes Hotel. He sent a cable to the boulevard des Capucines, promising that he would be back in Paris by 19 January. It ended with the words, 'I'm coming, Mist. I beg of you, please wait for me.' Léopold at first thought that maybe it might not be a good idea for his mother to be reminded of Maurice, but Fraisette, her sister-in-law, took it to her just the same. She began crying and said, 'When I do die, I'll be thinking of Maurice. He was the best of them all!' A few hours later, her condition deteriorated, and Léopold and another doctor diagnosed a cerebral haemorrhage. She lapsed into a deep sleep from which she never emerged and on 5 January 1956, a few minutes before noon, Mistinguett died.

Though Mistinguett had been eighty, Maurice was still absolutely devastated. Everyone had considered her immortal, and it took some time for the news to sink in. He cabled a message to France, followed by a personal one to the great star herself. As this was read out over the radio, millions of French people – many of whom had not even been born when Mistinguett was at the height of her success – wept with him.

You are not leaving,
You have not gone away.
You are changing, that's all!
You'll always be where life leads me,
Your face, your looks, your love,
These will break through the noisy shadows
Of places where business tries to replace love.
You are my lover, my mistress,
You are my greatest woman friend.
And you loved my mother!

Mistinguett was laid in state in the Madeleine, and for two days thousands of grieving admirers filed past her coffin. She was dressed in the pink gown she had worn during her last revue, and her hairdresser, Jean Clément, had fashioned her a simple head-dress out of carmine ostrich plumes. The next day she was buried in the churchyard at Enghien, and with her was buried the French music-hall. Though she would be eternally emulated by just about every female entertainer who set foot on the stages of the Casino, the Folies-Bergère and the Moulin-Rouge, she would never, never be replaced. Mistinguett had been the first, and she would be the last.

To a certain extent, Maurice was helped over the first hurdle of his grief by the French dancer-*chanteuse* Line Renaud. Known as the original 'Mademoiselle from Armentières', she had taken the whole of North America and Canada by storm with this song and 'Ma cabane au Canada', and her 'Ma petite folie' had been adapted by Bob Merril to become 'My Truly Fair', a monstrous hit for her and for Guy Mitchell. Line Renaud and her husband, Loulou Gasté, had recently bought a house in Las Vegas, overlooking the golf course, and Maurice spent several days here resting before flying to Los Angeles. Here he attended the Oscars ceremony, and was photographed chatting to Grace Kelly, who on the very day of Mistinguett's death had announced her engagement to Prince Rainier of Monaco. He was also photographed with Marilyn Monroe, and when asked by a reporter if being with a beautiful legend had made his old heart beat that little bit faster, he replied, 'It was like sniffing at the restaurant door, knowing that you can't afford to go inside and eat!' His opinion was not quite the same, however, as expressed in his journal. She was, he wrote, dimmer than her European counterparts, and although she evidently knew how to make men desire her, he could not help but feel anxious about her future.

There was also a brief but strictly professional liaison with a lesser-known but equally beautiful blonde, Barbara Laage, who was one of the stars in *The Happy Road*, directed in English and French versions by Gene Kelly. The film also featured the British actor Michael Redgrave. It told the story of two errant children (Bobby Clark and Brigitte Fossey) pursued by the mother of one and the father of the other. The reviews were generally poor, and the film did not do too well at the box office.

Before leaving Los Angeles, Maurice also spent some time with the film director Billy Wilder, still eager to work with him after his disappointment a few years before. The contract was negotiated for *Love in the Afternoon*, to be filmed in Paris with Gary Cooper and Audrey Hepburn during the autumn. He and his friends then flew back to France, to a homecoming usually reserved for kings. After settling in at La Louque, he officiated as godfather to François Vals's baby daughter, Brigitte, at the church in Montmorency – a happy event which was probably tinged with sadness, for at this church Mistinguett had also been baptized.

Shooting for *Love in the Afternoon* began on 20 August 1956, at the studios in Boulogne. Maurice considered Billy Wilder something of a latter-day Ernst Lubitsch, a genius for gentle, sophisticated comedies. If Gary Cooper had been a close friend during the early 1930s, while Maurice and Yvonne Vallée were trying to impress the Hollywood set, he did not appear to be so now. During the first day of shooting, he and Maurice hardly spoke at all, and even the genial Billy Wilder could not get the two together for an after-work drink with the rest of the cast. The reason for this was made clear some time later. In the film Ariane (Hepburn) falls in love with Frank Flannagan, a disreputable womanizer (Cooper), who is being watched by Ariane's private-detective father Claude Chevasse (Maurice). According to one source, Maurice could not stand to see a young woman as lovely as Audrey Hepburn languishing in Cooper's arms. 'The man's fifty-five years old, only twelve years younger than me!' he is alleged to have raved. And yet, a few months later he would tell Mary Pickford that he considered himself lucky to have been chosen to play Ariane's father, and not her grandfather! Maurice is also alleged to have been incensed by Billy Wilder's insistence that he should not sing in the film.

This 'problem' was rectified, however, while Maurice was going through the rushes of *Love in the Afternoon* – released in France simply as *Ariane*. He was approached by his friends Jacques Canetti and Jane Breteau, the director of the Alhambra, and offered what amounted to an open-ended contract. He accepted at once, and was surprised, and deeply moved, to learn a few days before the 28 September première that the music-hall had been renamed the Alhambra Maurice Chevalier, though in his memoirs he referred to it rather humbly as the Alhambra MC. His show – and it was this, and not a recital – was almost a carbon-copy of those he had put on in New York, though unlike in the Empire Room the clientele were mostly working-class. The first half was a selection of variety acts – the Georges Lafaye Marionettes, the then-popular Romano Brothers and Raymond Devos, who would soon be hailed as one of France's top comedians. For his *vedette-américain*, Maurice himself asked for Michel Legrand, who had made such an impression on American audiences. Michel's father, Raymond, had recorded with Edith Piaf during the war and he had also accompanied Maurice on his famous recording of 'Folies-Bergère'. Now it was his son who returned to the platform after the interval to back Maurice with twenty-four musicians, and the first-night audience was one of the most distinguished Paris had seen. Sitting on the front row were Line Renaud, Louis Jourdan, Michèle Morgan, Roger Vadim, Georges Guétary, Mouloudji, Jean-Pierre Aumont and, of course, Marlene Dietrich, who would not have missed seeing him for the world. Audrey Hepburn and Gary Cooper were also there, the latter putting in an appearance before flying back to Hollywood, 'just to show an old pal that there were no hard feelings', and Yves Montand and Edith Piaf sent telegrams. Maurice also seemed fitter and happier than ever before, though of course a great deal of his joviality could have been superficial since he was still mourning Mistinguett. Even so, artistically he was in sparkling form, striding on to the stage 'as if he owned' it, and pausing for no less than ten minutes as the audience of 3,000 rose to its feet to award him one of the most emotional welcomes he had ever known. His first song, which he had written to Fred Freed's music, said it all.

> *Tout près, à Marnes-la-Coquette,*
> *Dans un jardin touchant Paris,*
> *Habite un français qui projete*
> *De gagner de nouveaux amis.*
> *Rendez-vous à Paris,*
> *Le plus joli des beaux coins du monde,*
> *Où chaque minute, chaque seconde*
> *A son prix . . .*

> (Quite near, at Marnes-la-Coquette,
> In a garden on the edge of Paris,
> Lives a Frenchman who plans to win new friends.
> Rendez-vous in Paris,
> The loveliest, finest place in the world,
> Where each moment, each second
> Has its price . . .)

Henri Magna, writing for *Le Figaro*, enthused, 'Chevalier is the lover of Paris, and he should reassure himself that as a mistress she will always remain faithful!' Not everyone, however, was of the same opinion. Paul Gianoli, a twenty-five-year-old journalist working for *Paris-Presse* who had a particular penchant for attending first nights to see if the artiste under scrutiny could still stand up, went to see Maurice intending to give him a bad review. Half-way through Maurice's show, however, he realized that this would not be possible without actually lying. Therefore he gave an honest account of his evening, and the subsequent review was much appreciated, not least by 'the grand old man of the *chanson*'.

> I went to see this septuagenarian performing gymnastics in front of 3,000 people. I went to mock all the outdated songs of this has-been kitchen-hand who seems to have been dishing out the same dinners for thirty years. He sang, spoke, clowned around and juggled with hats and caps. Then he danced rock-and-roll! He parodied his contemporaries and the wooden spectators clung to every word. I was the only

one *not* to applaud. Then, something suddenly clicked inside
me, for Cocteau's 'Grand Sympathique' had won me over!
Feeling slightly ashamed in the middle of the delirious
applause I began wishing that I could have appreciated him
sooner.

Because of the success of *Love in the Afternoon*, and a repeat-
showing of *The Maurice Chevalier Show* on network television by
public demand, Maurice was asked back to New York for a series
of one-man shows, to follow immediately after the European tour
that had been planned for the spring of 1957. One of the conditions
in the contract was that if at all possible he should be accompanied
by Legrand, but this proved financially impossible. Not to be out-
done, Maurice went to see the directors of Philips and had them
record Legrand's orchestra on tape to be used as backing on the tour
– perhaps the first time such a thing had been done. Then he told
François Vals, who admitted that at the time he did not even know
what a tape-recorder looked like, that from now on he would be
responsible for each song starting on cue. There was to be some consolation for the hapless secretary, however. Maurice invited Madeleine to accompany them on the road, provided someone could be
found to look after Brigitte. This was arranged.

The *magnétophone* did cause one or two problems on its travels.
Maurice's first engagement was at the smart Gstaad Palace Hotel
in Switzerland, and when François set up the equipment for a
speedy rehearsal during the afternoon the acoustics sounded fine.
This changed during the evening when the hall was full and the
curtains were drawn across the windows; those spectators sitting
at the back could not hear him. At La-Chaux-de-Fonds everything
went so well that after his recital Maurice invited François on to
the stage and introduced him to the audience as 'mon Toscanini',
although this did not go down too well when he repeated the
process in Geneva – the audience there had just been told that the
great conductor had died. At another theatre, the management
actually went so far as to organize dressing-rooms for Michel
Legrand's musicians, only to be told that 'they' were contained in
the box under François Vals's arm. And at another a critic praised
Maurice for following Edith Piaf's example by 'hiding' the orchestra behind the backdrop and relying on his 'impeccable timing' to

come in on cue every time, especially when stopping in the middle
of a routine suddenly to recite a poem by Jehan Rictus. Only
once did this backfire, when someone 'cut out' the orchestra by
accidentally pulling the plug out of the socket!

From Switzerland, Maurice travelled to Belgium, Germany,
Holland, Sweden and Denmark. There was a brief but little
publicized tour of England and Ireland. From there it was on to
New York, where he opened in another six-week season at the
Empire Room. This had been sold out one month before his arrival. He also appeared in Dinah Shore's television show, singing
'Louise' and 'My Love Parade', and recorded his very first album at
sixty-eight, consisting of fourteen American songs from his early
films. At the Greek Theatre in Los Angeles, not an easy venue, he
sang for two hours in front of 5,000 people – his largest ever American audience – for seven evenings in succession. By this time, François and Madeleine Vals were so expert at operating the
tape-recorder that one music-hall authority, writing for *The Hollywood Reporter* actually criticized Maurice for not presenting his
orchestra to the audience after the performance. His secret was discovered, however, by Hy Gardner of the *New York Herald Tribune*.
Gardner accused Maurice of making his act too tight, so that there
was no room for improvisation – this was less important in France
than in England and America, where a great deal of his charm came
from his accent, and the way he had always 'discussed' his numbers
before performing them. Maurice did not take too kindly to being
criticized, but he did take Hy Gardner's advice to return to a piano
accompaniment and a few days later he engaged a young American
named Fred Stamer. The pair first appeared together a few days later
on a television show hosted by Lucille Ball and Desi Arnez.

It was Maurice's new American agent, Paul Kohner, who introduced him to Vincent Minelli during the summer of 1957, and it
was this meeting which resulted in his biggest film success since
Love Me Tonight – the phenomenal *Gigi*, which had already
proved a hit on the London stage with Leslie Caron interpreting
Colette's heroine in a non-singing role. The location shots, filmed
in Santa Monica and the Bois de Boulogne, were stunning, but the
Lerner and Loewe score was even more so. Leslie Caron may have
sung 'Say a Prayer for Me Tonight' to her cat, but few critics
would ever doubt that the best musical numbers went to Maurice:

'Thank Heaven for Little Girls', 'I Remember It Well' with the wickedly humorous Hermione Gingold, and a jaunty, light-hearted but nevertheless accurate song which could almost have been adopted as his new signature tune, for, as he explained, youth really *could* do a fellow in!

> How lovely to sit here in the shade,
> With none of the woes of man and maid,
> The rivals that don't exist at all,
> The feeling you're only two feet tall!
> I've never been so comfortable before!
> I'm glad that I'm not young any more!

Alan J Lerner was already a tremendous power in Hollywood. Back in 1951 he had written the score for *An American in Paris*, starring Gene Kelly, Leslie Caron and Georges Guétary. Five years later had come *Brigadoon*, also with Kelly and Cyd Charisse – Maurice had recorded one of its songs, 'It's Almost Like Being in Love'. *Gigi* was the brainchild of the same executive team, pro-duced by Arthur Freed and directed by Vincent Minelli. Lerner had been worshipping Maurice from afar for many years, but when he suggested that he be offered a part in the film, the others were very firmly against the idea. The excuse was that no part had been written, so Lerner quickly remedied this and the rest is, as they say, history. *Gigi* proved the biggest box-office draw of all the Arthur Freed musicals, grossing more than $15 million during its first year and practically running away with every award imaginable the following year. The première was attended by a host of celebrities, headed by the Duke and Duchess of Windsor, who had flown in especially from France.

Coinciding with the release of *Gigi* was *Artisan de France*, the seventh volume of memoirs which covered Maurice's life until the end of 1956. The book was dedicated to Mimi and Gigi Chevalier (Mireille and Gisèle), the two young daughters of his brother Paul's son René, who had married Lucette in 1947. Maurice invited them all to La Louque early in 1958, and of course a photographer was on hand to capture the happy family scene, the results of which were published in the magazine *Jours de France*. Charles Boyer and his wife also came over from Hollywood with their teenage son Michael. The trio spent much of their time strolling around the streets of Paris, and in particular the Flea Market at Clignancourt – unlike Hollywood, it was still possible to walk around without any fear of being mobbed by fans. Another visitor to Marnes-la-Coquette was the film-director Jean Negulesco, whom Maurice had met in Hollywood at a party given by Charles Boyer. Another was the American comedian Red Skelton, though the circumstances here were tragic. Skelton's young son, also named Red, had seen Maurice's television show in Hollywood. A few months later he had been diagnosed as suffering from leukaemia and with little time left had asked his father to take him to Paris to see his idol on the stage. When Maurice was told of this by Paul Kohner, his American agent, he invited the entire Skelton family to stay at La Louque. Shortly afterwards the boy died, and Maurice was heartbroken. Three other friends also died at around the same time: Christian Dior, the great director Sacha Guitry, and Erich von Stroheim, the bizarre but great actor who had starred with him in *Pièges*. He said, 'The list is getting longer. Soon I'll be the only one left.'

Maurice was also approached by the great Marcel Pagnol to star in a remake of his classic *La femme du boulanger*. Pagnol's original masterpiece, adhering closely to Jean Giono's novel, had proved a massive success in 1938, with the great French actor Raimu playing the central role. Maurice refused the part, probably not wishing to emulate him, but this did not prevent Pagnol from offering him another part created and made famous by Raimu, that of Panisse in a proposed remake of *Fanny*, from the *Marius* trilogy of 1932–3. Maurice replied that he would have to think about it.

He did not have to think twice, however, about accepting an invitation to appear in a television show loosely documenting his life: *Rendez-vous à Paris*, produced by Maurice Regamey and filmed at La Louque. One of his guest artistes was Van Dongen, the famous painter who, during the 1930s and 1940s, had executed superb portraits of Damia, Suzy Solidor, Manouche, Kiki de Montparnasse and dozens of other music-hall stars. The scene in which he appeared, naturally, called for a beautiful young girl and, naturally again, Maurice was asked to choose one. He opted for a youngster named Brigitte Bardot, who had recently caused a sensation in Roger Vadim's *Et dieu créa la femme*. 'That kid'll go far!' he enthused. Another 'kid' who would certainly go a long way also met Maurice at this time, courtesy of his adoptive mother, Hélène Mar, who, during the 1920s had enjoyed some success as the silent film star Eleen Dosset. When the lady heard on the grapevine that Maurice was auditioning for a group of children to appear in one of his sketches, she turned up at La Louque with one Jean-Philippe Smet, aged fifteen. Though Maurice liked the boy, he was not sure that his Elvis Presley hairstyle and mien would work well in his show. A few years later Jean-Philippe Smet would become Johnny Hallyday, the greatest French rock star of all time.

During the summer of 1958 Maurice returned to New York, where he appeared on *The Ed Sullivan Show* with Sophie Tucker, who was known all over the world as 'The Last of the Red-Hot Mamas'. It was all high-camp of course, with Maurice and Tucker duetting wonderfully but eccentrically on the already eccentric 'I Remember It Well', followed by Maurice's rendition of 'Some of These Days' and Tucker, complete with straw hat and cane, who positively murdered 'Mimi', on purpose, needless to say! He was also filmed with Jerry Lewis. The comedian invited him up on to the stage at the Deauville Theater and, with a cursory nod to the musical director, the pair improvised 'Shine on Harvest Moon'. The compliment was returned a few evenings later when Maurice asked Lewis to join *him* on stage at the Eden Roc. This caused the audience to whistle and stomp, so much so that Maurice assumed he must have offended them; even after entertaining the Americans for four decades he could not get used to the fact that whistling at an artiste was not a form of derision.

In Washington Maurice appeared in a benefit concert for the Variety Club hosted by Vice-President Richard Nixon. A few evenings later he sang 'I'm Glad I'm Not Young Any More' to the President's wife, Mamie Eisenhower – daring, perhaps, though much appreciated. Thirty-two years later, when the French were celebrating the centenary of Maurice's birth with an exhibition at the Théâtre des Champs-Elysées, Mr Nixon, who in the meantime had been President of the United States, wrote to François Vals (a letter which he has very graciously allowed me to refer to in this book). Mr Nixon began by expressing his delight at being asked to join the host of Chevalier fans worldwide paying tribute, and added,

> Mrs Nixon particularly recalls the occasion when he came to Washington to perform at a luncheon in honor of Mamie Eisenhower. I will never forget the time that I had the privilege of meeting him. *Gigi* is one of our favorite movies of all time and we never tire of seeing reruns which allow us to admire again his brilliant performance. You may recall that when my daughter Tricia was married at the White House, the first song the orchestra played after the wedding was 'Thank Heaven for Little Girls'. We shall always remember that during his lifetime he was a man who remained forever young.

In Hollywood Maurice resumed his negotiations with his friend Jean Negulesco and agreed to make *Count Your Blessings*. Based on Nancy Mitford's bestselling novel *The Blessing*, and adapted for the screen by Karl Tunberg, who had just scripted *Ben Hur*, it was the supreme example of an excellent film made 'bad' by adverse publicity and criticism. Co-starring Rossano Brazzi and the delectable Deborah Kerr, with good support offered by Patricia Medina and Mona Washbourne – not to mention the precocious child-star Martin Stephens, who would practically run away with *The Village of the Damned* one year later – it was hardly given a chance to work. Though most of the critics praised the actual performances of Maurice and Deborah Kerr, no one seemed to like the plot, and words such as 'dull' and 'tedious' peppered reviews. The film biographer John Douglas Eames said of the two stars, 'They are sparkling players in need of something sparkling to play.' Even so, Maurice enjoyed making the film and so did his entourage. Most of the location shots were filmed around the Vals's native Bordeaux, and Deborah Kerr simply loved staying at La Louque. 'The magic of the man was everywhere,' she has said in a recent interview.

Towards the end of 1958 there were two reconciliations of sorts. In October Maurice's chauffeur, Raph, left Marnes-la-Coquette to get married and the position was offered to Maurice's old friend, Félix Paquet, himself out of work and not in the best of health.

Maryse Paquet, now affectionately referred to as La Chatte –
which does not sound very endearing – was offered the position of
housekeeper-cook. The couple moved in at once.

In December Maurice was 'summoned' by President de Gaulle
to top the bill in *La nuit de la chancellerie*, a sumptuous gala at
the Palais de Chaillot. Also on the programme were the Belgian
chanteuse Annie Cordy, famed for her 'Cigarettes, Whisky and
Wild, Wild Women', Gilbert Bécaud, the comedian Raymond
Devos and a young singer called Philippe Clay who had written a
fascinating song, 'Le danseur de Charleston', which Maurice is
said to have turned down, advising Clay to give it to Marie Dubas.
This is what had happened. Marie had performed it in her last
season at the Pacra before becoming ill with Parkinson's Disease.
Adding culture to the bill was the ballerina Ludmilla Tcherina,
dancing the 'Dying Swan', and to add spice President de Gaulle
had asked for Charles Trenet!

Perhaps fortunately for all concerned, and most especially himself, Trenet pulled out of the proceedings at the last minute and
Maurice was the first to express his relief, giving the impression
that he had been terrified of appearing on the same stage as Trenet
in case Trenet stole the limelight from him. The truth is, he was
asked to step down. 'Le Fou Chantant' may not have known that
Maurice had been partly responsible for his being jailed during the
war for sex offences against minors, but he was well aware that
Maurice, like many others, knew that he was *still* offending and
being allowed to get away with it, simply because to expose him
would have lost Trenet's record company millions of francs in revenue. Roger Normand told me:

> At that time, Trenet was involved with a sixteen-year-old he
> had picked up at a well-known cruising area on the outskirts
> of Paris. Today such a thing would have been more or less
> acceptable, even between a man of forty-six and a sixteen-
> year-old, because sixteen is more or less adult. But in those
> days sixteen was a child, and Maurice told Trenet to his face
> how loathsome he thought he was – what would happen if he
> didn't back out of the show. So he did!

Trenet also despised Maurice's public comment, one which he

repeated in his next volume of memoirs, 'He's just a machine, a peculiar one which churns out poetry!' *La nuit de la chancellerie*, meanwhile, was a tremendous success, made even more so by Maurice's audacity. De Gaulle was sitting in the front row, along with several governmental aides and a host of Hollywood attendees, which included Sophia Loren, William Holden, Cary Grant and Yul Brynner. After singing 'Louise' in English – 'Just to prove to one and all that I *am* an educated man!' – he walked to the edge of the stage, leaned forwards and announced, 'Tonight we are very privileged to have with us the greatest Frenchman in France – and he is going to join us all with a chorus from "Ma Pomme"!' Only a man like Maurice could have got away with that.

After the show, all the artistes were asked to line up behind the curtain to be presented to the president. The others had to make do with the customary handshake and a distinctive but not necessarily genuine 'Well done!' When it came to Maurice's turn and Maurice attempted a polite little bow, de Gaulle shook his head and said, 'No, Maurice. You and I are *equals*!'

Variable Winds

In February 1959 Maurice flew to New York for a new season of concerts and film appearances. His first visit was to his friend Edith Piaf, who was far from well. During the previous September she and her new songwriter lover Georges Moustaki – his most famous number for her was 'Milord' – had crashed their car en route for Orly airport, and though everyone else in the car had walked away from the accident with just cuts and bruises, Piaf had suffered severe facial abrasions. The car itself had been a write-off. For three months the little singer had undergone a series of painful facial massages, determined not to cancel her proposed trip to the United States. Early in the New Year she had opened to an ecstatic press at the Versailles. When Maurice went to see her he found her looking frail, though her voice was as magnificent as ever. After the show he spent some time in her dressing room, where she introduced him to Georges Moustaki. He was not impressed.

Several evenings later, on 20 February, Piaf collapsed on the stage and was rushed to the Presbyterian Hospital on 168th Street. No one was more anxious than Maurice, and he cancelled his engagements for the next few days so that he could be close at hand. The surgeons had to fight to save her life, she was on the operating-table for four hours, and received several blood trans-fusions for a perforated stomach ulcer. For six days the hospital bulletins described her condition as critical. Her fans held over-night vigils in the street, praying for her recovery. Jean Cocteau said, from his home at Milly-la-Forêt, 'If Piaf dies, part of me will die with her.' Ironically, they would both die on the same day. Georges Moustaki deserted his benefactress to sun himself on the beaches of Florida, surrounded by pretty girls. But if Maurice was expecting to find the woman the Americans had dubbed 'Little Miss Courage' morose and feeling sorry for herself, he was in for a pleasant surprise. Piaf was already planning her comeback, memorizing new songs in her hospital bed and creating merry hell with her worried and hard-up entourage. She also had a new lover who had had a great deal to do with the healing process: Douglas Davies. He was a talented American painter, twenty years her junior, and Piaf had promised to take him back to France with her. Maurice told him, 'Piaf's my own little bantamweight champion. She'll pull through because she has guts!' Piaf did pull through, after an unexpected relapse, and she did take Douglas Davies to France. Their love affair, however, like most of the others, did not last.

A few weeks later, Maurice attended one of the most important soirées of his career: the Oscars ceremony at Hollywood's Pantage Theatre. He should have been used to the hype by now, even though he did not necessarily enjoy it the whole of the time. Nor did he always feel comfortable, at seventy, trying to live up to his *boulevardier* image. Some of the photographs taken of him entering the theatre with Sophia Loren clinging to his arm show him looking embarrassed. Half-way through the proceedings, 'by public demand', he sang 'Thank Heaven for Little Girls', and as he was finishing the song Rosalind Russell walked on to the stage mouthing the words, 'Hang on a minute, Maurice!' *Gigi* had already scooped the jackpot so far as Oscars were concerned: best film, best director, best screenplay, photography, editing and art direction, best scoring (by André Previn), and best costume design. Now, the actress led Maurice to the podium, where he was presented with the Honorary Award for thirty years of services to the film, theatre and music-hall industries. Rosalind Russell faced the audience and announced, 'This man should serve as an example to us all.'

After the Oscars ceremony, Maurice travelled to Dallas, Texas, where *The Maurice Chevalier Show* was one of the principal hits of that year's State Fair. At the end of July he flew to Vienna to film the exterior shots of Michael Curtiz's *Breath of Scandal*, with Sophia Loren and Isabel Jeans, one of the stars of *Gigi*. The production was regarded by critics and cinemagoers alike as a major disappointment.

Then it was Hollywood again, and Walter Lang's phenomenally successful *Can-Can*, with Louis Jourdan, Frank Sinatra, Marcel Dalio and Shirley MacLaine, and a superb score by Cole Porter which gave the world such classics as 'Just One of Those Things', 'I Love Paris', 'Montmartre' and Maurice's duet with Louis Jourdan, 'Live and Let Live'.

> Dress and let dress,
> But strip and let strip!
> And remember this line:
> 'Your business is your business,
> And my business is mine!'

The content of the film, and this song in particular, is said to have shocked the visiting Soviet premier Nikita Khrushchev and his wife, Nina, though one finds it hard to understand why, or why they should have turned up at the film lot, unannounced and accompanied by several presidential aides. Neither is it known exactly what was said, although when everyone was asked to line up for photographs they seemed happy enough, even if Maurice did prefer to stand in the background. The film also caused a heated argument between some of the stars and the European distributors when it was released in France in 1960. Some of the songs, including 'I Love Paris', had been left on the cutting-room floor. Worse still was the French release of *Gigi*. Not content with dubbing Leslie Caron's singing-voice with that of Marie France, a relative unknown, the French production team had covered Louis Jourdan's more than passable tones with those of Sacha Distel, an act which practically ruined his part in the film.

Maurice next appeared in the film *Pépé*, which was released a few months after *Can-Can*. It was directed by George Sidney, who took a leaf out of Sacha Guitry and Mike Todd's book by using a host of international stars in cameo roles; the lead parts were given to Cantinflas, who had proved such a hit in the latter's *Around the World in Eighty Days*, and Shirley Jones. Thus Maurice was a little lost in the company of Debbie Reynolds, Edward G Robinson, Zsa-Zsa Gabor, Bing Crosby, Sammy Davis,

Kim Novak, Tony Curtis and Jimmy Durante. His songs, however, did stand out from the rest. One was 'Mimi', and the other was the equally immortal Kurt Weill–Maxwell Anderson classic 'September Song'. It was a song which fitted Maurice like a glove and was considered by many American critics to have been the highlight of the film. In their infinite wisdom, the French distributors cut it out of the production when the film was released in France. Little wonder, then, that Maurice decided never to make another film in his homeland.

Early in February 1960 Maurice left France to conquer Australia, at the age of seventy-one, when the country was experiencing its hottest summer in decades. He and his company were met at Melbourne airport by the British actress Googie Withers and her husband, John McCallum. The couple were renowned for their hospitality and knowledge of Antipodean society. Thus Maurice was escorted to the principal tourist sites, museums, racecourses, parties and receptions, believing that his hosts' benevolence was sincere. This does not appear to have been the case. Googie Withers later said that her thanks for escorting Maurice 'all over Australia' was the tiniest bunch of violets she had ever seen. This was hotly denied by Madeleine Vals, as was the Australian actress Coral Browne's claim at the time that she had had a secret fling with Maurice some years before while he had been appearing at the London Hippodrome, and that after 'a torrid night of love' he had refused to give her the money for a taxi home. 'It was all pure invention. Some of these people did not wait until he was cold in his grave before attacking him,' Madeleine has said.

Australia *was* a great trial for Maurice, principally on account of the heat, although he did insist upon spending most of his free time strolling through the streets of Melbourne. 'There's so much greenery here,' he told a reporter, when visiting a hospital for handicapped children, accompanied by members of the Australian French Circle. He played for a month in Melbourne, always to packed houses, and followed this by another month in Brisbane and Sydney. He enjoyed every moment of the applause, even though he wrote in his journal, 'Tiredness, and this heat, is making these sixty shows difficult. Sometimes I feel like walking off the stage right in front of their eyes.'

Returning to La Louque, Maurice spent a few weeks checking

over the script for the eighth volume of his memoirs, *Soixante-quinze berges*, before travelling to Marseilles to work with the director Joshua Logan on the new film version of *Fanny*. Pagnol's masterpiece of dock life in the city had been filmed for Hollywood by James Whale in 1938, with Wallace Beery, Maureen O'Sullivan and Frank Morgan, under the title *Port of Seven Seas*. Pagnol himself, though satisfied with Charpin's portrayal of Panisse in the original French version, had already told Maurice that he had wanted him to play the character as a happy rather than a morose man. Then, of course, Charles Boyer had not been considered to play opposite him.

In 1954 David Merrick had staged the musical version of *Fanny* on Broadway, with an excellent score by Harold Rome (among his credits was his English adaptation of 'Je n'en connais pas la fin', which as 'My Lost Melody' had become Edith Piaf's theme-song during her visits to America). The critics, however, had not been over-impressed with the casting of an Italian singer (Ezio Pinza) and a German actor (Walter Slezak) in the central roles. And Joshua Logan did not wish to film it as a musical. His first stipulation, before negotiating the contracts, was that there should be no songs. 'Chevalier can't sing,' he is alleged to have remarked. In effect, the critics adored Maurice's Panisse and Boyer's César, although they were not sure that the role of Marius should have been given to the young German actor Horst Buchholz, or completely happy with the performance of the British actor Lionel Jeffreys, who played Monsieur Brun, not that there was anything wrong with it. Leslie Caron, who played Fanny, was on the other hand appreciated by everyone, not least of all Maurice, who never could resist a pretty face. Maurice himself criticized strongly the French version of the film, and with good cause, considering the cultural aspects of Pagnol's trilogy, for French cinemagoers were 'shocked' that the story ended before Panisse's death.

Fanny was also a magnificent but friendly battle of male egos, between Maurice and Charles Boyer on the one hand, and between the two of them and the dashing Horst Buchholz on the other. This was inadvertently transferred to the screen, giving the film much of its bite. Marius leaves his pregnant girlfriend, Fanny, and goes to sea in search of fame and fortune. She is rescued by the ageing Panisse, a rich merchant who marries her to give her baby a name. Marius then returns home to demand his wife and child, but is prevented from doing so by his father, César. The advance publicity for the film was tremendous, and Richard de Neut, whose Oscar predictions were regarded by many to be almost as important as the ceremony itself, stuck his neck out and said that both Maurice and the film would win awards. The film was in fact nominated, as was Charles Boyer, but that year the board was practically wiped clean by *West Side Story*.

Towards the end of January 1961 Maurice received another shock – a telephone call from France informing him of the death of his former rival Harry Pilcer. Since the Liberation, the man hailed as the greatest European dancer of the century had never stopped working, opening a succession of clubs and restaurants all over France. He had even made a triumphant film which had had nothing to do with dancing, playing opposite Tyrone Power in the 1947 adaptation of Somerset Maugham's *The Razor's Edge*. A nervous man, often plunging into the very depths of despair, he had never ceased to mourn the two great loves of his life: Gaby Deslys and Mistinguett. He had, however, never lost his appeal or popularity. His last appearance was at the Ambassadeurs in Cannes on 14 January, and he performed a dance he had devised to commemorate the fifth anniversary of Mistinguett's death. Two hours later he collapsed and died of a heart attack, aged seventy-four, just two years older than the man he had once referred to as 'the ponce in the straw hat'. Once again Maurice was reminded of his own mortality, and once again he considered retirement.

Pilcer's death was followed by that of Gary Cooper, after a long struggle against cancer. Marlene Dietrich attended the funeral and Maurice sent his condolences to Cooper's widow. Two months later another acquaintance, Ernest Hemingway, committed suicide. These tragedies affected Maurice badly, though he coped by immersing himself in his work. His next film, directed by Jean Negulesco and co-starring Angie Dickinson, was *Jessica*. In it he played a priest, a role which he later compared with Bing Crosby's in *Going My Way*. The location shots were filmed at Forza d'Agro, in Sicily, and may have cheered him up somewhat, though the title given to the film by the French, *La sage femme, le curé et le bon Dieu*, did not. He also hit the roof when told that the three René Rouzaud–Marguerite Monnot songs written for *Jessica* would be cut from the French version. 'Why do they keep on doing this to me?' he growled.

Why indeed? *In Search of the Castaways*, based on the story by Jules Verne and produced by Walt Disney at London's Pinewood Studios, saw him playing the eccentric Professor Paganel. Appearing with him in this often underrated adventure film were Michael Anderson Jnr, Wilfred Hyde-White, George Sanders and Hayley Mills, who at the age of fifteen was already a movie veteran. 'He called me *petit choux* and I called him *mon bijou*,' she recalled in a recent interview. Their big song in the film, 'Enjoy It', was, needless to say, removed in the French version, which was probably why Maurice decided not to sing at all in his next film. This was George Sherman's *Panic Button*, which also starred the phenomenally well-endowed actress Jayne Mansfield – she was photographed arriving for work one morning with a Chihuahua dog tucked into her cleavage, which may or may not have set Maurice's pulse racing. He certainly enjoyed being with her in Rome, and he is said to have been devastated by the news of her death in a car crash a few years later. He had no need to worry about the French 'amputating' this particular film – it was never released there!

As a *chanteur*, Maurice was afraid that the French might have forgotten him when he returned there in the middle of 1961. It was six years since his last major series of recitals, and he had been so busy with his American and British films that his singing career had been forced to take a back seat. Now, a whole new generation of song-stylists, comedian-*chanteurs* and singer-songwriters had sprung up. Jacques Brel had arrived from Belgium to become the most-fêted entertainer in France after Edith Piaf. George Brassens was not far behind him and a thirty-two-year-old *chanteuse* from Paris by the name of Barbara had just caused a sensation with her interpretations of their works, winning the prestigious Grand Prix du Disque. Today, she is the most important female entertainer in France. Another *chanteuse*, Isabelle Aubret, had recently won the European Song Contest with 'Un Premier Amour', and Françoise Hardy had reached the hit parades on both sides of the Channel with 'Tous les garçons et les filles'. These artistes and a number of others had coped well with the dawning of the era known in France as '*le yé-yé*', which towards the end of 1959, in the wake of Bill Haley, Gene Vincent and, of course, Elvis Presley, had set the whole of the country rocking. Other stars, such as the romantic singer Gloria Lasso, had objected so strongly that they had beaten a somewhat hasty retreat. Petula Clark, on the other hand, had been happy to adapt, and had been rewarded by a new generation of admirers, including Maurice.

The so-called temple of the French rock-and-roll scene was an establishment called the Golf Drouot, which was situated at the angle of the rues Drouot and Montmartre. It had one of the first juke boxes in France, on which youngsters could listen to the latest American 'tubes' – impressionable musicians such as Claude Moine, who would achieve immortality in France as Eddie Mitchell, Dick Rivers, who had taken his name from an Elvis Presley film role, and Johnny Hallyday, who in December 1959 had made his début in the programme *Paris-Cocktail*. Maurice had watched this, though he may have forgotten the young man who had turned up one day at La Louque with his adoptive mother, asking for an audition. Even so, adopting the maxim 'If you can't beat 'em, join 'em!' he visited the Golf Drouot to watch Mitchell 'in action'. The singer was backed by the group Les Chaussettes Noires, so called because they had been sponsored by a stockings manufacturer. Maurice was so impressed that before leaving he told Eddie Mitchell that maybe *he* should sing with Les Chaussettes Noires! A few weeks later he did exactly this. 'Le twist du canotier' was written for him by Noël Roux and Georges Garvarenz, and it became one of the bestselling records of the year. Maurice also managed to reach the hit parade with another 'unusual' song, Alain Goraguer and the recently deceased Boris Vian's 'Pan-pan-pan', which was part of a national campaign aimed at the production of potatoes.

Fun to perform and certainly original these two numbers may have been, but in reality they were little more than songs of the moment, which is why they have been largely forgotten by all but the more serious devotees of the Chevalier oeuvre. Maybe this is a great pity, though one cannot deny that the 'flipside' of 'Le twist du canotier' was far more important than any pop song, for it had been especially written for Maurice by his friend and fellow *enfant du faubourg* Charles Aznavour, who had just taken over the presidency of the retirement home at Ris-Orange.

Mômes de mon quartier,
Tout mon passé s'éveille,
Mômes de mes vingt ans . . .
Ménilmontant,
C'est loin, mais c'est si proche . . .

(Kids of my district,
All my past comes back to me,
Kids of my twenties . . .
Ménilmontant,
It's so far away, but it's so near . . .)

In November 1961 Maurice was approached by the British producer Robert Nesbitt, on behalf of Sir Bernard Delfont, and asked to top the bill at the Royal Variety Performance. Maurice said that this would be fine, and added, 'But I'll have to sing a song especially for the Queen Mother, won't I?' Such a thing would be very much a breach of protocol, and Maurice was asked to clarify his intentions. He would not, claiming that he had always got on well with the royal family, particularly with the Duke and Duchess of Windsor. He must have known the dissent such a remark would cause, since the subject of the abdication would still have rankled. In fact, the evening went remarkably well. Included on the bill were Frankie Vaughan, Jack Benny, George Burns, Shirley Bassey and his old friend Sammy Davis Jnr. Maurice eclipsed them all, and then sprang his surprise. During the last verse of his closing number he turned towards the royal box, raised his hat and concluded:

You must have been a beautiful baby,
For Majesty, look at you now!

Over the next few months, Maurice rested up at La Louque, working on his memoirs as usual, and selecting material for his forthcoming American tour. His agent there had offered him an open contract, so in effect he could name his own fee. Maurice, for once in his life, put his health and age before the almighty dollar and announced that his tour should not exceed eight weeks, and that if possible, New York should be given a miss on account of its fickle weather.

In the event, Hollywood was infinitely worse than New York could ever have been. When his plane touched down early in September, the town was hidden under heat smog. Madeleine Vals advised him to go straight to his hotel and stay there until the climate improved, but Maurice refused to do so, arguing that he never felt comfortable in a place unless he had taken a long stroll to get his bearings. In doing this he was taken ill and rushed back to his hotel suffering from a chill. This was only hours before the first of his seven performances at the huge, open-air Greek Theater, itself enshrouded in fog.

The evening was a near-disaster. In an attempt to re-create his famous 'a man alone' recitals of some years before, Maurice had asked for Fred Stamer to be placed to one side of the stage behind a semi-transparent screen. This was a mistake. He missed the cue for his first song, though this was not noticed on account of the applause. Then, during the next number – Cole Porter's 'Just One of Those Things', from *Can-Can* – he dried up completely and set off in the direction of the wings, where François and Madeleine Vals were watching with bated breath. What happened next was typical, considering his character and immense charm. Instead of walking off the stage he turned and headed back to the microphone, trying to laugh off the whole episode as some sort of joke. A young woman sitting near the stage then stood up and pointed, but instead of heckling she shouted, 'It's all right, Maurice! We love you!' This set off applause, which by the end of the next song had reached manic proportions with the entire audience of 4,500 on its feet, chanting, 'We love Maurice! We love Maurice!' For a moment he stood back, with tears in his eyes. He had won them over. The next morning one of the newspaper headlines read, 'Maurice Chevalier is Indestructible!' and this followed him around for the rest of the tour, which took in San Francisco, Seattle, Boston, Hartford, Philadelphia, Newark, five weeks in Chicago, and a superb recital in Washington before President Kennedy, for whom he sang Albert Willemetz's absurd but delightful 'Ma Louise'.

Quand je me vaporise,
Mon vaporisateur
Redit: 'Lou–Louise!'
Et parfum mon cœur.

(When I spray myself,
My atomiser
Says again: 'Lou–Louise!'
And perfumes my heart.)

During his 1955 trip to the United States, the American public had been deeply affected by the tragic death of James Dean. While Maurice was in Hollywood this time it was the turn of Dean's nearest female equivalent, Marilyn Monroe. She was found dead in her room after apparently committing suicide. Like James Dean, however, she would not be allowed to rest in her grave and rumours of who she had and had not taken as lovers began circulating at once. Maurice was not surprised to learn of Marilyn's demise at the age of only thirty-six – when writing about her in his journal he had more or less predicted that such a thing would happen – but he was very upset. 'Youth is precious,' he said simply. What he did not know at the time was that there was a good deal worse to come.

In October 1962 Maurice returned to France. He wrote, 'I need to recover my strength, to get myself in good fettle for next year, my seventy-fifth.' On 9 October Edith Piaf had married Théo Sarapo, a Greek hairdresser who, at twenty-seven, was nineteen years her junior. Prior to this Piaf, with her flair for discovering and launching new talent – her long list of protégés included Charles Aznavour, Yves Montand and Les Compagnons de la Chanson – had given Sarapo singing lessons and the pair had toured the Riviera before opening in a brief but triumphant season at the Paris Olympia. In the November they were invited to La Louque, even though one of Piaf's 'aides' was worried that there might be an argument over the fact that the couple's big song, Michel Emer's 'A quoi ça sert l'amour', had been publicly launched at Patachou's nightclub. Maurice's love for the greatest *chanteuse* of all time, however, was absolute. He and Mistinguett had been 'two dogs fighting over the same bone'; he and Piaf were 'two birds from the same nest in Belleville-Ménilmontant'. They spent some time alone, chatting together in Maurice's study, and when Piaf left he could not help but believe that for her time was quickly running out.

In January 1963 Maurice flew to Hollywood, where he appeared as himself in Melville Shavelson's *A New Kind of Love*, singing 'Mimi', which he had already sung twice on the screen. The two stars of the film were Paul Newman and Joanne Woodward. He then went on to New York, where, not surprisingly in the sub-zero temperatures, he went down with a chill and was prescribed antibiotics. His four-week stint at the Ziegfeld Theater was nothing short of a triumph of mind over matter, and the first time in more than fifty years that he had to perform without advance publicity – most of the newspapers and printers were on strike, and there were no posters. Toronto was not much better, and in Detroit his chill developed into influenza. Never before had he so looked forward to returning to Paris, but even then he rested only for a few days before flying to London on 9 April to star at the Saville Theatre in his now-legendary *An Evening with Maurice Chevalier*. At the airport, looking tired and, perhaps for the first time, showing his age, he agreed to give a press conference. Needless to say, many of the questions asked concerned the rumour that he was about to announce his retirement, a rumour he quickly scotched. 'I love my work and maybe that gives me a little youth. If it was a strain, I wouldn't do it,' he told Sydney Preston of the London *Evening Standard*.

It is alleged that during his twilight years Maurice would rather perform in Britain than in any other foreign country, for no other reason than its proximity to France should he be taken ill. It was an opinion he shared with his friend Piaf, who had once collapsed on stage in Stockholm and, terrified that she might die away from Paris, had chartered a DC10 to fly her home. The British critics certainly seemed to treat him differently from their American counterparts, concentrating more on his artistic abilities and less on his ability to stay on his feet. In those early days of Tommy Cooper, and Morecambe and Wise, his British fans also appreciated his wry, down-to-earth sense of humour which was why such sketches as 'Spectators' and 'Stations of Life' went down so well. The four-week London season also contained several new songs, as far-removed from his early Hollywood ones as they could have been. Out went much of the Leo Robin–Richard Whiting material, to be replaced by the more modern works of Cole Porter, Lerner and Loewe, Marguerite Monnot and Jean-Pierre Moulin. Songs like 'How to Handle a Woman', 'I Still See Eliza' and 'La tête du roi' were sung with comparative ease, and, of course, 'Thank Heaven for Little Girls' and 'I'm Glad I'm Not Young Any More' were *demanded*. There was also a belated tribute to Harry Pilcer in the form of one of his most famous songs, 'You Made Me Love You'. The surprise hit of the season was, however, none of these numbers perfectly arranged by Fred Stamer. It was 'Le twist du canotier', of which *The Times* quipped, 'It owes more to Mistinguett than it does to Johnny Hallyday.'

Among the first-night audience was the distinguished critic, Bernard Levin, who, of course, had seen all of this before.

> For once, brevity is the soul of enthusiasm. There is really little more to say than that '*Notre* Maurice' is back. He has not changed, despite his absurd insistence that he is older than he was last time. He does not reach after the high D, but then he never did. He does not try to knock the chandelier into the auditorium, though he never did that either. He is only, permanently, irreproachably himself – probably the greatest living solo performer in the world. He is still from the crown of his *canotier* to his blue suede shoes (I kid you not) *notre* Maurice, still the same and still unique.

Bernard Levin also criticized Maurice for not singing 'Valentine' – this was forfeited because he considered it too dated to follow 'Le twist du canotier' – threatening to inflict 'all the terrors of the earth' upon the hapless *chanteur* unless his famous song was returned to the fold. With his typical good humour – and one or two choice epithets – Maurice informed Levin that he would do this. And when asked by a reporter from the *Daily Mail* why he was still working, when he was obviously wealthy enough never to need to do so again, he retorted acidly, 'No other music-hall artist could do what I'm doing – a one-man show at the age of seventy-five. It's like making love, in a very pure way.'

While in London Maurice was approached by Yul Brynner and Melle Weersma, the representative of the United Nations Commission for Refugees, and asked to select one of his recordings for their *All-Star Festival* charity album. Bing Crosby and Louis Armstrong had already donated 'Up a Lazy River', and Edith Piaf – dangerously ill after giving her final performance in Paris at the Bobino just a few weeks before – had instructed Pathé-Marconi to hand over the previously unreleased 'Je m'imagine', which Nita Raya had written for her in 1960. The other artistes on the album included Mahalia Jackson, Nana Mouskouri and Ella Fitzgerald. Maurice told Brynner that for such an important cause a new song would have to be commissioned, and he immediately rang his friend Albert Willemetz, who was recovering from illness at Marnes-la-Coquette. He in turn got in touch with Joseph Kosma, and within a week Maurice had his song – one which, so far as is known, he never sang on the stage. The producers of the album were touched. Melle Weersma said, 'Maurice Chevalier, the kind, mature philosopher, has given us a charming, truly French allegory.'

> *La vie est une belle fille*
> *Qui sourit à qui sait l'aimer,*
> *Elle nous prend,*
> *Elle nous tortille,*
> *Uniquement pour nous faire primer . . .*

> (Life is a beautiful girl
> Who smiles at those who know how to love her,
> She takes us,
> She twists us,
> Just to get the better of us . . .)

In the middle of May Maurice returned to France. This time, he afforded his entourage the luxury of a two-month break, before setting off on a gruelling tour of South America and Canada which would have exhausted most men half his age. Rio de Janeiro, Sao Paulo, Buenos Aires, Lima and Montevideo were all taken in his stride, and this time Maurice kept out of the heat whenever possible. In Caracas, while a horde of press photographers and reporters rushed across the tarmac to meet his plane, he was 'arrested' by the airport police and whisked to his hotel in the back of a limousine. The reason for this was that the world-class footballer Di Stefano had been kidnapped by political sympathizers a few days before, and though he had subsequently been released, unharmed, the authorities had received an anonymous call suggesting that Maurice's life might be in danger. If Maurice was afraid, he certainly did not let it show during his performance, even though every moment of it was watched by the armed guards standing on either side of him in the wings.

From South America Maurice flew to Canada, and two week-long engagements in Montreal and Quebec. He was besieged with offers, and could easily have stayed in the country until the end of the year had it not been for two factors: the thought of having to cope with a harsh Canadian winter, and his imminent seventy-fifth birthday, which could be celebrated only in Paris, aided by the radio-station Europe 1, who played tributes to him for nineteen hours non-stop while relaying 'live' messages from the showbusiness profession, including transatlantic calls from Jerry Lewis, Sammy Davis Jnr and Ray Charles. He was also special guest at *La nuit du cinéma*, the annual event which he had boycotted during the war on account of its German sponsorship. Now he was welcomed on to the podium by seventy-five young 'lookalikes', all sporting straw hats and twiddling canes.

On 27 September 1962 Maurice opened at the Théâtre des Champs-Elysées in a series of twenty-five concerts. As usual, the first few rows of the stalls contained a liberal sprinkling of reporters and cynics who were there, primarily, to watch 'the grand old man of the music-hall make a spectacle of himself', as one of them put it, and as usual Maurice came up smelling of roses – literally so, for after his final curtain-call the stage was covered in flowers. A journalist from *Paris-Presse*, the publication which had often attacked him in the past, wrote, 'Maurice Chevalier is the most distinguished man that I have ever met in the music-hall!'

And yet, while receiving this adulation, Maurice could not but be affected by the tragedies that were going on around him. He had spoken to his great friend Edith Piaf on the telephone a few days before his Paris première. Her husband, Théo Sarapo, had hired a house near Mougins, and in the August she had lapsed into a hepatic coma which had necessitated her being rushed to a clinic in Cannes. Incredibly, just one week later, she discharged herself from here, and her husband moved her to Plascassier, near Grasse, where she had rallied together her closest friends: Charles Aznavour, Jacques Brel, her faithful household staff and a number of others. Then, on 9 October – her first wedding anniversary, no less – she lapsed into another coma. The next day her condition became so critical that her nurse asked the housekeeper to summon a priest. Sadly, she could not as a storm prevented her getting through on the telephone, and a few hours later Edith died of an internal haemorrhage, aged just forty-seven.

Maurice was one of the first to be informed of Piaf's death. The actual newsflashes did not go out until the following day on account of the singer's own insistence, some weeks before, that if she died, the people of Paris must never be told that she had 'deserted' them to pass away in some provincial village. Her body was therefore driven back to Paris in the back of an ambulance to be laid in state in the drawing room of her boulevard Lannes apartment. On the morning of 11 October the television producer Louis Mollion rang Jean Cocteau to arrange a radio broadcast – the poet had wanted to read a personal eulogy to his great friend. But this was not to be. By the time Mollion arrived at Milly-sur-Forêt Cocteau too was dead, having had a heart attack. Maurice was stunned. That evening he paid tribute to them both on stage at the Théâtre des Champs-Elysées. He said, 'Piaf has been beaten tragically by life, but she leaves behind her legend. Cocteau was an artiste whom one could love and admire because he never said a bad word about anyone. I shall miss them both.'

On 14 October Maurice met Marlene Dietrich at boulevard Lannes. Marlene, who in Piaf's own words had 'married' her by being witness at her wedding to Jacques Pills was now about to bury her. Her funeral, at the Père Lachaise cemetery, was the largest there has ever been in France – an estimated 2 million people lined the streets of Paris along the funeral route, and as the hearse passed many of them fell to their knees, making the sign of the cross. The emotion was quite extraordinary. Around the 97th Division another 40,000 clambered over the gravestones, causing a great deal of damage as a detachment from the Foreign Legion stood to attention and saluted – the year before, like the OAS after the fighting in Algeria, they had adopted 'Non je ne regrette rien' as their theme-song. Their massive wreath of purple wildflowers was inscribed, '*A leur Môme Piaf – La Légion.*' Maurice's wreath read, 'Sleep in peace, courageous little Piaf.' And he, like so many of the singer's friends and admirers, was horrified by the Pope's decision to deny her a requiem mass and Christian burial, proclaiming she had lived a life of public sin. Then, from Père Lachaise Maurice and Marlene moved on to Milly-sur-Forêt and the more private though no less emotional funeral of Jean Cocteau.

1963 ended with another tragedy, this time not a personal one, although it nevertheless affected Maurice badly. On 22 November he was rehearsing for a television show in New York when a series of newsflashes informed the world that President Kennedy had been assassinated by Lee Harvey Oswald in Dallas. He is alleged to have sent flowers and a letter of condolence to Jackie Kennedy, not before the funeral but after, expressing his admiration for the way in which she had coped with her tragedy. He told an American reporter, 'Her composure should be an example to us all. Madame Kennedy will always be the Mother Courage of America.'

Few people were surprised when, in the wake of so many dramas, severe depression set in. From Maurice's point of view, it seemed such a waste having such talented flames extinguished prematurely while he was just 'staggering along', having passed his allotted three-score-and-ten years. Marlene Dietrich told me,

Every day I would switch on the radio or the television and expect to hear that he'd killed himself. That's how depressed he had become. So I told him in no uncertain terms that he would have to get a grip on himself, and I am so pleased that he listened to me. Chevalier may have been at that age when most of us retire, but we didn't want to let him go – not just yet!

Le Grandpère de la Chanson Française

Revitalized by a quiet Christmas spent at La Louque, surrounded by his family and friends, and glowing within after spending an evening dining with President de Gaulle and his wife, who had addressed him as Maître, Maurice set off on yet another world tour. This took him to Germany, Belgium, Holland and Scandinavia, and yet again he ended up in the United States, which he was fond of referring to as his second home. The Americans had a new president, Lyndon B Johnson, though Maurice is thought not to have admired him as much as he admired Eisenhower or Kennedy. One man he did admire, though, and tremendously so, was Martin Luther King, who on 28 August 1963 had helped to organize America's largest ever civil rights demonstration – almost a quarter of a million non-violent protesters, including Marlon Brando, Bob Dylan and Burt Lancaster, had attended the rally at the Lincoln Memorial to hear King deliver his famous 'I have a dream' speech. During his tours of America Maurice had never ceased to be appalled by the scale of racial prejudice there and so, when he was invited to Chicago's Palmer House to pose for photographs alongside a racial integration committee, he set aside his usual political neutrality and announced to the small gathering of press, 'Racial discrimination, when men kill each other because of the colour of their skin, is an inhuman vice which should be stopped.' Unfortunately, his comments never reached the major newspapers, the ones which had criticized him during the war, and at the time of the McCarthy witch-hunt.

After performing in Saint Louis, Indianapolis and Denver –

always to packed houses, although by now the anecdotes between songs were getting longer – Maurice flew to Honolulu to view the base at Pearl Harbor. He then returned to New York, where he was asked to top the bill in an important television series of the day, *The Bell Telephone Hour*. Undecided what to sing, bearing in mind the twenty-minute time limit, he opted to do a lengthy medley of French *chansons*, ones made famous not by himself but by his fellow artistes. Thus he sang 'La goualante du pauvre Jean', 'Sous les ponts de Paris', 'I Wish You Love' and, of course, 'La vie en rose', setting a precedent, for it would henceforth be expected of him every time he walked on to an American stage. He also found time to appear in a film, *I'd Rather Be Rich*, a remake of *It Started with Eve* with Charles Laughton and Deanna Durbin. Directed by Jack Smight, it also starred Sandra Dee and Robert Goulet, but from Maurice's point of view the film was important because it reunited him on the screen with his old 'sparring-partner' from *Gigi*, Hermione Gingold. The film was generally well received by the critics, and was not unsuccessful at the box office, though it could never be regarded as one of Maurice's better forays into the world of cinema.

Undoubtedly the greatest tragedy of Maurice's twilight years – more traumatic even than the combined deaths of Piaf and Cocteau – was the death on 7 October at Marnes-la-Coquette of the man he had called his second heart, Albert Willemetz. This was a private grief for Maurice, but also a great loss to France. Though seventy-seven, Willemetz had continued writing until the day of his death. During the 1920s and 1930s he and his partner Henri Christiné had practically monopolized the French operetta stage, and his works – 'Valentine', 'Mon homme', 'J'en ai marre', 'C'est vrai' and 'Dans la vie faut pas s'en faire', along with dozens of others – had travelled the world like choice wines. Maurice said, 'The world won't be the same without him, and part of me has followed him up there.'

Upon his return to Paris towards the end of 1964 Maurice found a whole pile of contracts waiting for him to sign. The actor Jean-Louis Barrault, internationally renowned for his portrayal of the mime artiste Baptiste in Marcel Carné's *Les enfants du paradis*, asked him to appear in a series of recitals at the Théâtre de France. Other offers were from the Casino, the Théâtre des Variétés, the

Théâtre des Champs-Elysées and the Alhambra. For a few days he deliberated over which one to choose; the money was not as important as the symbolism of the venue, and he could of course, practically have written his own contracts, as he had done in America. In the end he turned down every one of these engagements. 'I much prefer representing my country overseas,' he announced, which must have left many people feeling slightly puzzled. He did, however, enter the Festival studios to record a novelty number with Giglola Cinquetti, that year's winner of the Eurovision Song Contest: 'L'italiano'. This was a light-hearted look at an old man learning a new language from a pretty young girl, and it was written by Hubert Giraud and Noël Roux, who also supplied 'La tendresse'. These were released on an EP with Guy Béart's 'Un enfant écrit' and another oddity by Edith Piaf's former orchestra-leader Jean Léccia, 'Mon cœur est un juke-box'. Needless to say, these songs added lustre to the hit-parade material of the year and were played non-stop by radio stations throughout Europe.

1965 was an extremely busy year for Maurice, who seems to have been getting his second wind. In Munich he appeared in a television spectacular with the actress Lilli Palmer, and this was followed by a triumphant two-hour-plus recital in Hamburg. In Paris the entrepreneur Georges Cravenne engaged him as guest of honour in a sumptuous gala at Maxim's. This was aimed at launching Régine Zylberberg, a thirty-five-year-old Belgian-born *chanteuse*. An instant but not unexpected phenomenon, she would become known as 'The Queen of the Night' and, after a very short time, would command only the very best songwriters. Frédéric Bottom, Barbara and Charles Aznavour supplied her with material, as did Serge Gainsbourg. In later years she would enhance her reputation by opening a string of nightclubs around the world.

Maurice then toured America, taking in Puerto Rico, Washington, Miami and Boston, and ending up in New York, where he appeared in a television show singing the songs of Cole Porter. Next it was Hollywood, where he signed a contract with Walt Disney to make *Monkeys Go Home*, visited Disneyland, and met his friend Charles Aznavour – all in the same day!

Unfortunately, Maurice's penultimate film was not his best. It co-starred Dean Jones and Yvette Mimieux, and was not released in France. Much more important was his series of recitals, organized and produced by Alexander Cohen, and presented at the Alvin Theater in New York in April 1965. Among the dozens of personalities gracing the first-night audience, Maurice signalled out one in particular, Jacqueline Kennedy, and spent a few moments alone with her in his dressing-room. Their exact conversation is not known, though she is said to have thanked him for singing one of her late husband's favourite songs, the French-language version of 'One Hour with You'.

> *J'aimerais vivre une heure près de toi,*
> *Te voir sourire à moi rien qu'à moi,*
> *Je te dirais mille choses,*
> *Que l'on n'ose qu'à mi-voix . . .*

> (I would like to live one hour close to you,
> To see you smile only for me,
> I would tell you a thousand things,
> That one only would say to oneself . . .)

Maurice's 1965 American tour, like its predecessor, was not without its tragic moments. His old army pal Maurice Yvain, the composer of so many of his most famous songs, died at Suresnes, aged seventy-four. Though the loss was perhaps not as deeply felt as that of Albert Willemetz, who had also been a neighbour, it did come as a blow. 'Maurice has gone, and so has that part of my youth,' he said.

Far, far worse was the tragedy which befell his friend Charles Boyer, who during the autumn of 1965 spent some time in Paris during the filming of the epic *Is Paris Burning?*, in which he had a cameo role. Boyer's twenty-year-old son Michael, whom Maurice himself had described as 'a chip off the old block', seemed to be heading for a flourishing television career after being appointed associate-producer for *The Rogues*, the successor to Dick Powell's *Four Star Playhouse*. Unfortunately, the project, which had almost certainly been 'arranged' by Charles Boyer, fell through and the actor tried to make up for the disappointment by offering his son an apartment in Los Angeles for his twenty-first birthday. That he was a very mixed-up young man goes without saying; and when a reporter inquired about his son on the Paris film-lot Boyer remarked, 'I am trying to help my son to find himself.' A few days later, on 23 September, Charles Boyer received a telephone call informing him that Michael was dead; the young man had committed suicide. Charles Boyer was devastated, and so was Maurice. He was unable to attend Michael's funeral, but he did send flowers, and of course the Boyers were invited to spend a few days at La Louque – an invitation which was politely turned down. The couple would never get over their son's death. Twelve years later, Pat Boyer would die of cancer, and, unable to cope on his own, Charles too would end his own life.

For Maurice 1965 was also a year for helping young artistes who had emerged after or broken away from the now-dying age of the '*yé-yé*'. The first of these was Salvatore Adamo, a twenty-one-year-old singer-songwriter who had been born in Sicily but brought up in Belgium. Adamo had won an amateur song contest on Radio-Luxembourg with a song called 'Si j'osais', and on the strength of this he had been offered a recording contract. This had led to another hit record and a meeting with Bruno Coquatrix of the Paris Olympia – the only major theatre in Paris which had never boasted the name Maurice Chevalier on its famous façade. Adamo opened there in January, and Maurice was so impressed that he considered it essential for the young man's talents to become as widely known as possible. He therefore telephoned the director of New York's Carnegie Hall to inform him of Adamo's 'enormous potential, *should* he be engaged' – something which the director did, apparently on the strength of Maurice's name. Needless to say, the Americans liked him. 'He's a natural – not as sickly as Sacha Distel,' one critic said. 'But then again, he isn't a patch on Chevalier!'

Early in 1966 Maurice recorded a series of eight television programmes, *Maurice de Paris*, which were produced by Jean-Paul Sassy and Gisèle Boyer. In the February he again flew to America, where he was affected by the intense heat in Puerto Rico, and by the cold in Chicago. At Dayton Beach he lost his voice during the afternoon of his concert, though miraculously it returned in time for him to perform. Back in Paris, he paid a visit to the studios at Decca and recorded an entire album of Disney children's songs in a single session. Most of these he sang again a few days later at La Louque, in front of two camera crews, one for France and the other for CBS.

On 18 April the radio station France Inter spent the entire day with him, from 9.45 in the morning until 10 at night. They had already had a *Journée Barbara* for the great *chanteuse*; now it was Maurice's turn. The singer Georges Chelon, one of the many guests who paid tribute to him, called him '*Le grandpère de la chanson française*'. During the evening he was guest of honour in the then legendary programme *Les quatre-cents coups*, and sitting upon a table – he said this was his way of holding court – he received friends and colleagues one by one, and said a few words into the microphone. He was particularly interested in 'the artistes of tomorrow' – a few of whom were beginning to become household names then, though they may not be remembered now. In the age of the beatnik, Antoine was a young singer from Madagascar who sang ceaselessly about his mother's insistence that he should get his hair cut. Sheila, privately referred to as '*une mangeuse du micro*', had begun her career at the Golf Drouot singing ditties such as 'L'école est fini'. Maurice smiled at her now and called her '*très mignon*', but he was only being kind. Some of the youngsters, of course, had genuine talent and all of them went on to better things, at home and abroad. He had seen Françoise Hardy many times on the television, but so far as is known had not met her before. Her big song in France was 'Tous les garçons et les filles', but he particularly admired 'Autumn Rendezvous', which had been played a lot in America during his last visit. He told her, 'You have a talent which is quite extraordinary. You'll go a long way because you're not noisy like some of the others.' Hughes Aufray he knew well. A great fan of Bob Dylan, Aufray had attracted a cult following with the French adaptations of songs such as 'Mr Tambourine Man' and 'Blowing in the Wind'. Like Adamo, Hughes Aufray had also begun his American career through Maurice's intervention; a few discreet telephone calls and he had appeared on numerous television shows in New York, and he had been one of the stars of the famous 'April in Paris' ball. Maurice told him, 'You did well in America because you are a very elegant young man.' Aufray pointed to Maurice's white hair, and reciprocated, 'And you were the perfect Santa Claus. That's why I love you – that's why we all love you!'

None of these young artistes, however, quite compared with a nineteen-year-old girl from Avignon who shortly before had made her début in the television show *Le jeu de la chance*. This was the age of the Piaf 'soundalikes', two years after the great singer's death, and from it emerged three young ladies of quite singular talent. Georgette Lemaire had recorded an album containing several songs written by Piaf's team of Charles Dumont and Michel Vaucaire; 'Et si c'était vrai' had been a minor hit for her in England. Betty Mars, perhaps the most original of the trio, had actually begun singing in the streets of Paris and in 1974 would provide the soundtrack for Guy Cazaril's film about Piaf's life. The third artiste, and the most internationally successful, was Mireille Mathieu. In her autobiography, *Oui, je crois!*, she recalled the first time Maurice invited her to visit La Louque.

A respectable housemaid opened the door, and a butler showed us into the hall where we were greeted by a life-size painting of Chevalier. The flesh and blood original was waiting in the salon, fresh-faced and with a pearl in his tie, surrounded by his household: Félix Paquet and his wife Maryse, and François and Madeleine Vals, all of them smiling. Then Maurice kissed me and said, 'There's a great difference between Piaf and you. Piaf walked among the shadows, but you walk in the sunshine!'

Maurice fell for Mireille Mathieu in a big way, resulting in perhaps the most important platonic relationship of his later years. Her big songs were 'Mon credo' and 'Qu'elle est belle', which had been produced under the strict gaze of her impresario and mentor Johnny Stark, the man responsible for Johnny Hallyday in the early 1960s. She also resembled Piaf – tiny and slim – and came from a similar background, the eldest in a poor family of twelve. Maurice promised to help her, and he did. During the summer of 1966 he telephoned Bernard Delfont in London and told him, 'This girl has talent. Piaf herself would have loved her.' A few weeks later she sang 'Mon credo' on *Sunday Night at the London Palladium* and within minutes the television switchboard was jammed with calls wanting to hear more. The following week she appeared again, and soon afterwards reached the British hit parade with 'La dernière valse', the French adaptation of the Les Reed–Barry Mason classic which had precipitated Engelbert Humperdinck to world fame. In fact, Mireille and Humperdinck would appear together many times in the near future. As for now, in spite of Johnny Stark's alleged insistence that his protégée was not quite ready for the move, Maurice decided that he would take his very own 'Mimi' to New York, where he had been engaged for a four-week season. Both did well. Mireille was a big hit on *The Ed Sullivan Show*, even if the great showman could not pronounce her name, and Maurice opened at the Waldorf Astoria a few days later, when the city's music-halls had been hit by a musicians' strike. One evening, even Fred Freed, recently restored to the fold, was not allowed on stage. Maurice took this in his stride, telling the management, 'Fine, so I'll sing without any accompaniment!' He did exactly this, and promptly brought the house down. A correspondent for the *New York Times* wrote, 'In a simple but glorious evening, the Great Maurice enabled us to forget the tension between our two countries.' (He was referring to General de Gaulle's decision for France to leave the North Atlantic Treaty Organization.)

There was also a new song, one which expressed his admiration for the greatest love of his life: Paris.

> *Votre firmament c'est très gentil,*
> *C'est charmant, plein d'agrément . . .*
> *On y sens flotter une odeur de sainteté,*
> *Le premier, le seul, le vrai paradis*
> *C'est Paris!*

> (Your firmament is very kind,
> It's charming, filled with pleasure . . .
> There one senses floating an air of sanctity,
> The first, the only, the true heaven,
> It's Paris!)

At around this time Maurice announced his plans for the future. His entourage and his admirers knew only too well that he would not go on for ever, even though his performances were no less energetic than they had been since his 'reconquest' of America; no one, however, liked to use the word 'retirement', least of all Maurice himself. Some of his critics had, of course, misinterpreted an earlier decision 'to go on singing until I drop' as a sign of his meanness – while he could earn huge fees he would still keep on working, whether he was fit to do so or not. This was pure tripe. Like Edith Piaf, Judy Garland and, to a certain extent, Frank Sinatra, Maurice was well aware of the fact that the stage was in his blood and that the applause of his public was his life-force. Had he stopped singing at such a critical phase in his career, life would have had little or no meaning. Even so, he did begin dreaming of one final, massive all-embracing tour of the world, taking in every country he had loved, and finishing with a series of recitals at the Théâtre des Champs-Elysées to coincide with his eightieth birthday in September 1968. This decision also coincided with the one made by Jacques Brel, some forty years his junior, to retire from his frenetic public performances in order to concentrate more on songwriting and making films.

In September 1966 Brel was invited to La Louque. Here, he told Maurice why he had decided to retire – a combination of stage fright and having, in a musical sense, done everything. He said, 'Every time I face an audience, I die a thousand times.' It was also suggested that Brel had been thinking of offering Maurice a song – the way he had offered one to Edith Piaf, three weeks before her death – but that he declined, thinking Maurice would turn him down. This is a great pity, as one imagines Maurice singing a pastiche in the vein of 'Ne me quitte pas' inordinately well. Brel opened at the Olympia on 6 October, saying to a reporter three days later, 'Thank God I won't have to die again!' Twelve years to the day he did die, of lung cancer. There was also a tragic link between the great Belgian singer and another friend, Walt Disney. Maurice had given up cigarettes some years before, and the fact that Brel chainsmoked – sometimes getting through as many as five packs a day – worried him. Eventually, he would have a lung removed, but this would not deter him from the habit which would ultimately kill him. Disney likewise did not survive long after having his lung removed; he died in the December of 1966, aged sixty-five. Maurice said, 'Disney and I were perhaps the last of the world's great optimists. Who's going to inspire me, now that he's gone?'

During the Christmas period Maurice reflected on the various ups and downs of his lengthy life and career. He had been asked to perform in Japan, a country he had never visited in spite of his being one of the top record-sellers there. Repeated demands had also come in from South Africa, Canada and, of course, England and the United States. Maurice decided that his farewell tour would take in as many countries as possible, but only the ones where people had already seen him. 'I'm too old to take on any uncalculated risks,' he said, referring to the Far East. Therefore the offer from Japan was turned down.

On 16 January 1967 Maurice arrived in Johannesburg, and as usual, instead of resting after the long flight, he booked into the Hyde Park Hotel and immediately went 'walkabout'. In an act which was not political but human, he strolled through Soweto, greeting his coloured admirers while being cautious not to say anything which might have been misconstrued by the predominantly white press. The racial discrimination disgusted him. 'Even the toilets are marked "black" and "white", he was heard to say. The attitude and climate of South Africa were, however, bad for him. After just two days he succumbed to an attack of laryngitis and had to see a doctor, who prescribed antibiotics and advised him to cancel or at least defer his opening night. Maurice had been reprimanded by the medical profession before for failing to compromise where his health was concerned, and once more he decided that only he knew best. This time, fortunately, he was aided by an audience which was more sympathetic than a Parisian one might have been. His age and his supposed frailty were taken into account, and no one was expecting a miracle when he stepped on to the stage, but they got one all the same, one which went on for more than two hours. 'Chevalier is as indestructible as the Table Mountain,' one newspaper reported.

The Farewell Tour

Dear Monsieur Chevalier,
   On behalf of the kids (all of us), thank you so much for everything. You are a beautiful person, and will never get old, only more beautiful.
   Love. All of us.

This poignant little message, expressing exactly the Americans' profound admiration for Maurice, was scribbled on the back of a ticket by a female student and handed to him after he had sung to the gathering at California's Berkeley University in October 1967, and it made him cry. This was just the beginning of what would be the most emotional period of his life. In Hyannis Port, Massachusetts, he had again met Jacqueline Kennedy, and there had been a lengthy chat with ex-president Truman after his recital in Independence, near Kansas City. In Los Angeles he had 'bumped into' Marlene Dietrich and Ingrid Bergman. Each artiste, friend or acquaintance was treated as though he would never see them again. In Washington he appeared at the vast Constitution Hall, an establishment usually reserved for classical recitals, and the day after a famous concert given by Leonard Bernstein and the New York Symphony Orchestra, alone on the stage, he eclipsed even Bernstein and brought the house down. In New York, such was the demand for tickets at the Lincoln Center on 19 November that 150 chairs were set out on the stage behind him. This caused problems at the end of his show when he was given a standing ovation. He said, 'I thought they were going to rush me, so I panicked. Then I realized that they were only trying to smother me, with love!'

While in New York Maurice broke with his own tradition and, before leaving for France, spent four days showing the Vals and Fred Freed around the city. He was observed doing 'ordinary things' of the sort Americans obviously thought impossible for their own stars – shopping, stopping off at a bar for a drink, and even giving money to an old tramp. Then it was Christmas at La Louque before starting all over again. 'I've still got fifty-five cities and eighteen countries to go before I finally hang up my boots,' he said at the airport. He was also asked why, in spite of his alleged over-fondness for money, he had turned down $100,000 for a series of advertisements for confectionery. 'I've not done anything like that in France, so I won't be doing it here,' he snapped.

Early in January 1968 Maurice flew to Helsinki, the opening venue on a European tour which would cover thirty cities, including Stockholm, Copenhagen, Amsterdam and Vienna, in just over one month. He later confessed that nothing had moved him quite so much as his reception in Britain. His arrival at the Savoy Hotel on Sunday, 11 February, was likened to a 'second coming' by one reporter, and the press conference which followed was both excitable and sincere. More than once, Maurice's voice broke and he had to pause and sip a glass of water. But if these 'representatives' of his public were under the illusion that he would be back in the near future, Maurice soon put them in their place by his candid responses to their questions.

'My so-called eternal youth? When I was younger I used to drink more, live more and love more. That is why I've got the flame of youth inside me!'

'Do I like London? What a question! London and America enabled me to become the International Frenchman!'

'No, I won't pose for photographs wearing my *canotier*. It doesn't seem right that a man of eighty should put on a straw hat and clown around!'

'Why am I retiring? Because I am eighty, and therefore I feel that I should call it a day. Maybe I would like to do a final film, if they can find a part for an old man like me. Or maybe they should make a film *about* me while I'm still here – if they can find someone to play me!'

'Why am I saying goodbye? Because I'm at an age where saying goodbye is the most honest thing that I can do!'

A few days later, the man whose press handouts proclaimed him to be 'The Most Popular Frenchman in the World' opened in a one-week season at the London Palladium. 'Valentine', 'Louise' and 'Ma pomme' were all there, as were one or two of his songs from the war – 'Ça s'est passé un dimanche' and 'Ça sent si bon la France'. There were also several examples of Maurice's new repertoire, the contents of which certainly belied his age. Offering an imitation of his pop-star friend Antoine, he sang Henri Bourtayre's 'Oui au whisky'! Then, to show that he was not behind the times when it came to musical fashion, he sang a French adaptation of one of the Beatles' most famous songs, except that 'Yellow Submarine' was given a coat of paint to be transformed into 'Le sous-marin vert'. He apologized on behalf of his songwriter. 'The French word for "yellow" is "jaune". Unfortunately, it's very difficult to find a word which rhymes with that.' There was also the jaunty 'Sourire aux lèvres', written for Maurice by Michel Rivgauche, who was renowned for his works for Edith Piaf, and arranged by one of the greatest orchestra leaders in Europe, Caravelli.

> *Il faut garder le sourire aux lèvres,*
> *Pour voir la vie d'un p'tit air allègre!*
> *C'est la p'tite fleur d'la bonne humeur,*
> *Qui pousse dans les cœurs!*

> (One must keep a smile on one's lips,
> To see life with a lively air!
> It's the little flower of good humour,
> Which grows within our hearts!)

Publicly, Maurice's good humour and broad, still-saucy smile were omnipresent, though privately it was another matter. Out of the spotlight he suffered from lengthy periods of depression and self-doubt. The burden of being the 'Ambassador of France' often weighed heavily upon his shoulders, particularly as he had no clear indication of what he would do with himself once the curtain came down for the last time. His next volume of memoirs, *Quatre-vingt berges*, had just been published in France and he was well into what he anticipated would be the last, *Môme à cheveux blancs*. 'There'll be no more after this one,' he told a British reporter. 'I mean, what will I have to write about after ten lengthy volumes?'

Following the London Palladium, Maurice made a lightning tour of Britain, taking in Manchester, Bournemouth, Glasgow, Cardiff and Coventry, where, after singing 'Thank Heaven for Little Girls', he descended into the audience to shake hands with his admirers. Then it was back to La Louque, where, during the evening of 4 April he switched on his television set in time to catch the newsflash announcing the murder in Memphis of Martin Luther King, who, in recognition of his tireless quest for world peace, had recently been awarded the Nobel Prize. Maurice was devastated; but worse still, King's assassination had sparked off racial unrest all over America, and Maurice was scheduled to fly to Orlando on 9 April, the actual day of the minister's funeral. His friends begged him to cancel, but, as in the past, this was out of the question. 'Something inside tells me that I've got to go,' he said to François Vals. On the evening of 10 April, he watched an edited version of the ceremony on an American news report and at once made comparisons between King's widow and Jacqueline Kennedy. 'In spite of what's happened, she wants to continue her husband's work,' he enthused. 'What a brave woman she must be!'

The tension caused by the events in Memphis were certainly felt all over America, and took some of the edge off Maurice's concerts, particularly in Washington and Baltimore, where there were spasmodic outbreaks of violence. There were, of course, lighter moments. In Florida he spent an enjoyable afternoon looking around Disney World. On 21 April, in New York, he was presented with a special Tony Award by Audrey Hepburn for his work on the American stage. Then it was on with the tour – Flint, Baltimore, Chicago, Detroit, Westbury and eventually back to New York, and the plane back to Paris, where there were problems of a different kind. The country was paralysed by strikes on account of the students' insurrection, and as Air France could not guarantee a flight, Maurice had to fly to Brussels. Several weeks later, when he must have been wondering what could possibly happen next, he learned of the assassination on 6 June of Senator Robert Kennedy in Los Angeles.

In July the tour resumed. Maurice flew to Brazil in what was the hottest season of the year. His concerts in Rio de Janeiro and Porto Alegre were handled well, though by the time he opened in Sao Paolo he was reported to be looking decidedly tired. This tiredness affected his performance, and half-way through the first half he had to be escorted back to his dressing room. He was driven back to his hotel and a doctor was summoned, but after an extensive examination he was declared to be suffering from no more than fatigue. The next evening he strode on to the stage with the energy of a man half his age and opened with 'Tout va bien pour moi'!

On 6 August Maurice opened in a week-long season at the Buenos Aires Opera House. After the première he was invited to dine at the restaurant run by Jo Bouillon, the former bandleader and ex-husband of Josephine Baker. His gastronomic interests had earned him the nickname 'Joe Soup', which although merely an English translation of his name, he found most unflattering. Maurice had always nurtured a great feeling for Bouillon, in spite of his 'unfortunate' choice in women. In 1935 they had recorded together, and probably would have done so more often had it not been for Josephine. Bouillon had also lined up a pleasant surprise for his old friend – seated at the dinner table was Léopold de Lima, Mistinguett's son, now aged sixty-seven but still running his own medical practice. 'Popol was the kid Maurice ought to have fathered,' Mistinguett had once said, probably forgetting that Maurice had been only twelve years old at the time!

And the tour continued. Montevideo, Santiago, Lima, Panama, Mexico, Quebec, and finally Montreal, where in the vast Town Hall he gave what the Canadians declared was the greatest performance of his entire career. He was even asked to stay in the country to celebrate his eightieth birthday on 12 September – not that his French admirers would have allowed such a thing!

This 'gala to end all galas' took place at the Lido in Paris and was organized by his friend Georges Cravenne. Maurice was almost mobbed outside the theatre and spent a long time shaking hands, hugging acquaintances, and blowing kisses at the crowd. Barring the obvious showbusiness personalities, most of his audience was surprisingly young. Within the famous music-hall, the equally famous Bluebell Girls filed on to the stage – forty of them, each carrying a cake lit with two candles. Maurice was so moved that it took him several minutes to find the courage to speak. While in America he had recorded his ultimate contribution to the film industry – the theme-song for Disney's *The Aristocats*, and since returning to France he had been amused to find himself referred to as 'Doctor Sunshine'. He said, 'If that's how you feel about me, then I now know that I've achieved my goal!'

Maurice also appeared in a one-hour television interview, *Les grandes confidences*, which was filmed at La Louque. The producer was Frédérique Hébrard, the wife of the actor Louis Velle, with whom he had made *J'avais sept filles* in 1954. Maurice called her one of the most cultured women he had ever met. He had also known her father, the biographer André Chamson, an important figure of the French Resistance. The programme went out at the end of the month, while Maurice was performing in Palma in what would be his last show outside France. Even so, there were many who genuinely believed that he would go on for ever, particularly when he sang a recent composition by Pierre Delanoë, who, after Vincent Scotto, was the most prolific songwriter in France, with some 3,000 songs to his credit, including 'Et maintenant', his collaboration with Gilbert Bécaud.

> *Quand j'aurai cent ans,*
> *Quand le Bon Dieu me fera des avances,*
> *Je dirai: 'Attends!*
> *J'suis amoureux et ma vie recommence!'*

> (When I'm a hundred years old,
> When God advances towards me,
> I'll say: 'Wait!
> I'm in love, life's beginning again!')

Anyone who was anyone in Paris was sitting in the audience at the Théâtre des Champs-Elysées when Maurice opened in his final season on 1 October 1968: Henri Varna, Manitas de Plata, Charles Trenet (who had labelled him 'The Eiffel Tower of Song'), Marcel Pagnol, the jockey Yves Saint-Martin, Fernandel, the boxer Georges Carpentier, and the Duke and Duchess of Windsor, to name but a few. There would be only seventeen recitals, but every one was highly charged with emotion and the first night was taped and issued on an album. When Maurice walked on to the stage, carrying his ever-faithful straw boater, everyone rose and applauded him madly for fifteen minutes. This idolatry lasted another two hours. His voice breaking, he announced, 'I'm going to try my best to earn your kindness tonight, but oh, what a funk I'm in!' This brought loud guffaws of laughter, though Maurice was deadly serious – facing an audience, even an occasionally hostile one, was for him as easy as breathing, but the in-between periods still brought on fits of panic that he would one day find himself unable to sing any more. At the Théâtre des Champs-Elysées all this was placed behind him as he launched into his first song, 'La marche de Ménilmontant'. From then on it was plain-sailing all the way through to the interval, which was only there, he said, so that the *audience* could take a breather! For his second half, he summoned up all the wizardry and expertise of his seven decades of theatrical experience, giving the audience the inevitable 'Prosper' and 'Valentine', the Cole Porter medley, and Fred Freed's sparkling, fresh arrangements of 'Louise' and 'Paris je t'aime'.

> *Pour les caresses de mille maîtresses,*
> *Elles m'oublieront bien vite,*
> *Et pourtant,*
> *Moi d'leurs baisers j'm'souviendrais*
> *Bien longtemps!*
> *Paris je t'aime d'amour!*

(As for the caresses of a thousand lovers,
They'll forget me quickly enough,
And yet,
I'll remember their kisses for a long long time!
Paris, I give you my real love!)

The standing ovation after Maurice's performance lasted more than half an hour and ended with some 2,000 fans chanting along with him, '*Tout va bien pour moi, tout va bien pour vous!*' Afterwards he was asked by Jacques Canetti if, the next evening, the television cameras might be allowed inside the theatre. 'You will have to wait until tomorrow. Maybe then I'll be in better fettle,' Maurice replied. For the next two weeks he gave the same answer – a great, great pity.

On 21 October Maurice Chevalier sang in public for the last time. During the morning he spent an hour or so opening letters and telegrams. Alain Delon, Charles Aznavour, Gilbert Bécaud and Yves Montand all conveyed their best wishes. So did Jacques Brel, temporarily out of retirement to star in the French adaptation of *The Man of La Mancha*, which had recently opened in Brussels. Strangely, there was also a letter from a former 'enemy', Georges Brassens, himself unable to see Maurice because of illness. And to show that he had no hard feelings, Maurice sent a telegram to Jacqueline Kennedy congratulating her on her marriage to Aristotle Onassis, though secretly he did not approve, sharing the view of many people that in remarrying she had insulted the memory of the dead president. Thus at 5.30 pm – it was a Sunday and by tradition there was no evening performance – Maurice said farewell to his public. He concluded, 'The word "goodbye" is too sad. Therefore from the bottom of my heart I would simply like to say "*au revoir*".' This he did with a moving song by Jean Dréjac and Fred Freed.

> *Public mon bel emblème,*
> *Public mon beau miroir,*
> *Ça fait trois fois vingt ans qu'on s'aime,*
> *Est-ce la fin d'un beau poème?*
> *Qui sait? Mais je vous dis quand même:*
> *'Au revoir!'*
> *Merci pour la balade,*
> *Merci pour les grands soirs,*
> *Je vous dédie ma sérénade . . .*

> (Public, my fair emblem,
> Public, my lovely mirror,

It is three times twenty years that we love each other,
Is it the end of a beautiful poem?
Who knows? But all the same I say to you:
'Au revoir!'
Thank you for the run,
Thank you for the great evenings,
I dedicate my serenade to you . . .)

In the avenue Montaigne outside the theatre, a large crowd had gathered to see Maurice in his car. Many were in tears; only the optimists assumed that he would soon be back. After all, had he not done this sort of thing before, the rest at La Louque, spent writing his memoirs or strolling around the park? It is true that there were numerous receptions, official functions and suchlike over the next few weeks: visits to the racecourse at Longchamp to see Yves Saint-Martin, who was François Vals's cousin; the première of Brel's *L'homme à La Mancha* in the December; the annual *La nuit du cinéma* with his friends Claude Dauphin and Mireille Mathieu; the première of *Funny Girl*, where he was photographed escorting Barbra Streisand – it was an extremely important film, he declared, because Fanny Brice and Mistinguett had shared the same theme-song, 'Mon homme'. Hardly a week went by without his photograph appearing in a newspaper or on the television news, though not everything said about him was kind – particularly the remarks about his 'rapacious demands' for 70 per cent of the box-office receipts at the Théâtre des Champs-Elysées, money which in all honesty he deserved. One event which was conveniently 'overlooked' by the French press was Maurice's involvement with the Petits Frères des Pauvres shortly before Christmas 1968, when he, François Vals and Félix Paquet distributed money and gifts to several destitute families in and around Paris.

Maurice was, of course, inundated almost daily with offers of work from all over the world, some of which he must have found very hard to turn down. But as he had said back in October, 'I would rather finish now, while I'm still lucid, than go on until I'm past it!'

The tenth volume of Maurice's memoirs, *Môme à cheveux blancs*, was published in France in 1969, and a little later in Britain

and America under the title *I Remember It Well*. Many readers
were surprised by his frank, philosophical comments.

> I am a simple man, the man of my one-man shows. Anything
> that does not go along with this side of my character makes
> me profoundly unhappy. When I go to noisy parties, I feel
> like a peasant at a palace reception, nervous and tight around
> the collar. The only places I feel really comfortable are *chez
> moi* with the people I trust, or all alone on stage, where I can
> be myself with a theatre full of people who have come to see
> me, just me, my white hair, my past and my present.

He was lonelier than he had ever been, and a sad old man.
His brother Paul died in August, aged eighty-three, and his great
spiritual comforter, Père Boulogne, passed away on 17 October.
He was cheered up no end, however, at the end of the month by
President de Gaulle's thank-you letter for the book which Maurice
had sent him a few weeks before. The letter began 'Cher Maître'
and, besides praising his 'magnificent talent', included the phrase
'your exceptional artistic radiation served France well', referring
to the war years, an extremely important antidote for anyone who
still suspected him of nefarious activities.

On 20 November Maurice was invited to a reception at one
of Paris's oldest music-halls, the Alcazar. The occasion was the
celebration of the seventieth birthday of Duke Ellington, with
whom he had made his début as a recital artiste forty years before.
It was also a charity event, with the proceeds going to l'Union des
Artistes. The other guests included the painter Salvador Dali, and
the singers Régine and Nicoletta – the latter had just recorded a
cover-version of the Shirley Bassey song 'Does Anybody Miss
Me?'; and in so doing had gained Maurice's admiration. A part
of the programme was relayed to millions of listeners on *Le Pop-
Club de José Artur*, on France Inter radio station.

Early in the New Year he flew to Holland to publicize the Dutch
translation of his memoirs. At signings in Amsterdam and Rotter-
dam, when asked to sing he courteously declined. He did, however,
show some interest in the Cinémathèque France's special series of
screenings of his early Hollywood films, even if his attitude
towards them had changed. *One Hour With You* was dismissed

as 'agreeable but dated'. Worse still, he declared, was *The Merry Widow*, in which he thought he had over-played his role 'with horrible consequences'. And after forcing himself to watch *Folies-Bergère* and *The Love Parade*, he announced that he had had enough. He was selling himself short, of course. His admirers, many of whom had not even been born when these fine films were made, applauded every scene.

And then, when everyone was least expecting it, Maurice was to find one final, all-embracing happiness, a soul-mate who would bring him peace of mind, satisfaction that in spite of adversity life was still worth living, and above all the love and devotion for which he had craved, it would seem, for so many years. He wrote in his journal:

> At the age of eighty-two I am certain that I have found a feminine hand to consolidate my new way of life, and someone in whom I can truly believe. A hand to hold my own, until the very end if need be. I have recently rediscovered a friend from the old days. Because life has not treated her kindly, I would like to help her. I find her more sincere than *any* of the women in my past.

The 'feminine hand' belonged to Odette Meslier, the pretty ex-Bluebell Girl who in 1952 had danced around Maurice during his 'Valentine' sketch in the revue *Plein feu*. The couple had in fact met again at the Alhambra in 1957, since when Odette had married and given birth to a handicapped daughter, Pascale. When she wrote to Maurice in April 1970 she was separated from her husband and living with her parents. Inevitably, the mother and child were invited to La Louque one afternoon, and Maurice was astonished at the way they fitted in with his preconception of perfect family harmony. He decided that more than anything in the world, he would like to help.

Meanwhile, the final volume of Maurice's memoirs, *Les pensées de Momo*, was published in France by Presses de la Cité. He was invited to a series of signings in America, and though he was determined never to go on stage again, he was still eager to travel the world for as long as he could, helping to nurture the legend which he himself had created. Prior to this he was guest of honour in *La joie de vivre*, commemorating the Marseilles goalkeeper Jean-Paul Escale. Then in June he and François Vals flew to Washington, where *I Remember It Well* was one of the major features at the Book Convention. It was a brief but nevertheless successful visit, culminating in a press conference and an appearance on *The David Frost Show*. Maurice is also said to have enjoyed the experience of being able to travel abroad 'just like any other passenger', without any kind of pre-publicity, although, of course, as soon as he stepped off the plane in New York he had been recognized and surrounded by dozens of fans.

Never before, however, had he been so pleased to return to La Louque. Odette and Pascale had been installed in an apartment in the park at Marnes-la-Coquette, and over the next few weeks Maurice spent much of his time with them, organizing physio and speech therapy sessions for the little girl. In spite of his new-found contentment, however, the summer months did bring lengthy periods of depression on account of a growing obituary list. François Mauriac and General Koenig died suddenly. The operetta star Luis Mariano lost his long battle against cancer. Jacques Pills, who had married Lucienne Boyer, Edith Piaf and, some said, Josephine Baker, died of a heart attack. A few weeks later Piaf's second husband, Théo Sarapo, was killed in a car crash just outside Limoges. This came as a particular blow to Maurice. After Piaf's death, Sarapo had inherited debts of 7 million francs and had been forced to work very hard to pay them off, and not always in the friendliest of atmospheres. It was even suggested, but subsequently disproved, that his death might have been no accident. Finally, there were the deaths of the actor Bernard Noël and Maurice's personal physician Michel Fouquet, and the unexpected suicide of Lucien Morisse, the artistic director of the radio-station Europe 1.

'I feel so vulnerable, so feeble,' he wrote, on the eve of another publicity trip to the United States. He was certainly under the weather, probably due to the virus which had affected his throat, and the long flight could not have done him much good. His first official engagement was at the Hadley School for the Blind, where he learned that *I Remember It Well* was about to be transcribed into Braille. From there he flew to New York, where he gave interviews on several television and radio chat-shows, including a second appearance on *The David Frost Show*. There was also a splendid cocktail party at Brentano's Bookstore on Fifth Avenue, complete with red carpet, where he was reunited with his friend Alan Jay Lerner and introduced to Joan Crawford, of whom Mistinguett had told him, some forty years before, 'That woman has the makings of a good bitch!' He was photographed charming his friends and former acquaintances, always sporting his sunny, sincere smile, telling jokes, or reminiscing over some witty anecdote. Behind the mask of joviality, however, there lurked a tragic figure. The man whom writer and producer Jean-Christophe Averty had called '*mon gros père*' was unwell and secretly unsure of himself. Few people knew that shortly before the ceremony a doctor from the French Hospital had given him an injection to ensure that he stayed on his feet.

When he returned to France towards the end of the year Maurice was suffering from insomnia and acute bouts of nervous tension. Before, he had always laughed off his 'slight indispositions'. Now he was worried. 'I got out of these depressions when I was younger,' he wrote. 'The thing is, I keep forgetting that soon I will be eighty-three.' Neither was he helped by the letter he received from his old friend Charles Boyer, himself on the verge of neurosis since the death of his son. Unable to cope with his loss, and wishing to spend as much time as possible with Patricia, his wife, Boyer had renounced his acting career and had begun searching far and wide for a new home. At first there was talk of his moving to a house in Marnes-la-Coquette, something that would have benefited himself and Maurice enormously. As Marlene Dietrich has said, 'Every time I went to see Chevalier, he was always alone, apart from that man who lived at the house. I never saw anyone from his family, and he *never* mentioned them at all.' But Boyer decided that he could never live anywhere that reminded him of Michael and a little later he bought a house in Switzerland for the summer, and a house in Majorca for the winter. So far as is known, the two friends never met again.

At around this time Odette Meslier's estranged husband died and she found herself free to move into La Louque – though she was not free from scandalmongers or from media interference. Maurice was also well into what would have been his twelfth volume of memoirs, to which he had given the title *On est comme on naît*. The book was eventually completed and deposited with a publisher in Paris, but Maurice asked for the script back: according to François Vals, it was not the most uplifting of tomes on account of Maurice's general state of mind. His mood is not thought to have been helped by the now possessive Félix Paquet, who had more or less become Maurice's guardian, vetting all visitors to La Louque, including the family, Janie Michels and the Vals, who, since Maurice's retirement, had begun spending more time at their house in Sèvres. Marlene Dietrich, who was 'allowed past the barrier', has said that at this point in his life she had never seen him looking so sad. Exactly why Paquet behaved so strangely is not known, but things got progressively worse. François has said that Maurice used to love his weekly visits to Sèvres to dine with the Vals family, but that because of Paquet's iron rule these trips stopped early in 1971. The only brief spell of 'freedom' was when Maurice and François came to London to promote *I Remember It Well*. He looked unwell, but he was just as jovial as ever.

The bestselling book in France in 1971 was Henri Charrière's *Papillon*, telling of his imprisonment on and subsequent escape from the fortress at Devil's Island. It had also been turned into a very successful film starring Steve McQueen. The year before, a woman called Simone Berteaut, claiming to be the half-sister of Edith Piaf, had written a warts-and-all account of Piaf's life which had all but outsold the Bible. Both authors were denounced as fakes by many critics and, it would seem, by Maurice. On 6 March he watched a programme about Charrière on the television; what happened next is recorded in François Vals's recollections of his twenty years with Maurice, as told to the writer Pierre Berruer.

> Maurice clenched his jaws. Suddenly he rose, banged on the table, and exploded. 'Today, in order to be someone, you've got to be a convict!' The Paquets were surprised. Maurice didn't usually lose his temper like that. Then he glared at them from the corner of his eye and stormed off to his room.

It is impossible to know whether this outburst had any real bearing on the events of the next few hours. In retrospect, the episode seems to have been blown out of all proportion. However, the following morning, a Sunday, Maryse Paquet waited for the call from Maurice's room announcing that he was awake and wanting his breakfast. This was usually taken upstairs at 8.30. After an hour, when there was still no sign of life, Maryse thought it wise to investigate. She found Maurice unconscious. On the table next to his bed was an empty barbiturates bottle; he had also tried to cut his wrists. An ambulance was called, and he was rushed to the American Hospital at Neuilly, followed by François Vals and the Paquets. Afraid of being alone, and possibly of the fact that he considered himself a shadow of his former self and a would-be burden on those who loved him, he had wanted to die, to join La Louque, his beloved mother, who had never ceased to be in his thoughts. Maryse Paquet had also found a note scribbled in his handwriting. It ended, 'Please forgive me. You are all in my will. We will see each other again, up there. I kiss you all.'

For two days Maurice lay in a coma. The doctors were not too worried about the cuts on his wrists as these were superficial. The fact that the barbiturates had probably been swallowed more than nine hours before hospitalization, however, gave everyone grave concern. Mercifully, the media did not interfere. They were not informed of Maurice's illness until he had come out of the coma, and the public did not find out what had really happened until 24 January 1972, by way of a scurrilous report in the French publication *Minute*. For the time being, '*le grandpère de la chanson*' was undergoing medical tests after a nasty bout of influenza. Then, on the last day of March, he was allowed to return to La Louque, and the incident on 7 March was pushed to the back of everyone's minds.

For several months Maurice seemed to rally. There were short walks through the park with Odette Meslier, and the occasional visit from his spiritual adviser, Père Carré. He expressed a desire to see Marlene Dietrich. She was unable to visit, because of her Scandinavian tour, but wrote him two moving letters. In the July he was informed of the death of yet another showbusiness friend, Louis Armstrong. On 12 September, his eighty-third birthday, he received a visit from Jerry Lewis. This would be one of the last genuinely happy days of his life, of which precious little remained. Slowly but surely, he was becoming a recluse. A few weeks later he developed a liver complaint, said to have been brought on by barbiturate poisoning. This trouble quickly spread to his kidneys, and he was convinced that he was close to death. On 26 October he summoned his lawyer and redrafted his will, making Odette Meslier his sole legatee and leaving substantial bequests to François and Madeleine Vals, the Paquets, Janie Michels, Nita Raya, his nephew René and his wife Lucette, and several others.

Maurice's last outing, ironically, was typically unselfish. Reminiscing about his childhood, he had decided to take Odette and Pascale to his former favourite haunt, the Cirque d'Hiver. It was here, on the evening of 12 December, that he complained of feeling unwell and asked to be taken home. Early the next morning he was re-admitted to the American Hospital, where his doctor's worst suspicions were confirmed: a blockage of the kidneys. That same day he was transferred to the Hôpital Necker and placed on a dialysis machine. Because of his advanced age there could be no question of a transplant. It was simply a matter of time.

Still very much aware of what he was saying and doing – and so far as is known, not in any great pain – Maurice was informed that Marlene Dietrich had asked to see him. He told one of the doctors that this would not be a good idea: he did not wish his great friend to see him so close to death, as she very kindly explains in the preface to this book. His other friends and close relatives saw him only through a glass partition. Then, during the evening of 1 January 1972 Père Carré was summoned to his bedside to offer him the last rites. At 7.30 the great Chevalier slipped away.

A few weeks before he had given François Vals a number of envelopes to be distributed on New Year's Day, 'no matter what happens to me', hardly aware that this would be his final act of benevolence. These were to be handed out to his loved ones. Each envelope contained several banknotes and the now heartrending message, 'Happy New Year, my children!'

Epilogue: 5 January 1972

Every year since the death of Mistinguett on this very day in 1956, Maurice had spent some time alone in front of her photograph contemplating what might have been had things turned out differently between them. Now, on the sixteenth anniversary of her death, he was being laid to rest in the churchyard at Marnes-la-Coquette, next to La Louque, his beloved mother, whose remains had been transferred here just a few years before.

Maurice's funeral was not a large one compared to those of his contemporaries such as Edith Piaf, Mistinguett, and Josephine Baker. He had specifically requested this his obsequies should not be turned into a showbusiness extravaganza. Even so, more than 1,000 people huddled together in the bitter cold outside the church, while Père Carré's moving testimony was relayed through loud-speakers. He announced, 'Maurice Chevalier attained perfection by remaining a simple man – a man who sacrificed everything for the sake of his art.'

The 'guest-list' within the church resembled one of Maurice's opening nights: Princess Grace of Monaco was dressed in black mink; Marcel Pagnol and Michel Simon represented the film world; there was the poet Louis Amade; and on behalf of the Folies-Bergère, the widow of Paul Derval; from the sporting world there were Georges Carpentier and the jockey Yves Saint-Martin; There were representatives from the National Assembly and the United States government; and from the world of the music-hall Tino Rossi, Marcel Amont, the comic Fernand Raynaud, and a host of others. Several representatives from the Hadley Institute for the Blind had flown over especially from America. Most important of all, however, were the members of Maurice's family – the blood relations, of course, and others who had entered his life at varying stages of his career. In Maurice's estimation, there had never been any real division between the two: Lucette and René, who continue to preserve his tradition in such a way that everyone who meets them goes away feeling uplifted and proud to have known them; François and Madeleine Vals, who for twenty years had known no other life than the one *chez Maurice*; Odette Meslier, the maligned, uncrowned saint who had brought warmth to his last months; Janie Michels, who as a cherished friend had stood by him long after their love affair had ended; Nita Raya, who had helped him through the very worst of his traumas; the Paquets, and Yvonne Vallée, his ex-wife, who sent a wreath.

At the time of writing, Maurice's 'family' are still very much alive – some quietly so, whilst others, such as his niece and nephew and the Vals, actively promote his memory and good name. And it is a good name, in spite of those cynics, scandalmongers and critics who have attempted to defame him by saying otherwise.

Marie Dubas died only weeks after Maurice on 21 February, the day Maurice normally would have arranged to place flowers on Fréhel's grave, this being the anniversary of her death. Damia died in 1978. My beloved godfather, Roger Normand, died at Ris-Orangis in February 2000. Michel Guyarmathy of the Folies-Bergère and Sylvie Galthier are also gone, as are old 'enemies' Charles Trenet and Georges Guétary. Félix Paquet, in a fit of pique, flung himself from an upstairs window and the tabloids had a field-day, claiming that many years earlier Maurice had had a troubled clandestine relationship with his butler, and that Paquet had been blackmailing Maurice to ensure his silence. Just about everyone who knew the pair dismissed the claim as hogwash.

Perhaps the last word should be left to his friend Marlene Dietrich, who said of him: 'Maurice Chevalier? He was a *decent* man, and you'd better not foget it!'

The Recordings of
Maurice Chevalier

There exists no complete discography of Maurice Chevalier's recorded output, which is alleged to have begun around 1908 with the release of 'On the level you're a little devil'. The singer himself did not like making records – like all visual artistes he was only at his best before live audiences – and prior to the French 'shellac-boom' of 1934, few lists were kept of studio visits. If a pressing was found to be unacceptable, either by the artiste or the engineer, it was discarded. Thus, Maurice's early songs are still being discovered. The following, therefore, is but a rough guide of what is and has been available in France and Britain over the last decade.

Maurice Chevalier 1928–1948: 'Valentine'; 'Mimi'; 'Paris je t'aime'; 'Quand un vicomte'; 'Prosper'; 'Donnez-moi la main'; 'Ma pomme'; 'Paris sera toujours Paris'; 'Le chapeau de Zozo'; 'Ah! si vous connaissiez ma poule'; 'Ça fait d'excellents Français'; 'La Choupetta'; 'Ça c'est passé un dimanche'; 'Ça sent si bon la France'; 'La fête à Neu-Neu'; 'La chanson du maçon'; 'Marche de Ménilmontant'; 'Un p'tit sourire'; 'Mam'zelle'; 'Fleur de Paris'; 'La chanson populaire' EMI PM517

The Collection: 'Louise'; 'Paris je t'aime'; 'Mimi'; 'Mon cœur'; 'On Top of the World Alone'; 'Bonsoir, Goodnight Chérie'; 'Oh Come on, Be Sociable'; 'Walking my Baby Back Home'; 'Hello Beautiful'; 'Mais où est ma Zou-Zou?'; 'Mama Inez'; 'Sweepin' the Clouds Away'; 'All I Want is Just One Girl'; 'Singing a Happy Song'; 'What Would You Do?'; 'Le chapeau de Zozo'; 'Ma pomme'; 'The Rhythm of the Rain' OBJECT 0086

Une fois vingt ans: 'Marche de Ménilmontant'; 'Appelez ça comme vous voulez'; 'Ah! si vous connaissiez ma poule'; 'Place Pigalle'; 'Femmes de France'; 'Nouveau bonheur'; 'Paris je t'aime'; 'Prosper'; 'Pour les amants'; 'Quai de Bercy'; 'C'est en flanant dans les rues de Paris'; 'Ça sent si bon la France'; 'Mon cœur'; 'Ma régulière'   EMI CHTX 240355

Deux fois vingt ans: 'Ma pomme'; 'Il pleurait'; 'Mimile'; 'Donnez-moi la main'; 'Quand on r'vient'; 'Mon p'tit Tom'; 'Dites-moi ma mère'; 'On est comme on est'; 'Quand un vicomte'; 'Ça s'est passé un dimanche'; 'Vous valez mieux qu'un sourire'; 'Moi-z-et elle'; 'Paulette'; 'Notre espoir'   EMI CHTX 240356

Trois fois vingt ans: 'La chanson du maçon'; 'Le régiment des jambes Louis XV'; 'La polka des barbus'; 'La cane du Canada'; 'Arthur'; 'Fleur de Paris'; 'Les mirlitons'; 'Valentine'; 'L'amour est passé près de vous'; 'Prenez le temps d'aimer'; 'Au paradis'; 'Le chapeau de Zozo'; 'Un p'tit air'; 'Y'a d'la joie'
EMI CHTX 240170

Quatre fois vingt ans: Chevalier discusses various aspects of his life aided by some of the above songs.   EMI SHTX 340732

Valentine: 'Paris je t'aime'; 'Mais non, mais non madame'; 'Ma pomme'; 'La java en mineur'; Ça fait d'excellents Français'; 'La symphonie des semelles de bois'; 'Dans la vie faut pas s'en faire'; 'Couplets de "Là-haut"'; 'Je m'donne'; 'Si vous n'aimez pas ça'; 'Vingt ans'; 'C'est Paris'; 'Marche de Ménilmontant'; 'Valentine'
EMI C048-50656

The Maurice Chevalier Collection: 'Balance-là'; 'Quand on r'vient'; 'Wait Till You See Ma Chérie'; 'Louise'; 'My Love Parade'; 'Paris Stay the Same'; 'Up on Top of a Rainbow'; 'All I Want is Just One Girl'; 'Livin' in the Sunlight, Lovin' in the Moonlight'; 'You Brought a New Kind of Love to Me'; 'My Ideal'; 'Moonlight Saving Time'; 'Mimi'; 'Qu'auriez vous fait?'; 'Oh, that Mitzi'; 'The Poor Apache'; 'Prosper'; 'La romance de la pluie'; 'I Was Lucky'; 'You Took the Words Right Out of My Mouth'
DEJA VU DV2100

Maurice Chevalier's Paris: 'What Would You Do?'; 'You Brought a New Kind of Love to Me'; 'Le chapeau de Zozo'; 'Livin' in the Sunlight, Lovin' in the Moonlight'; 'The Rhythm of the Rain'; 'Ma pomme'; 'You Look so Sweet, Madame'; 'You've Got That Thing'; 'Oh, that Mitzi'; 'Singing a Happy Song'; 'Paris Stay the Same'; 'Valentine'; 'Wait Till You See Ma Chérie'; 'Tzinga-doodle-day'; 'Mimi'; 'Quand un vicomte'; 'Donnez-moi la main, Mam'zelle'; 'My Love Parade'; 'All I Want is Just One Girl'; 'Les mots qu'on voudrait dire'; 'Louise'; 'Personne ne s'en sert maintenant'
CONIFER TQ156

Rendez-vous à Paris avec Edith Piaf et Maurice Chevalier: Piaf sings: 'Amour du mois de mai'; 'Si tu partais'; 'Les cloches sonnent'; 'Une chanson à trois temps'; 'Sophie'; 'Le geste'. *Chevalier sings:* 'Y'a pas si loin'; 'Rendez-vous à Paris'; 'Folies-Bergère'; 'Deux amoureux sur un banc'; 'Dans la vie faut pas sans faire'; 'C'est ca Paname'
RCA ITALIA LPM 10117

De Valentine à Yellow Submarine: 'Valentine'; 'Louise'; 'Nouveau bonheur'; 'Mimi'; 'Mon cocktail d'amour'; 'La romance de la pluie'; 'Quand un vicomte'; 'Prosper'; 'Donnez-moi la main'; 'Le chapeau de Zozo'; 'Ma pomme'; 'Ah si vous connaissiez ma poule'; 'Un p'tit air'; 'Y'a d'la joie'; 'Il pleurait'; 'Appelez ça comme vous voulez'; 'Ça fait d'excellents français'; 'Paris sera toujours Paris'; 'Ça ç'est passé un dimanche'; 'Notre espoir'; 'Ça sent si bon la France'; 'La chanson du maçon'; 'Marche de Ménilmontant'; 'La symphonie des semelles en bois'; 'Fleur de Paris'; 'Le Twist du canotier' (*with Les Chausettes Noires*); 'Sourire aux lèvres'; 'Le sous-marin vert'; 'Broadway'; 'Oui au whisky'
PATHÉ–MARCONI 7907601

Au temps du Charleston: 'Si vous êtes'; 'Quand je suis chez toi'; 'Mon cœur'; 'Moi j'fais mes coups en d'ssous' (*all with Yvonne Vallée*); 'Montrez-le moi' (*with Pizella*); 'Pour vous mesdames'; 'Mais où est ma zouzou'; 'Je l'sens'; 'Un petit mouvement'; 'Je ne dis pas non'; 'La leçon de Charleston'; 'Marguerite'; 'Moi-z-et elle'; 'Oui mais'; 'Ma régulière'; 'Sans avoir l'air d'y toucher'; 'Quand on revient'; 'Cœur d'artichaut'; 'Mon p'tit Tom'; 'Ça m'est égal'
MUSIC MEMORIA 50–715

The Films of Maurice Chevalier

The following were not released outside of France. They are mostly shorts or filmed music-hall sketches. All are silent, sometimes with added musical sound, and few are complete. Even so they are extremely important because they show Chevalier as the pre-Americanized 'apache' from Ménilmontant.

Trop crédule [1908, France]
Director: Jean Durand. No other details.

Par habitude [1911, France]
Director: Max Linder, who possibly starred. No other details.

Un marié que se fait attendre [1911, France]
Director: Louis Gasnier. No other details.

La mariée récalcitrante [1912, France]
Director: Louis Gasnier. No other details.

La valse renversante [1914, France]
Director: Charles Pathé. Also starred Mistinguett, Félix Mayol.

Le mauvais garçon [1922, France]
Director: Henri Diamant-Berger. Also starred Albert Préjean, Nina Myral, Marguerite Moreno, Denis Legeay.

Gonzague [1923, France]
Director: Henri Diamant-Berger. Also starred Marguerite Moreno, Albert Préjean and Florelle.

L'affaire de la rue de Lourcines [1923, France]
Director: Henri Diamant-Berger. Also starred Georges Milton and Florelle.

Jim Bouge, boxeur! [1923, France]
Director: Henri Diamant-Berger. Also starred Albert Préjean, Jane Myro, Florelle.

The following are Chevalier's American and European films. Some of the early ones were released in French versions with American actors having been replaced by their nearest French counterparts. Similarly, some French songs were dubbed over English ones, and vice-versa. Alternative prints of most of Chevalier's films also exist with certain songs/scenes cut, usually due to censorship or copyright problems.

Hello New York! (Bonjour New York!) [1928, USA]
Director: Robert Florey. With Yvonne Vallée. This was a publicity short made by the executives at Paramount, and shown in cinemas amongst newsreel clips, advertising *The Innocents of Paris*. Some prints include his test for Jesse Lasky/Irving Thalberg in Paris.

The Innocents of Paris (La chanson de Paris) [1929, USA]
Director: Richard Wallace. With Frances Dee, Russell Simpson, David Durand, Sylvia Beecher. Songs: 'Louise'; 'Valentine'; 'It's a Habit of Mine'; 'Wait Till You See Ma Chérie'; 'On Top of the World Alone'.

The Love Parade (Parade d'amour) [1929, USA]
Director: Ernst Lubitsch. With Jeanette MacDonald, Jean Harlow, Lupino Lane, Virginia Bruce, Lilian Roth, Ben Turpin. Songs: 'The Grenadiers March'; 'My Dream of Love'; 'Mon cocktail d'amour'; 'Soyons communs'; 'Personne ne s'en sert maintenant'; 'Paris je t'aime'; 'Pour faire plaisir à la reine'; 'My Love Parade'.

Paramount on Parade [1930, USA]
This was the film company's answer to a 'live' music-hall show. Ernst Lubitsch and Elsie Janis were but two of thirteen directors, and the film was released in five prints: English, German, French, Swedish and Spanish. Chevalier appeared in the American version with Evelyn Brent, Jean Arthur, Clara Bow, Gary Cooper, Fredric March and Fay Wray, and in the French version with Alice Tissot, Marguerite Moreno, Saint-Granier and Boucot. One sequence, 'Sweeping the Clouds Away', was in Technicolor. Songs: 'En plus grand'; 'Ça fait toujours plaisir'; 'Sweeping the Clouds Away' ('Je veux ma place au soleil'); 'All I Want is Just One Girl'.

The Big Pond (La grande mare) [1930, USA]
Director: Hobart Henley. With Claudette Colbert, Nat Pendleton, Maude Allen. Songs: 'Livin' in the Sunlight, Lovin' in the Moonlight'; 'You Brought a New Kind of Love to Me' ('Nouveau bonheur'); 'Je ne peux pas vivre sans amour'; 'La vie est belle'.

Playboy of Paris (Le petit café) [1930, USA]
Director: Ludwig Berger. With Frances Dee (American version). With Yvonne Vallée, Françoise Rosay (French version). Songs: 'My Ideal' ('Mon idéal'); 'En flanant dans les squares de Paris'; 'Dans la vie, quand on tient le coup'.

The Smiling Lieutenant (Le lieutenant souriant) [1931, USA]
Director: Ernst Lubitsch. With Miriam Hopkins, Claudette Colbert; Charlie Ruggles. Music and songs by Oscar Strauss: 'One More Hour of Love'; 'It's Always Love in the Army'; 'While Hearts are Singing'.

One Hour With You (Une heure près de toi) [1932, USA]
Directors: George Cukor, Ernst Lubitsch. With Jeanette MacDonald, Roland Young, Charlie Ruggles, Barbara Leonard (American version). With Jeanette MacDonald, Lily Damita (French version). Music and songs by Oscar Strauss: 'Oh cette Mitzi'; 'What would you do?' ('Qu'auriez-vous fait?').

Love me Tonight [1932, USA]
Director: Rouben Mamoulian. With Jeanette MacDonald,

Myrna Loy, C Aubrey Smith, Charles Butterworth, Charlie Ruggles. Songs by Rodgers & Hart: 'How Are You'; 'The Son of a Gun is Nothing But a Tailor'; 'Love me Tonight'; 'Mimi'; 'Isn't it Romantic'; 'Lover'; 'The Poor Apache'.

A Bedtime Story (Monsieur bébé) [1933, USA]
Director: Norman Taurog. With Edward Everett Horton; Babe LeRoy, Gertrude Michael. Song: 'Monsieur Bébé's Lullaby'.

The Way to Love (L'amour guide) [1933, USA]
Director: Norman Taurog. With Ann Dvorak, Sylvia Sydney, Edward Everett Horton (American version). With Jacqueline Francell, Marcel Vallée (French version). Songs: 'En flanant dans les rues de Paris'; 'A Little More, a Little Less'; 'Près de vous tout me parait si doux'.

The Merry Widow (La veuve joyeuse) [1934, USA]
Director: Ernst Lubitsch. With Jeanette MacDonald, Donald Meek, Una Merkel, Edward Everett Horton, Herman Bing, Shirley Ross, Akim Tamiroff (American version). With Jeanette Mac-Donald, Danielle Parola, Marcel Vallée, Jean Perrey (French version). Songs by Lorenz Hart, set to music by Lehár: 'Heure exquise'; 'Ah les femmes, femmes, femmes'; 'Je m'en vais chez Maxim'; 'Vylia's Song'.

Folies-Bergère [1935, USA]
Directors: Roy del Ruth (USA); Marcel Achard (Fr). With Merle Oberon, Ann Sothern (American version). With Fernand Ledoux, Sim Viva, Nathalie Paley (French version). Excepting 'Valentine', songs by Jerome Kern: 'Rhythm of the Rain' ('Romance de la pluie'); 'It was Written'; 'Le joyeux chapeau de paille'; 'Singing a Happy Song'.

The Beloved Vagabond (Le vagabond bien-aimé) [1935, GB]
Director: Curtis Bernhardt. With Margaret Lockwood, Betty Stockfeld (British version). With Hélène Robert, Fernand Ledoux, Madeleine Guitty, Betty Stockfeld (French version). Songs: 'Le bon système'; 'Madame'; 'You Look so Sweet'; 'Tzinga-doodle-day'; 'Quand un vicomte'.

L'homme du jour [1936, France]
Director: Julien Duvivier. With Elvira Popesco, Josette Day, Mona Dol, Marguerite Deval. Songs: 'Ma pomme'; 'Prosper'; 'Y a d'la joie'; 'Mon vieux Paris'.

Avec le sourire [1936, France]
Director: Maurice Tourneur. With Léon Morton, André Lefaur, Mary Glory, Jean Temerson. Songs: 'Y a du bonheur pour tout le monde;' 'Le chapeau de Zozo'; 'Les mots qu'on voudrait dire'; 'Ah, qu'il est beau!'

Break the News [1938, GB]
Director René Clair. With Jack Buchanan, Felix Aylmer, June Knight, Martha Labarr. Music by Cole Porter.

Pièges [1939, France]
Director: Robert Siodmack. With Marie Déa, Erich von Stroheim, Mady Berry, Pierre Renoir, Jean Temerson. Songs: 'Il pleurait'; 'Mon amour'. During the German Occupation all the scenes featuring von Stroheim were cut on Goebbels' orders.

Sept jours au paradis [1945, France]
Director: unknown, though alleged to have been Robert Siodmack. Chevalier's co-stars not known. The film was abandoned, although he did later record the theme-song, 'Hello!'.

Le silence est d'or [1947]
Director: René Clair. With Dany Robin, François Perrier, Marcelle Derrien, Gaston Modot. Music and theme by Georges van Paris: 'Pour les amants c'est tous les jours dimanche'. The film won the Grand Prix du Festival de Bruxelles, and at Locarno Chevalier won the prize for best actor. The American version was accompanied by a running commentary by Chevalier and contained the song 'Place Pigalle'.

Le roi [1949, France]
Director: Marc-Gilbert Sauvageon. With Annie Ducaux, Alfred Adam, Sophie Desmarets, Félix Paquet. Songs: 'Bouquet de Paris';

'C'est fini'; 'La Cachucha'; 'La barbe' (this song performed by
Robert Murzeau).

Ma pomme [1950, France]
Director: Marc-Gilbert Sauvageon. With Vera Norman; Félix
Paquet, Sophie Desmarets, Raymond Bussieres. Songs: 'Clodo-
Sérénade'; 'T'en fais pas fiston'; 'Ma pomme'; 'Y'a tant
d'amour'.

A New Kind of Love [1950, USA]
Director: Billy Wilder. With Marlene Dietrich. This film, which
was to be a 'Hollywoodized' account of Chevalier's life, centred
around the song of the same name and Edith Piaf's 'La vie en
rose', was cancelled when Maurice was prevented from entering
America by the McCarthy witch-hunt.

Chevalier de Ménilmontant [1953, France]
Director: Jacques Bratier. This was a short film documenting the
quarter of Paris where Chevalier grew up, and featured some of
the 'locals'. Song: 'La marche de Ménilmontant'.

Schlagerparade [1953, West Germany]
Director: Erik Ode. This film, not released in France, featured a
number of European stars including Lys Assia (who won the very
first Eurovision Song Contest), Germaine Damar, Walter Giller.
Chevalier sang 'Deux petits cœurs' and danced the be-bop to Stan
Kenton's band.

Cento anni d'amore (Un siecle d'amour) [1953, Italy]
Director: Lionelli de Felice. With Vittorio de Sica. Chevalier
appeared with Alba Arnova and Jacques Sernas in the sketch
'Amour 5'. No other details.

J'avais sept filles [1954, France]
Director: Jean Boyer. With Louis Velle, Paolo Stoppa, Delia Scala,
Annick Tanguy. Chevalier's first complete film in colour. Songs:
'Demain j'ai vingt ans'; 'C'est l'amour mais oui!'. The film
represented France in the *Punta de l'Este* festival, but won no
prizes.

Love in the Afternoon (Ariane) [1956, USA]
Director: Billy Wilder. With Audrey Hepburn, Gary Cooper, Olga Valery. Theme music: 'Fascination'; 'L'âme des poètes'.

The Happy Road [1956, USA]
Director: Gene Kelly. With Gene Kelly, Barbara Laage; Brigitte Fossey, Bobby Clark, Michael Redgrave, Jean-Pierre Cassel. Song: 'The Happy Road' ('La route joyeuse').

Gigi [1957, USA]
Director: Vincente Minnelli. With Leslie Caron, Hermione Gingold, Louis Jourdan, Isabel Jeans, Jacques Bergerac, Eva Gabor. Score and songs, Alan J Lerner, Frederick Loewe: 'Thank Heaven for Little Girls' ('C'est une chance qu'il y ait des petites filles'); 'It's a Bore' ('C'est la barbe'); 'The Parisians' ('Les Parisiens'); 'She's Not Thinking of Me' ('Tout cela n'est pas pour moi'); 'Gigi'; 'The Night They Invented Champagne' ('Ceux qui inventèrent le champagne'); 'I'm Glad I'm Not Young Any More' ('Quel plaisir de vieillir'); 'Say a Prayer for Me Tonight' ('Prie pour moi ce soir'); 'Gossip'. The last song was not included in the French version, where the voices of Sacha Distel, Marie France and Jane Marken were dubbed over those of Louis Jourdan, Leslie Caron and Isabel Jeans. The film won ten Academy Awards, including an honorary award for Chevalier.

Count Your Blessings [1958, USA]
Director: Jean Negulesco. With Deborah Kerr, Rossano Brazzi, Tom Helmore, Martin Stephens; Mona Washbourne, Patricia Medina.

Breath of Scandal [1959, USA]
Director: Michael Curtiz. With Sophia Loren, John Gavin, Angela Lansbury, Isabel Jeans. Song: 'Smile in Vienna'.

Can-Can [1959, USA]
Director: Walter Lang. With Frank Sinatra, Shirley MacLaine; Louis Jourdan; Juliette Prowse, Marcel Dalio. Songs by Cole Porter: 'Live and Let Live'; 'It's All right With Me'; 'Come Along With Me'; 'You do Something to Me'; 'Just One of Those Things';

'Let's Do It'; 'I Love Paris' (cut from French version); 'Mont-martre'; 'C'est magnifique'.

Pépé [1960, USA]
Director: George Sidney. With Cantinflas, Dan Dailey, Shirley Jones, Bing Crosby, Bobby Darin, Cesar Romero, Kim Novak, Tony Curtis, Jay North, Sammy Davis Jnr, Zsa-Zsa Gabor, Jimmy Durante, Greer Garson, Janet Leigh, Edward G Robinson, Judy Garland (voice only). Songs: 'Hooray for Hollywood'; 'Pépé'; 'Mimi'; 'South of the Border'; 'That's How it Went, All Right'; 'Lovely Day'; 'September Song'; 'That Far Away Part of Town.' The last two songs were cut from the French version.

Fanny [1960, USA]
Director: Joshua Logan. With Leslie Caron, Charles Boyer, Horst Buchholz, Raymond Bussières, Lionel Jeffries.

One, Two, Three, Four (Les collants noirs) [1960, GB]
Director: Terence Young. This film comprised of four ballets with music by Bizet, Thiriet, Constant and Damase. Chevalier intro-duced *The Twenty-Four Hour Widow* (with Cyd Charisse); *Cyrano* (with Moira Sheara and Roland Petit); *Carmen* (with Zizi Jeanmaire and Roland Petit); *La Croqueuse de Diamants* (with Zizi Jeanmaire).

Jessica (La sage-femme, le curé et le bon dieu) [1961, USA]
Director: Jean Negulesco. With Angie Dickinson, Sylvia Koscina, Marcel Dalio. Songs by Marguerite Monno and Dusty Negulesco. Songs: 'Will You Remember'; 'It is Better to Love'; 'La bella Jes-sica'; 'Vesper Song'. All these songs were cut from the French version.

In Search of the Castaways [1961, USA & GB]
Director: Robert Stevenson. Producer: Walt Disney. With Hayley Mills, Wilfred Hyde-White, Michael Anderson Jnr, George San-ders. Songs: 'Let's Climb'; 'Castaway'; 'Enjoy It'. The last two songs were cut from French version.

Panic Button [1962, USA]
Director: George Sherman. With Jayne Mansfield; Eleanor Parker; Michael Connors. This film was not released in France.

A New Kind of Love [1963, USA]
Director: Melville Shavelson. With Paul Newman, Joanne Woodward, Thelma Ritter, George Tobias, Eva Gabor. Chevalier appeared in a guest role interpreting 'Mimi'. Other than the title, this film had nothing to do with the proposed film of 1950.

I'd Rather be Rich [1964, USA]
Director: Jack Smight. With Sandra Dee, Andy Williams, Hermione Gingold, Robert Goulet, Charlie Ruggles. Song: 'I'd Rather be Rich'.

Monkeys Go Home [1965, USA]
Director: Andrew MacLaglen. Producer: Walt Disney. With Yvette Mimieux, Dean Jones, Bernard Woringer. Not released in France.

The Aristocats [1970, USA]
Director: Woolie Reitherman. Producer: Walt Disney. An animated film featuring the voice of Chevalier, who sang Robert Sherman's 'The Aristocats' over the credits.

Retrospectives and Tributes

To pun one of Maurice's most popular songs, it is a case of, 'Thank heaven for small mercies!' as far as tributes go – there is just one remarkable film in his native France, and a half-hearted, poorly researched two-part radio series in Britain.

MAURICE CHEVALIER: *Ma vie en canotier*
Director: Philippe Fortin; producer: Alain Armani; concept/narration: Jacques Plessis. Contributors: Lucette & René Chevalier, Charles Aznavour, Charles Trenet.

This is a jewel of a production which no Chevalier enthusiast should be without, mindless of the somewhat cheesy input from 'enemy' Trenet, who attempts to monopolize the proceedings from start to finish. There are rare clips of the great man: with his mother, with Edith Piaf, playing tennis at Bougival with Mistinguett, sparring with champion boxer Marcel Cerdan, mimicking Tino Rossi and Michel Simon, hilariously impersonating Mayol with 'Viens Poupôle'. The most important aspect of the film is that it displays what a tremendous visual artist Chevalier was – the fact is that, excellent as they are, studio recordings of classics such as 'Prosper', 'Quand un vicomte' and 'Valentine' barely skim the surface of his phenomenal talent. Here he performs 'Marche de Ménilmontant' with a gang of street kids. 'Ça fait d'excellent français', performed to an audience of appreciative soldiers, completely disproves the widely publicized fact that Chevalier lost much of his popularity after being wrongly accused of collaboration during World War II. There are extracts from many of his films, including *La valse renversante* (1914) with Mistinguett, and a clip of him singing 'La romance de la pluie', which Gene Kelly subsequently adapted for his legendary tableau *Singin' in the Rain*. Better still is a complete promo-type sequence of Chevalier performing 'Sur l'avenue Foch'. The video was released at the same time as Jacques Plessis's equally engaging *Mistinguett: ma vie en revues.*

Other songs: 'Paris Tour Eiffel'; 'Rue de retrait'; 'Sans avoir l'air d'y toucher'; 'Les mirlitons'; 'La tour'; 'Châpeau de paille'; 'Y'a de la joie'; 'Moi je fais mes coups en dessous'; 'On est comme on est'; 'En famille'; 'L'enrôlement'; 'Dans la rue'; 'Quand on revient'; 'Dans la vie faut pas s'en faire'; 'Les faubourgs'; 'Ma pomme'; 'Le peintre'; 'Le français moyen'; 'Qu'est-ce qui revient?'; 'L'oscar'; 'Les 80 berges'; 'Vieux canotier chapeau de paille'; 'Un p'tit air'.

MAURICE CHEVALIER: *The Man with the Straw Hat and the Crazy Accent*
BBC Radio 2, 107 minutes. Narrated by Michael Freedland, 1997.

Songs: 'Valentine'; 'Paris Stay the Same'; 'Louise'; 'Dites-moi'; 'Ma mère'; 'Madelon'; 'Ma pomme'; 'Folies-Bergére'; 'Ça c'est Paris' (Mistinguett)' 'The Poor Apache'; 'Parlez-moi d'amour'; 'My Love Parade'; 'Rosie'; 'Rosie' (Al Jolson); 'Oh, cette Mitzi!'; 'Mon idole'; 'Girls, Girls, Girls'; 'Louise'; 'Momo'; 'La vie en rose'; 'La marche de Ménilmontant'; 'You Must Have Been a Beautiful Baby'; 'Thank Heaven for Little Girls'; 'I'm Glad I'm Not Young Anymore'; 'I Remember it Well'; 'Titine'; 'Au revoir'; 'A New Kind of Love'.

Contributors: Maurice Chevalier (archives); Charles Aznavour, Ginette Spanier, Ronald Kennedy (archives), David Price-Jones, Alan J Lerner, Billy Milton, Thérèse de St Falle, Janie de la Chapelle, Leo Robin, Rouben Mamoulian.

'A largely unhappy man who thought time and time again of ending it all . . . a lover who thought no one loved him enough . . . so tight with his money he was downright mean . . . a compulsive depressive.'
    Thus is Chevalier described and all too frequently maligned in what is a scissors-and-paste profile where the production team too obviously know little about their subject – rather like record com-

panies who put out nostalgia CD compilations and, instead of taking the trouble to search the archives for more unfamiliar material, include only those songs that fans already have in abundance. What makes it special are the interviews with Chevalier himself – the last conducted for the BBC's *Be My Guest* in December 1971, just three weeks before his death. He speaks fondly of his early British music-hall influences (Harry Lauder, George Robey, Harry Wheldon) and of his mother – a saint for whom, had he been forced to choose between her and his career, he would have chosen her every time. He remembers Mistinguett (annoyingly and persistently referred to as 'Mizz' by Freedland). Curiously he refers to soldier-lover Martin Kenny (though not by name), the man who gave him the idea of his trademark straw hat and tuxedo. Finally he speaks of his own greatness, but humbly so and with absolutely no element of *la gross tête*.

The production then starts to fall apart with a wealth of supposition and unfounded allegation. We hear of how Chevalier, during his first mental breakdown early in 1927 and when he was facing hostile audiences in *Whitebirds*, is alleged to have told his wife Yvonne Vallée (when they were not yet married!) how he was planning to send his mother to a country retreat so that he would be free to shoot himself! He is also said to have confessed to Thérèse de St Falle, his publisher, that he had *not* loved Mistinguett and Marlene Dietrich – the first because she was 'too old', and the other 'too German'! Even more preposterous are the conclusions about Chevalier's collaboration drawn by 'Occupation of France, historian David Price-Jones. They are largely based on the assumption that if the Duchess of Bedford believed Chevalier to be a collaborator, then he must have been one and there was no requirement for evidence of this! Price-Jones further argues that by not condemning Nazis and by performing to French prisoners in Germany, then Chevalier was actually acknowledging that the Nazis had had the whiphand. Obviously the historian, who goes on to say that France had forty-*million* collaborators (in other words her entire population), would have come to the same conclusion about Edith Piaf, Lucienne Boyer, Damia, Fréhel and countless other unsung celebrity would-be martyrs! Ginette Spanier angrily disagrees, declaring Chevalier one of the bravest men she ever knew for risking his life by smuggling Jews into the

Free Zone.

The programme ends with more stretching of the truth: Chevalier wanting to be elected to the prestigious Comédie Française and being rejected on account of his so-called wartime activities; him telling friends how embarrassed he felt to be seen in public with last love Odette Meslier and how towards the end of his life Chevalier shot himself and had to be smuggled out of La Louque, wrapped in a blanket and bleeding, by the faithful François Vals who maintains that, like Yvonne Vallée, he had refused to even speak to anyone connected with this production. Though the programme is to be commended for including a few rare complete songs (including Jacques Brel's 'Titine') it should be definitely taken with an extremely large pinch of salt.

Selected Bibliography

Pierre Berruer: *Maurice Chevalier raconté par François Vals*, Plon, 1988.

David Bret: *The Piaf Legend*, Robson, 1988; *The Mistinguett Legend*, Robson, 1990.

Jacques Canetti: *On recherche jeune homme aimant la musique*, Calmann-Lévy, 1978.

Charles Castle: *The Folies-Bergère*, Methuen, 1983.

Maurice Chevelier: *Ma route et mes chansons*
I *La Louque*, 1946; II *Londres–Hollywood–Paris*, 1947; III *Temps gris*, 1948; IV *Par-ci, par là*, 1950; V *Y'a tant d'amour*, 1952; VI *Noces d'or*, 1954; VII *Artisan de France*, 1957; VIII *Soixante-quinze berges*, 1963; IX *Quatre-vingt berges*, 1967; all published René Julliard. X *Môme à cheveux blancs*, 1969; XI *Les pensées de Momo*, 1970; both published by Presses de la Cité.

Colette: *L'envers du music-hall*, Flammarion, 1913.

Charles B Cochran: *Showman Looks On*, Dent, 1945.

Jean Cocteau: *Le foyer des artistes*, Plon, 1947; *La Comtesse de Noailles, oui et non*, Libraire Académique Perrin, 1963.

Jaques Damase: *Les folies du music-hall*, Edn Spectacles, 1960.

Paul Derval: *Folies-Bergère*, Editions de Paris, 1954.

John Douglas Eames: *The MGM Story*, Octopus, 1975.

Janet Flanner: *Paris Was Yesterday*, Viking Press, 1972.

Claude Fléoutier: *Un siècle de chansons*, PUF, 1988.

Martin Greif: *The Gay Book of Days*, W H Allen, 1985.

Lynn Haney: *Josephine Baker: Naked at the Feast*, Robson, 1981.

Jaques-Charles: *De Gaby Deslys à Mistinguett*, Gallimard, 1925; *De Dranem à Maurice Chevalier*, Fayard, 1930; *Cent ans de music-hall*, Jeheber 1956; La revue de ma vie, Arthème Fayard, 1958.

Claudine Kirgener: *Maurice Chevalier; Itinéraire d'un inconnu célébre*, Vernal & Lebaud, 1988.

Robert de Laroche & François Bellair; Marie Dubas, Candeau, 1980.

Peter Leslie: *A Hard Act to Follow*, Paddington Press, 1978.

Mireille Mathieu; *Oui, je crois!* published by Laffont.

Mistinguett: *Memoirs and Confessions*, compiled and edited by Hubert Griffith, Hurst & Blackett, 1958; *Toute ma vie*, (two volumes) René Julliard, 1954.

Roger Peyrefitte: *Manouche*, Grove Press, 1974.

Edith Piaf: *Au bal de la chance*, Jeheber, 1958.

Gene Ringold & Dewitt Bodeen: *The Films and Career of Maurice Chevalier*, Citadel Press, 1972.

André Rivollet: *Maurice Chevalier; De Ménilmontant au Casino de Paris*, Grasset, 1927.

Larry Swindell: *Charles Boyer*, Weidenfeld & Nicolson, 1982.

Permissions

The author would like to thank the following for giving him permission to include extracts from the songs of Maurice Chevalier and his contemporaries: Cyril Shane Music, 'Toi, toi, toi', 'Le sourire aux lèvres'; Warner Chappell Music, 'Dîtes-moi, ma mère, 'Isn't it Romantic,' 'Up on Top of a Rainbow', 'Hymne à l'amour', 'I'm Glad I'm not Young Anymore', 'Live and Let Live'; 'The Poor Apache', © Famous Music Corp., USA Warner Chappell Music Ltd/International Music Publications used by permission; The late Maryse Damia, 'Y'a tant d'amour'; Paramount ASCAP, 'Le Madelon de la victoire', 'Maréchal nous voilà', 'Un air de chanson populaire'; François Bellair, 'Ce soir je pense à mon pays'; SACEM, Paris, 'Au fond de tes yeux', 'Rendez-vous à Paris, 'Quand j'aurais cent ans', 'Mômes de mon quartier', 'La vie est une belle fille'; Ascherberg, Paris, 'Mon homme'; Campbell Connelly, 'Valentine', 'Louise'; Feldman, Paris, 'Paris je t'aime'; BIEM, 'Y'a d'la joie', 'Ma pomme'; TRO Essex Music, 'Reste'; Editions Salabert, Paris, 'Notre espoir', 'Une heure près de toi'; Francis Day, 'Ça sent si bon la France', 'La chanson du maçon'; Editions Paul Beuscher, Paris, 'Fleur de Paris'; Editions Tutti, Paris, 'Il pleurait'; Southern Music Publishing Co., 'Toujours aimer', 'La marche de Ménilmontant', 'Chapeau de paille', 'C'était moi', 'Au revoir'.